PROVERBS, THE HIDDEN COVENANT: ACCESS TO HEAVEN'S ECONOMY

REMNANT WARRIOR
PUBLISHING

Author: Dr. Russell Welch

Published by Remnant Warrior Publishing
A Division of Wind Walker Enterprise, LLC
11349 Skimmer Ct Jacksonville Florida 32225

This Book was written in 2018, and published in 2026

"If you enjoy this book, would you be so kind as to help us remain in the top listing by leaving a positive Book review."

I decree that this book is a divine Kingdom seed—rooted in the biblical pattern of Isaiah 55:11, where the Lord declares that His Word "shall not return void, but shall accomplish what I please." It is infused with Holy Ghost fire, forged in the secret place like Jeremiah's burning word shut up in the bones, and commissioned to break through every cultural barrier, religious stronghold, and hardened heart. Just as the early apostles carried scrolls of revelation that turned cities upside down (Acts 17:6), this work carries the same apostolic thrust —an anointing that pierces darkness, plants truth, and awakens destiny in those ordained to receive it. Wherever it is sown, it will release a supernatural harvest of righteousness, revival, and revelation, echoing Jesus' promise that the seed of the Kingdom becomes a tree of transformation for the nations. This is not ink on paper —it is a scroll from heaven, a prophetic instrument aligned with the eternal counsel of God, and it will not return void.

~Dr. Russell Welch

DEDICATION

This book is dedicated to the mentors the Lord has graciously placed in my life—men who did more than teach, advise, or correct, but who modeled covenant faithfulness through their lives. Each one carried a measure of wisdom that shaped my understanding of sonship, stewardship, and obedience, and each impartation became a stone laid along the ancient pathways I now walk.

From my early days, **Dallas Henry**, whose counsel anchored me in reverence and discipline, to my current days, **Samuel Brassfield**, and all in between, those whose faithfulness and clarity continues to sharpen my discernment, I honor the lineage of wisdom entrusted to me. You did not merely speak truth; you lived it. You corrected when necessary, encouraged when timely, and trusted the work of God in seasons when clarity was still forming.

Your investment was not transactional—it was covenantal. You gave time, prayer, correction, and example without demanding return, and the fruit of that generosity continues to multiply. This work stands as a testimony to the power of faithful mentorship and the quiet strength of those who build sons rather than platforms.

May the legacy you imparted continue to bear fruit in generations yet to come.

INTRODUCTION

The Hidden Covenant in Plain Sight**

For generations, the book of Proverbs has been treated as a collection of wise sayings—helpful, practical, and morally instructive. But beneath its surface lies something far older, far deeper, and far more powerful than most believers have ever realized. Proverbs is not merely wisdom literature; it is a covenant document, a treasury of Heaven's economic laws concealed in poetic form. It is the Father's instruction manual for sons and daughters learning to walk in His ways, steward His resources, and participate in His Kingdom. Hidden in plain sight is a blueprint for supernatural increase, sustainable prosperity, and generational blessing—accessible not through formulas, but through relationship.

The wisdom of Proverbs is not transactional; it is relational. It does not offer quick fixes, shortcuts, or techniques for manipulating outcomes. Instead, it reveals the inner architecture of Heaven's economy, where increase flows through alignment, honor, righteousness, and identity. Every verse is a doorway into the Father's heart, teaching His children how to live in the world without being shaped by its systems. Proverbs is the language of covenant—an invitation to step out of the scarcity of the world and into the abundance of Heaven.

For too long, the Church has approached finances from

the posture of servants rather than sons. Servants strive, perform, and fear loss. Sons inherit, rest, and walk in confidence. Proverbs was written for sons—those who carry the Father's name, reflect His character, and steward His resources with wisdom. When read through the lens of sonship, Proverbs becomes a map for accessing Heaven's economy, revealing how identity shapes stewardship and how covenant shapes increase.

This book is not about getting rich. It is about getting aligned. It is about rediscovering the ancient pathways that lead to stability, clarity, and supernatural provision. It is about learning how Heaven's economy actually works—and why it operates so differently from the world's. Proverbs teaches that wealth without wisdom collapses, but wisdom without wealth is incomplete. Heaven's design is that sons carry both.

The hidden covenant woven through Proverbs is not mystical or obscure. It is revealed through patterns—diligence, discipline, generosity, honor, counsel, righteousness, and integrity. These are not moral virtues alone; they are economic laws. They govern the flow of resources, the expansion of influence, and the preservation of increase. When sons walk in these patterns, they step into a rhythm of life where provision comes without sorrow, and increase comes without striving.

This book will take you into the heart of that covenant. It will show you how Proverbs reveals the Father's economic system, how wisdom functions as Heaven's first currency, and how identity grants access to what effort alone can never produce. You will see why some prosper and others collapse, why some steward well and others waste, and why Heaven entrusts more to those who walk in alignment with its laws.

You are not entering a financial manual. You are entering a revelation. A rediscovery. A return to the ancient paths.

Proverbs is not a book of advice. It is a covenant invitation.

And Heaven's economy is waiting for sons who will walk in its ways.

CHAPTER ONE — THE FEAR OF THE LORD: THE FOUNDATION OF COVENANT ACCESS

Reverence as the Gateway to Wisdom

The fear of the Lord is presented in Proverbs as the starting point of true knowledge and the gateway into covenantal access, not as a trembling servile terror but as reverent awe that reorders the heart (Proverbs 1:7). This reverence creates a posture in which sons and daughters receive instruction and are shaped by wisdom rather than shaped by the world's urgencies. When reverence governs the inner life, decisions are filtered through Heaven's priorities and not through immediate appetite or cultural pressure. The early church fathers recognized this posture as formative; Augustine taught that reverence opens the soul to divine instruction and prepares the heart to receive wisdom. Reverence is therefore practical: it changes how one stewards time, money, relationships, and influence. When reverence becomes habit, covenant access begins to unfold in ordinary life.

Reverence cultivates humility, and humility is the soil in which wisdom grows, for Proverbs links lowliness of heart with the gaining of understanding (Proverbs 3:34; 11:2). Sons and daughters who practice reverence do not posture for favor; they posture for alignment, and that alignment attracts the Father's provision. This is not about performance but about posture—an inner orientation that says, "I belong to You and will steward what You entrust." Historical voices like John Chrysostom emphasized that reverence produces moral formation and practical prudence in daily affairs. Reverence therefore becomes a daily discipline of the soul, shaping speech, work, and generosity. When humility and reverence combine, wisdom becomes accessible and practical.

Reverence also functions as a protective boundary against the seductions of quick gain and the anxiety of scarcity, because it reorients trust toward the Father's provision (Proverbs 10:22). The one who fears the Lord is less likely to chase shortcuts that compromise integrity, and more likely to steward resources with long-term vision. This protective quality of reverence is visible in the lives of those who practice discipleship rather than mere technique; their choices reflect covenantal thinking. Early Christian writers noted that reverence produces a steady soul that resists the frenzy of the marketplace and the panic of comparison. Reverence therefore preserves both character and resources. When fear of the Lord governs choices, provision is preserved and multiplied.

Reverence opens the ears to instruction and the heart to correction, which Proverbs repeatedly links to life and flourishing (Proverbs 1:5; 9:9). Sons and daughters who receive correction without offense grow in discernment and avoid costly mistakes that drain influence and resources. The discipline of receiving counsel is a fruit of reverence and a practical expression of covenant humility. Augustine and Chrysostom both counseled that the wise welcome correction as a means of formation rather than a threat to status. This posture produces resilience and clarity in seasons of testing. When correction is embraced, wisdom deepens and access to Heaven's economy becomes more reliable.

Reverence reframes success as stewardship rather than self-exaltation, and Proverbs warns that pride precedes ruin while humility precedes honor (Proverbs 16:18; 22:4). Sons and daughters who fear the Lord measure success by faithfulness to covenant responsibilities rather than by external applause. This covenantal metric protects influence from corruption and preserves legacy for future generations. The early fathers taught that true honor is given by God to the humble, and that human acclaim is a poor substitute for covenantal approval. Reverence therefore aligns motives with eternal priorities. When success is stewarded in reverence, increase carries no sorrow.

Reverence is cultivated through practices that shape the soul: listening to Scripture, silence, prayerful reflection, and disciplined discipleship communities that model wisdom. Proverbs itself is an instrument for forming reverence, calling readers to internalize patterns of thought that reflect Heaven's order (Proverbs 8:10–11).

Discipleship, not mere information, is the means by which reverence becomes habit and not merely a concept. The early church practiced rhythms that formed reverence—regular reading, communal counsel, and moral formation—so that doctrine became life. These practices are accessible today and produce the same fruit of steady wisdom. When reverence is practiced, covenant access becomes lived reality.

COVENANT BEGINS WITH ALIGNMENT

Covenant access in Proverbs is always tied to alignment with the Father's ways; covenant is relational and requires posture, not performance. Alignment begins in the inner life where motives are examined and reoriented toward God's priorities rather than personal ambition. Sons and daughters who align their hearts with Heaven's values steward resources differently, choosing long-term fruit over short-term gain. The Scriptures teach that committing one's works to the Lord establishes plans and secures provision (Proverbs 16:3). Early Christian teachers emphasized that alignment with God's will produces both moral formation and practical blessing. When alignment is chosen, covenant pathways open.

Alignment is expressed in daily stewardship: how time is spent, how speech is used, and how resources are allocated. Proverbs instructs that wise planning and ordered living protect increase and prevent waste (Proverbs 21:5). Those who align their planning with wisdom create margin and structure that allow blessing to be sustained rather than squandered. Discipleship communities historically taught practical disciplines—accountability, shared counsel, and mutual correction—

that kept leaders aligned and protected their influence. Alignment therefore is communal as well as personal. When daily rhythms reflect Heaven's order, covenant access is reinforced.

Alignment also means choosing the counsel of the wise over the applause of the crowd, because many counselors bring safety and clarity (Proverbs 11:14; 15:22). Sons and daughters who seek wise counsel avoid the pitfalls of pride and impulsive decisions that lead to loss. The early fathers urged believers to surround themselves with mentors and elders who embody wisdom, recognizing that formation is relational. This relational alignment produces better decisions and preserves resources. When counsel is sought and heeded, covenant access is safeguarded.

Alignment requires integrity in speech and action, for Proverbs links truthful lips and honest scales with blessing and favor (Proverbs 12:22; 11:1). Sons and daughters who practice integrity build trust with both Heaven and people, and trust becomes a currency in the economy of covenant. Historical witnesses in the church taught that integrity is the visible sign of an inwardly aligned heart and that it opens doors of influence. Integrity therefore is not merely moralism but a practical economic principle. When integrity governs transactions, covenant access flows without friction.

Alignment includes honoring authority and relationships, because honor opens doors and creates favor in human and heavenly spheres (Proverbs 3:9–10; 18:16). Sons and daughters who practice honor treat people and assignments with reverence, and that posture invites responsibility and blessing. The early church modeled honor through submission to elders and mutual respect, which preserved unity and multiplied influence. Honor is thus a relational strategy that protects covenant access. When honor is practiced, opportunities multiply.

Alignment is sustained by disciplines that guard the heart: prayer, Scripture, silence, and the company of the wise. Proverbs calls for a life shaped by instruction and correction, and discipleship is the means by which alignment becomes habitual (Proverbs 1:8–9). The early fathers emphasized the role of spiritual disciplines in forming character and protecting leaders from compromise. These disciplines are practical and accessible, and they produce steady growth over time. When disciplines are embraced, covenant alignment becomes a way of life.

Fear of the Lord vs. Fear of Lack

The fear of the Lord and the fear of lack are two opposing spirits that produce radically different economies in a person's life; Proverbs contrasts them repeatedly. Fear of lack drives hoarding, anxiety, and impulsive decisions that erode influence and joy, while the fear of the Lord produces trust, generosity, and wise stewardship. Sons and daughters who live under covenantal fear are freed from scarcity thinking because their identity secures provision beyond immediate circumstances. Scripture affirms that the blessing of the Lord brings wealth without painful toil and that divine blessing adds no sorrow (Proverbs 10:22). Early Christian writers observed that those formed by reverence live with a different economy—one of trust and steady increase—rather than frantic accumulation. When fear of the Lord replaces fear of lack, provision flows without strain.

Fear of lack often masquerades as prudence, but Proverbs exposes its fruit: anxiety, compromise, and short-term thinking that damages legacy (Proverbs 28:22). Sons and daughters must learn to distinguish prudent planning from scarcity-driven manipulation, and reverence sharpens that discernment. Discipleship trains the heart to trust God's timing and to steward resources with generosity rather than clutching. The early fathers counseled that a heart formed by reverence is not careless but is courageous in giving and wise in planning. This courage produces a different kind of prosperity—one that is sustainable and relational. When fear of lack is replaced, generosity becomes natural.

Fear of the Lord produces a posture of dependence that paradoxically increases capacity, because dependence invites divine partnership rather than self-reliance. Proverbs teaches that committing plans to the Lord establishes them and that wisdom multiplies what is entrusted (Proverbs 16:3; 8:10–11). Sons and daughters who depend on the Father make decisions that honor covenant priorities and thus unlock supernatural favor. Historical voices in the church noted that dependence on God produces both humility and boldness, a combination that attracts responsibility. Dependence therefore is an economic strategy rooted in identity. When dependence governs choices, covenant access expands.

Fear of lack often leads to shortcuts that compromise integrity, but the fear of the Lord protects reputation and influence by prioritizing righteousness over rapid gain. Proverbs warns that dishonest gain is fleeting and that integrity preserves wealth (Proverbs 13:11; 20:17). Sons and daughters who fear the Lord refuse to trade long-term trust for short-term advantage. Discipleship communities historically guarded leaders from compromise by providing accountability and correction. This communal protection preserves both character and resources. When integrity is chosen over shortcuts, covenant access remains intact.

Fear of the Lord reorients the imagination toward abundance and stewardship rather than scarcity and consumption, and this shift changes how resources are used and multiplied. Proverbs teaches that generosity and wise stewardship produce increase and that scattering often results in greater capacity (Proverbs 11:24–25). Sons and daughters who imagine abundance steward differently: they invest in people, legacy, and Kingdom purposes rather than merely accumulating. Early church examples show communities that practiced radical sharing and saw provision multiply through mutual care. This pattern is covenantal and replicable. When imagination is shaped by reverence, resources are deployed for eternal impact.

Fear of lack can isolate and produce secrecy, but the fear of the Lord invites transparency and shared responsibility, which are essential for covenant flow. Proverbs commends counsel, shared wisdom, and communal discernment as safeguards for prosperity (Proverbs 15:22; 24:6). Sons and daughters who practice transparency invite wise counsel and multiply stewardship capacity through collaboration. The early fathers emphasized the communal nature of formation and the economic benefits of shared wisdom. This communal posture protects against the hidden sins that destroy influence. When transparency replaces secrecy, covenant access is strengthened.

HOW REVERENCE UNLOCKS DIVINE PROVISION AND WISDOM AS HEAVEN'S FIRST ECONOMY

Reverence unlocks divine provision because it aligns the heart with the Father's priorities, and Scripture repeatedly links honor and firstfruits with overflowing provision (Proverbs 3:9–10). Sons and daughters who honor God with their substance and firstfruits position themselves under covenant promises that produce abundance without sorrow. This is not a formulaic transaction but a relational principle: honor expresses trust and opens channels of blessing. Early Christian teachers recognized that honoring God and living in reverence invited God's favor in practical life and ministry. Reverence therefore functions as both posture and practice that unlocks provision. When honor is practiced, provision follows as a natural consequence.

Wisdom is presented in Proverbs as Heaven's first currency, more valuable than silver or gold and the multiplier of every resource (Proverbs 8:10–11). Sons and daughters who pursue wisdom invest in the primary asset of Heaven's economy, and wisdom converts small resources into lasting fruit. This economy values discernment, timing, and relational capital above mere accumulation. Historical voices like Augustine and Chrysostom treated wisdom as formative and practical, not merely theoretical, and they urged believers to prize instruction above riches. Wisdom therefore is both treasure and tool in covenant life. When wisdom is pursued, resources are multiplied with purpose.

Divine provision often arrives through ordinary channels—relationships, counsel, disciplined labor, and faithful stewardship—because reverence shapes how these channels are stewarded. Proverbs teaches that the diligent and faithful are entrusted with more and that blessing often follows steady, wise labor (Proverbs 10:4; 12:24). Sons and daughters who practice reverence do not despise small beginnings but steward them with excellence. The early church modeled faithful labor and mutual support as means of sustaining communities and multiplying resources. This ordinary pathway is the covenantal pattern for sustainable increase. When ordinary faithfulness is practiced, provision becomes steady.

Reverence also unlocks favor in human relationships because honor and humility attract trust and responsibility, and Proverbs links honor with influence (Proverbs 18:16; 22:1). Sons and daughters who practice reverence are more likely to be entrusted with opportunities and to be recommended by leaders. The early fathers observed that humility and honor opened doors for ministry and multiplied influence across communities. Favor therefore is not manipulation but the natural fruit of a reverent life. When relationships are honored, covenant access is amplified.

Wisdom as Heaven's currency reshapes risk and reward calculations by prioritizing long-term fruit over immediate gratification, and Proverbs repeatedly warns against the seduction of quick gain (Proverbs 20:21; 21:5). Sons and daughters who think covenantally accept seasons of preparation and resist schemes that promise rapid wealth at the cost of integrity. Discipleship forms the patience and discernment necessary to navigate seasons wisely. Historical examples in the church show that those who built slowly and wisely left enduring legacies. Wisdom therefore protects both resources and reputation. When long-term thinking governs decisions, covenant increase endures.

Finally, reverence and wisdom together create a spiritual economy where provision is both supernatural and practical: supernatural because it is released by covenantal favor, and practical because it flows through disciplined stewardship and wise planning. Proverbs teaches that blessing without sorrow comes from the Lord and that wisdom multiplies what is entrusted (Proverbs 10:22; 8:10–11). Sons and daughters who live in reverence and pursue wisdom participate in an economy that honors God, blesses others, and preserves legacy. The early church's witness confirms that covenantal living produces both spiritual depth and practical provision. When reverence and wisdom unite, Heaven's economy becomes accessible and sustainable.

CHAPTER TWO — WISDOM AS WEALTH: THE FIRST CURRENCY OF HEAVEN

Wisdom Precedes Riches in Proverbs

The book of Proverbs consistently places wisdom before wealth, teaching that the proper ordering of the inner life produces outward increase rather than the reverse (Proverbs 8:10–11; 3:13–16). Wisdom is presented as a personified voice calling from the heights, inviting sons and daughters into a way of living that yields fruit over time rather than instant gain. This ordering reframes prosperity as the byproduct of formed character and right judgment rather than the primary aim of life. Early Christian teachers observed the same pattern: formation of the soul precedes fruitful ministry and sustainable provision, and figures like Augustine and Gregory of Nyssa argued that true riches are those that flow from a rightly ordered heart. When wisdom is sought first, decisions about work, giving, and influence are governed by long-term stewardship rather than short-term appetite. The covenantal economy of Heaven rewards those who prize wisdom above immediate accumulation.

Proverbs teaches that wisdom is not merely intellectual information but practical skill for living, a kind of applied insight that governs daily choices and long-range planning (Proverbs 4:7; 8:12). Sons and daughters who pursue wisdom invest in discernment, timing, and relational capital, and these investments compound over seasons. This practical wisdom shapes how resources are stewarded, how risk is evaluated, and how opportunities are multiplied. Historical witnesses in the early church emphasized that wisdom is formed through discipleship and practice, not merely through study, and they commended communities that cultivated habits of discernment and prudence. When wisdom becomes habit, small faithful choices accumulate into significant capacity. The economy of Heaven multiplies what is stewarded with wisdom.

Proverbs contrasts the fleeting nature of ill-gotten gain with the durability of wealth produced by wisdom, warning that quick riches often lead to loss while steady increase endures (Proverbs 13:11; 21:5). Sons and daughters who prefer wisdom over schemes avoid the moral and practical pitfalls that destroy influence and legacy. This contrast is not a condemnation of enterprise but a caution about the posture behind enterprise: whether it is driven by covetousness or covenant. Early church voices noted that communities which built slowly and wisely preserved unity and multiplied resources for generations. When wisdom governs enterprise, prosperity becomes sustainable and generational. The hidden covenant rewards patience and prudence.

Proverbs frames wisdom as a protective principle that preserves reputation and influence, linking discretion with long life and honor (Proverbs 19:11; 22:1). Sons and daughters who cultivate discretion avoid impulsive speech and reckless decisions that erode trust and diminish capacity. This protective aspect of wisdom is economic because reputation is a form of relational capital that opens doors and invites responsibility. The early fathers taught that moral formation and prudence were essential for leaders entrusted with resources and people. When reputation is preserved through wisdom, opportunities for stewardship increase. The covenant economy entrusts more to those who are proven in character.

Wisdom precedes riches because it aligns the heart with Heaven's priorities, and alignment produces decisions that attract favor rather than friction (Proverbs 3:5–6). Sons and daughters who trust the Lord and seek His counsel make choices that reflect covenant values and therefore invite supernatural partnership. This alignment is cultivated through disciplines—Scripture, prayer, silence, and discipleship—that form the inner life to recognize God's voice. Historical Christian practice shows that communities committed to these disciplines experienced multiplied provision through mutual care and wise stewardship. When alignment becomes the norm, wealth follows as a natural expression of covenant faithfulness. The first currency of Heaven is therefore the wisdom that shapes faithful living.

Proverbs invites readers to prize wisdom above material gain because wisdom secures both present flourishing and eternal fruit, and the text repeatedly declares that wisdom's returns exceed silver and gold (Proverbs 8:10–11; 16:16). Sons and daughters who choose wisdom over immediate profit build lives that are resilient in trials and generous in blessing. This priority transforms the way resources are used: from consumption to investment in people, legacy, and Kingdom purposes. Early church leaders affirmed that true riches are measured by spiritual fruit and communal flourishing rather than by personal accumulation. When wisdom is treasured, the economy of Heaven becomes the operative reality in daily life. The covenant invites sons to value what endures.

UNDERSTANDING AS A MULTIPLIER

Understanding in Proverbs functions as a multiplier because it enables discernment that turns small resources into lasting fruit rather than fleeting gain (Proverbs 2:6–8; 4:5–9). When a person gains understanding, they see patterns, seasons, and relational dynamics that others miss, and this insight allows them to steward with foresight. Sons and daughters who cultivate understanding make choices that compound: they invest in people, protect reputation, and avoid entanglements that drain capacity. The early church recognized understanding as a gift that matured through practice and counsel, and elders were valued for their capacity to multiply community resources through wise governance. When understanding is applied, the smallest seed can become a harvest. The multiplier effect of understanding is therefore a covenantal principle.

Understanding reshapes risk assessment by distinguishing between prudent risk and reckless speculation, and Proverbs commends the one who considers the path of his feet and watches his ways (Proverbs 4:26–27). Sons and daughters who exercise understanding do not confuse faith with foolishness; they take courageous steps informed by counsel and timing. This discernment protects resources and preserves momentum through seasons of uncertainty. Historical examples in the church show that leaders who combined bold faith with sober understanding stewarded communities through famine and persecution. When understanding governs risk, provision is preserved and multiplied. The covenant economy favors those who balance faith with wisdom.

Understanding multiplies influence because it produces clarity in communication and strategy, enabling leaders to mobilize people and resources toward shared purposes (Proverbs 15:22; 24:6). Sons and daughters who speak with understanding attract counsel and cooperation rather than confusion and division. This clarity becomes a form of leverage in relational economies where trust and alignment determine access. Early Christian communities that practiced shared discernment multiplied their capacity to care for the vulnerable and to sustain mission. When understanding shapes leadership, networks expand and resources flow. The multiplier effect is relational as well as practical.

Understanding also multiplies stewardship by improving timing and allocation, for Proverbs links seasons and preparation with harvest (Proverbs 6:6–8; 20:4). Sons and daughters who understand seasons sow and rest at the right times, preserving margin and maximizing yield. This seasonal wisdom prevents waste and ensures that resources are available when opportunity arrives. The early fathers taught that prudent preparation and wise allocation were marks of mature communities that endured hardship. When timing is honored through understanding, increase is optimized. The covenant economy rewards those who steward with seasonal insight.

Understanding multiplies legacy because it orients decisions toward generational impact rather than immediate gratification, and Proverbs commends the one who leaves an inheritance for his children's children (Proverbs 13:22). Sons and daughters who think in terms of legacy invest in structures, relationships, and character that outlast them. This generational perspective multiplies the fruit of present stewardship into future capacity. Historical Christian practice of mentoring, communal care, and planned stewardship preserved resources across generations. When understanding governs legacy, the covenant continues to bless beyond a single lifetime. The multiplier of understanding secures continuity.

Finally, understanding multiplies spiritual and material fruit because it integrates knowledge with application, turning insight into effective action rather than mere information (Proverbs 1:5; 2:2–6). Sons and daughters who combine learning with obedience see their knowledge produce tangible blessing and influence. Discipleship is the vehicle that converts instruction into formed character and competent stewardship. Early church teachers emphasized that knowledge without practice is incomplete and that formation requires both teaching and lived example. When understanding is lived out, the covenant economy multiplies what is entrusted. The multiplier effect of understanding is therefore both practical and spiritual.

KNOWLEDGE AS THE STEWARD OF INCREASE

Knowledge in Proverbs is portrayed as a stewarding capacity that organizes resources, relationships, and opportunities for fruitful multiplication (Proverbs 24:3–4; 10:4). Knowledge without wisdom can be dangerous, but knowledge shaped by discernment becomes a powerful tool for stewardship. Sons and daughters who cultivate knowledge about markets, people, seasons, and spiritual dynamics are better equipped to steward what God entrusts. The early church valued learned leaders who combined scriptural understanding with practical governance, and they invested in training that prepared elders for responsible oversight. When knowledge is stewarded by wisdom, increase is protected and expanded. The covenant entrusts responsibility to those who prove capable.

Knowledge organizes systems that preserve margin and prevent collapse, because Proverbs links planning and counsel with stability (Proverbs 21:5; 15:22). Sons and daughters who apply knowledge to create structures—budgets, teams, rhythms, and accountability—prevent the chaos that often accompanies growth. This organizational knowledge is not merely technical; it is moral and relational, ensuring that systems serve people and purposes rather than becoming idols. Historical Christian communities that developed sound practices for care and resource distribution survived seasons of scarcity and multiplied their witness. When knowledge shapes systems, stewardship becomes sustainable. The covenant economy rewards competent management.

Knowledge also functions as a translator between vision and execution, converting prophetic insight into practical steps that produce measurable fruit (Proverbs 16:3; 20:18). Sons and daughters who steward knowledge can take a broad vision and break it into actionable plans that others can follow. This capacity to operationalize vision multiplies influence because it enables teams to move together with clarity. Early church leaders who combined visionary insight with administrative skill multiplied the reach of their mission and preserved unity. When knowledge bridges vision and action, covenant purposes advance. Stewardship requires both dream and discipline.

Knowledge protects against deception by sharpening discernment and exposing schemes that promise rapid gain at the cost of integrity, and Proverbs warns repeatedly against the seduction of dishonest profit (Proverbs 11:1; 20:17). Sons and daughters who steward knowledge are less likely to be ensnared by false promises because they can evaluate offers through the lens of covenant priorities. Discipleship communities historically provided the context for testing counsel and verifying claims, protecting leaders from isolation and error. When knowledge is communal and tested, stewardship remains pure. The covenant entrusts resources to those who can discern.

Knowledge multiplies generosity because it reveals effective ways to deploy resources for maximum Kingdom impact, and Proverbs commends the generous soul that refreshes others (Proverbs 11:24–25). Sons and daughters who steward knowledge invest in people and projects that produce lasting fruit rather than transient applause. This strategic generosity multiplies influence and opens doors for further stewardship. Early Christian practice of shared resources and strategic care multiplied provision across communities and seasons. When knowledge guides generosity, the covenant flow increases. Stewardship becomes both wise and generous.

Finally, knowledge as steward requires humility, because Proverbs links teachability with life and favor (Proverbs 9:9; 12:1). Sons and daughters who steward knowledge remain learners, receiving correction and counsel that refine their capacity. Discipleship is the environment where knowledge is tested, corrected, and matured into reliable stewardship. The early fathers emphasized that leaders must remain teachable to avoid the pride that destroys influence. When knowledge is stewarded with humility, the covenant entrusts greater responsibility. Stewardship is therefore both competent and humble.

WHY WISDOM IS MORE VALUABLE THAN GOLD AND HOW SONS INHERIT WISDOM

Proverbs declares that wisdom is more precious than rubies and that nothing desired compares with her, framing wisdom as the primary treasure of Heaven's economy (Proverbs 3:14; 8:11). Sons and daughters who prize wisdom above material accumulation orient their lives toward what endures and multiplies across seasons. This valuation changes priorities: resources are used to cultivate character, train leaders, and build structures that outlast a single generation. Early Christian teachers echoed this priority, urging believers to seek spiritual riches that produce communal flourishing rather than personal luxury. When wisdom is treasured, the covenant economy entrusts both spiritual and material increase. The hidden covenant rewards those who choose the primary currency.

Wisdom's superiority to gold is practical as well as

spiritual because wisdom preserves wealth while gold alone can be squandered, and Proverbs contrasts the fleeting nature of ill-gotten gain with the durability of wise increase (Proverbs 13:11; 21:20). Sons and daughters who invest in wisdom protect their resources from the erosive effects of impulsive decisions and cultural pressure. This protection is economic because it preserves capital, reputation, and relational trust that open future opportunities. Historical examples show that communities that prioritized formation and prudence survived crises and multiplied their witness. When wisdom guards wealth, legacy is secured. The covenant favors those who steward with prudence.

Wisdom is transferable through discipleship, and Proverbs emphasizes instruction, correction, and the passing of understanding from one generation to the next (Proverbs 4:1–9; 13:22). Sons inherit wisdom not by accident but through intentional formation: teaching, example, and communal practice. Discipleship is the mechanism by which knowledge becomes character and by which households and communities preserve covenant patterns. Early church structures—catechesis, mentoring, and communal rhythms—served precisely this function, ensuring that wisdom was transmitted and not lost. When discipleship is practiced, sons inherit both insight and responsibility. The covenant continues through formed generations.

Sons inherit wisdom by proximity to the wise and by participation in covenant communities that model right living, because Proverbs commends the company of the prudent and warns against the path of fools (Proverbs 13:20; 22:24–25). Sons who dwell among the wise absorb patterns of speech, decision, and stewardship that shape their capacity. This proximity is cultivated through discipleship relationships—mentors, elders, and peers who model covenantal living. Historical Christian practice of apprenticeship in ministry (here reframed as discipleship) ensured that leaders were formed in both doctrine and practice. When sons are formed in community, wisdom becomes inheritance rather than mere instruction.

Sons inherit wisdom through tested responsibility, for Proverbs links faithfulness in small things with greater trust and reward (Proverbs 28:20; 27:23–27). Those who prove faithful with little are entrusted with more, and this pattern is the covenantal logic of stewardship. Discipleship provides the context for proving faithfulness: small tasks, accountability, and increasing responsibility that reveal character. The early church multiplied leaders by entrusting them with responsibility and observing their stewardship over time. When faithfulness is proven, the covenant entrusts greater stewardship. Wisdom is therefore both taught and tested.

Finally, sons inherit wisdom as they cultivate a posture of reverence and teachability, because Proverbs repeatedly links the fear of the Lord with the beginning of wisdom and with life (Proverbs 1:7; 9:10). A teachable heart receives correction, seeks counsel, and values formation over acclaim. Discipleship disciplines—listening, silence, Scripture, and communal accountability—create the environment where teachability flourishes. Early Christian writers insisted that humility and reverence were prerequisites for true understanding and effective leadership. When sons remain teachable, wisdom becomes their inheritance and Heaven's economy becomes accessible. The hidden covenant entrusts its treasures to formed hearts.

CHAPTER THREE — THE HIDDEN COVENANT OF SONSHIP

Covenant Identity Versus Orphan Striving

The hidden covenant of sonship begins with identity: sons are invited into inheritance, not hired to perform for favor, and this identity reshapes every economic posture (Proverbs 2:21–22). Sons who know their place in the Father's house steward differently because their decisions flow from belonging rather than from proving, and belonging reframes risk, generosity, and legacy.

Orphan thinking, by contrast, produces frantic striving, short-term gain, and protective hoarding that erodes influence and joy over time. The wisdom of Proverbs consistently contrasts those who live by covenantal trust with those who live by anxious self-reliance, showing that identity determines outcome more than technique. Early Christian teachers observed that communities formed by a sense of family stewarded resources with mutual care rather than competitive accumulation, and they urged formation into familial identity as the antidote to scarcity. When sons embrace covenant identity, their stewardship becomes relational, generous, and sustainable.

Covenant identity changes language and imagination: sons speak in terms of inheritance, stewardship, and legacy rather than entitlement, scarcity, or survival, and this vocabulary shapes behavior. Proverbs teaches that the heart's orientation precedes outward fruit, so the words a person uses reveal the economy they live in (Proverbs 4:23). Sons who rehearse covenant language cultivate trust, patience, and long-term vision; their speech aligns with Heaven's priorities and opens relational doors. Historical witnesses in the church noted that language formed communities—household terms produced household practices that multiplied care and provision. Discipleship trains the tongue to name covenant realities and to declare stewardship rather than scarcity, and this practice rewires decision-making. When vocabulary shifts, the imagination follows and the economy of the heart changes.

Covenant identity also reframes failure and loss: sons interpret setbacks through formation rather than finality, seeing correction as part of inheritance preparation rather than as disqualification. Proverbs links correction with life and growth, and sons who accept correction remain teachable and entrusted (Proverbs 3:11–12). Orphan thinking treats loss as threat and often responds with defensive shortcuts that compromise integrity. The early fathers counseled that spiritual formation includes seasons of pruning that prepare heirs for greater responsibility, and they modeled communities that restored rather than expelled those who stumbled. Discipleship provides the context for restoration and for proving faithfulness over time. When setbacks are interpreted covenantally, they become training grounds for stewardship.

Covenant identity shifts the posture toward resources: sons view resources as entrusted rather than owned, and stewardship becomes a sacred trust rather than a personal trophy. Proverbs repeatedly links faithful stewardship with increased responsibility, showing that trust precedes entrustment (Proverbs 28:20). Those formed in sonship steward with generosity, accountability, and long-term thinking because they know they will give account as heirs. Early Christian communities practiced shared ownership and mutual care as expressions of familial identity, and these practices preserved resources across seasons. Discipleship cultivates the habit of entrusting resources to Kingdom purposes rather than hoarding them for personal security. When resources are seen as trust, stewardship becomes faithful.

Covenant identity reorients ambition: sons pursue purposes that extend legacy and bless others rather than personal acclaim, and Proverbs commends the one who seeks understanding and leaves an inheritance for children's children (Proverbs 13:22). Ambition shaped by sonship invests in structures, people, and institutions that outlast a single lifetime. Orphan ambition seeks immediate recognition and often sacrifices long-term fruit for short-term applause. Historical Christian practice shows that leaders formed in family-like communities built institutions—schools, hospitals, care systems

—that multiplied blessing across generations. Discipleship forms ambition into stewardship, aligning drive with covenant priorities. When ambition is reoriented, legacy becomes the measure of success.

Covenant identity produces a different posture toward authority: sons honor and submit within covenant structures because submission is not servile but relational, and Proverbs links honor with favor and influence (Proverbs 3:9–10). Sons who practice honor create environments of trust where resources are multiplied through delegated responsibility. Orphan posture resists authority or manipulates it for personal gain, fracturing trust and diminishing capacity. Early church fathers taught that healthy submission within family and community preserved unity and multiplied stewardship. Discipleship models relational authority that forms character and prepares heirs. When authority is honored, covenant access is reinforced.

THE FATHER'S ECONOMIC SYSTEM

The Father's economic system, as revealed in Proverbs, operates on principles of covenant trust, relational exchange, and moral order rather than on market coercion or transactional manipulation (Proverbs 11:24–25). This system rewards generosity, integrity, and faithfulness because those virtues preserve channels of blessing and invite supernatural partnership. Sons who live within this system experience provision that is both practical and supernatural: practical through wise stewardship and supernatural through favor that opens doors beyond human effort. Early Christian communities embodied this system through mutual aid, shared resources, and sacrificial giving that sustained mission and multiplied witness. Discipleship trains hearts to participate in this economy by forming habits of giving, accountability, and communal care. When the Father's system is embraced, resources flow in ways that defy worldly logic.

The Father's economy values character over capital, and Proverbs repeatedly elevates righteousness and wisdom above wealth, showing that moral formation secures long-term increase (Proverbs 16:8; 8:10–11). Sons who prioritize character attract trust and responsibility, and trust becomes a form of relational capital that opens opportunities. Orphan systems prioritize capital accumulation without formation, producing brittle wealth that collapses under pressure. Historical witnesses in the church recorded that communities which invested in character formation preserved their witness and multiplied resources across persecution and scarcity. Discipleship is the mechanism by which character is formed and by which capital is stewarded for Kingdom ends. When character is prized, the Father's economy entrusts more.

The Father's economic system is covenantal in its reciprocity: giving and honor produce relational returns that are not transactional but covenantal, and Proverbs teaches that generosity often results in unexpected increase (Proverbs 11:25; 19:17). Sons who give from identity rather than obligation release flows that return in multiplied forms—favor, opportunity, and provision. Orphan exchange treats giving as loss and hoards for security, cutting off relational returns. Early church practice of radical sharing demonstrated how covenant reciprocity multiplied provision for entire communities. Discipleship forms the heart to give without calculation, trusting the Father's covenantal return. When reciprocity is practiced, the Father's economy moves.

The Father's system protects the vulnerable as a sign of covenant health, and Proverbs repeatedly links justice for the poor with blessing and stability (Proverbs 14:31; 22:9). Sons who steward within covenant responsibility care for the weak, and this care preserves social and spiritual capital that sustains communities. Orphan economies neglect the vulnerable and create instability that eventually undermines prosperity. Historical Christian witness shows that communities attentive to the poor survived crises and attracted favor because they embodied covenant compassion. Discipleship trains hearts to see stewardship as communal care rather than private accumulation. When the vulnerable are honored, the Father's economy demonstrates its life.

The Father's economic system is strategic: it multiplies through networks, counsel, and delegated stewardship rather than through isolated accumulation, and Proverbs commends many counselors for safety and success (Proverbs 11:14; 15:22). Sons who build wise networks increase capacity because counsel prevents costly mistakes and opens collaborative opportunities. Orphan strategies isolate decision-making and often repeat errors that drain resources. Early church structures —elders, deacons, and communal oversight—created networks that multiplied care and preserved resources. Discipleship forms leaders who can both receive counsel and steward networks responsibly. When strategy is communal, the Father's economy expands.

The Father's economic system is patient and generational: it prizes long-term fruit over immediate gratification, and Proverbs honors those who prepare and leave inheritance for future generations (Proverbs 13:22; 21:5). Sons who think generationally invest in formation, institutions, and relationships that outlast them. Orphan thinking seeks immediate reward and often sacrifices continuity for speed. Historical Christian institutions that planned for the long term

—schools, hospitals, charitable systems—left legacies that multiplied blessing across centuries. Discipleship cultivates the patience and foresight necessary for generational stewardship. When patience governs planning, the Father's economy endures.

INHERITANCE AS ACCESS

Inheritance in the hidden covenant is not merely material transfer but access to authority, wisdom, and relational networks that enable stewardship at a higher level, and Proverbs frames inheritance as both reward and responsibility (Proverbs 13:22). Sons who receive inheritance gain not only resources but also mentorship, reputation, and delegated authority that accelerate stewardship capacity. Orphan models reduce inheritance to private wealth, severed from responsibility and formation, which often leads to waste. Early church practice emphasized the passing of spiritual authority and formation from elders to younger leaders, ensuring that inheritance included character and competence. Discipleship is the conduit through which inheritance is transmitted as access rather than as entitlement. When inheritance is rightly understood, it becomes a platform for multiplied stewardship.

Inheritance grants access to relational capital: names, reputations, and networks that open doors for influence and provision, and Proverbs links a good name with favor (Proverbs 22:1; 18:16). Sons who inherit relational capital steward it by honoring those relationships and by extending trust to others. Orphan approaches treat reputation as a commodity to be exploited, which corrodes trust and closes doors. Historical Christian communities passed on reputational trust through mentoring and public testimony, preserving networks that sustained mission. Discipleship trains heirs to steward relational capital with humility and accountability. When relational inheritance is honored, access multiplies.

Inheritance includes access to wisdom passed down through teaching, correction, and example, because Proverbs emphasizes the transmission of understanding from one generation to the next (Proverbs 4:1–9). Sons who inherit wisdom are equipped to make decisions that multiply resources and preserve legacy. Orphan cultures often neglect formation, leaving heirs with capital but without the discernment to steward it. Early church catechesis and mentoring ensured that spiritual and practical wisdom accompanied material provision. Discipleship remains the primary vehicle for transmitting wisdom as inheritance. When wisdom is inherited, stewardship becomes competent and faithful.

Inheritance also confers delegated authority: sons are entrusted with responsibilities that expand as they prove faithful, and Proverbs links faithfulness in small things with greater trust (Proverbs 28:20; 27:23–27). This delegated authority enables heirs to steward larger spheres of influence and to multiply impact. Orphan models either hoard authority or abdicate it, both of which stunt communal growth. Historical Christian practice of ordination, mentorship, and progressive responsibility prepared leaders to receive and exercise authority wisely. Discipleship provides the testing ground for delegated trust. When authority is delegated through formation, inheritance becomes active stewardship.

Inheritance opens access to covenant promises that are relational rather than transactional, and Proverbs shows that blessing often follows covenantal obedience and honor (Proverbs 3:9–10; 10:22). Sons who live in covenant alignment find doors opening that are not explained by human effort alone. Orphan thinking attempts to manufacture blessing through manipulation, which severs the relational channels that produce covenant favor. Early church testimony records instances where faithful communities experienced multiplied provision through obedience and mutual care. Discipleship cultivates the posture that aligns heirs with covenant promises. When promises are accessed relationally, provision flows.

Inheritance requires stewardship training to convert access into sustainable increase, because resources without formation often lead to ruin, and Proverbs warns against the folly of unwise management (Proverbs 21:20; 23:4–5). Sons who receive inheritance must be formed in disciplines of planning, generosity, and accountability to preserve legacy. Orphan approaches assume entitlement and neglect formation, producing squandered wealth and fractured communities. Historical Christian structures provided training and oversight to heirs, ensuring continuity of mission and care. Discipleship is the environment where stewardship skills are practiced and proven. When training accompanies inheritance, access becomes enduring.

WHY SONS PROSPER DIFFERENTLY AND COVENANT RESPONSIBILITIES OF SONS AND DAUGHTERS

Sons and daughters prosper differently because their economy is identity-driven: belonging precedes blessing, and Proverbs repeatedly shows that the heart's orientation determines the flow of provision (Proverbs 10:22; 3:5–6). Sons who operate from identity steward with generosity, patience, and long-term vision, and these postures attract both human favor and divine partnership. Orphan economies, driven by fear and performance, produce brittle success that often collapses under pressure. Early Christian communities that embraced familial identity multiplied care and sustained mission across hardship. Discipleship forms the inner posture that produces different outcomes. When identity governs action, prosperity aligns with covenant.

Sons and daughters prosper differently because they are entrusted with delegated authority as they prove faithful, and Proverbs links faithfulness with increased responsibility and honor (Proverbs 28:20; 22:29). This pattern of entrustment creates a ladder of stewardship where small faithfulness leads to greater spheres of influence. Orphan systems either centralize power or distribute it without formation, both of which undermine sustainable growth. Historical church practice of mentoring and progressive responsibility prepared leaders to steward larger trusts. Discipleship provides the context for proving faithfulness and receiving delegation. When trust is earned, prosperity expands responsibly.

Sons and daughters prosper differently because their giving is covenantal rather than transactional: generosity becomes a channel for relational returns and for the multiplication of resources, and Proverbs commends the generous soul (Proverbs 11:24–25). Sons and daughters who give from identity release flows that return in favor, opportunity, and multiplied provision. Orphan giving is often calculated and defensive, which chokes relational reciprocity. Early Christian communities practiced radical sharing that sustained entire neighborhoods and multiplied witness. Discipleship trains hearts to give without calculation and to steward generosity strategically. When giving is covenantal, prosperity becomes communal.

Sons and daughters prosper differently because they prioritize wisdom and formation over quick gain, and Proverbs elevates wisdom as the primary treasure that secures both present and future fruit (Proverbs 8:10–11; 4:7). This priority produces decisions that compound over time rather than schemes that promise rapid wealth at the cost of integrity. Orphan strategies chase speed and often sacrifice continuity for immediate reward. Historical examples show that communities investing in formation left enduring legacies. Discipleship cultivates the patience and discernment necessary for wise prosperity. When wisdom is prized, prosperity endures.

Sons and daughters prosper differently because they steward reputation and relational capital, recognizing that a good name opens doors and invites responsibility, and Proverbs links reputation with favor (Proverbs 22:1; 18:16). Sons who protect reputation through integrity attract partnerships and opportunities that multiply stewardship capacity. Orphan approaches exploit reputation for personal gain, which corrodes trust and closes doors. Early church leaders modeled reputational stewardship through consistent character and public accountability. Discipleship forms leaders who value trust above applause. When reputation is stewarded, prosperity is sustainable.

Sons and daughters prosper differently because they accept covenant responsibilities: care for the vulnerable, justice in commerce, and legacy thinking that secures future generations, and Proverbs repeatedly ties blessing to righteous action (Proverbs 14:31; 21:5). Sons and daughters who embrace these responsibilities participate in an economy that blesses both giver and receiver and that preserves social and spiritual capital. Orphan economies neglect responsibility and create instability that eventually undermines prosperity. Historical Christian practice of institutional care—hospitals, schools, relief—demonstrated how covenant responsibility multiplies blessing across society. Discipleship trains heirs to carry responsibility with humility and competence. When responsibility is embraced, prosperity becomes testimony.

Sons and daughters prosper differently because they form communities of wisdom and counsel that protect against isolation and error, and Proverbs commends many counselors for safety and success (Proverbs 11:14; 15:22). Sons and daughters who build wise networks multiply capacity because counsel prevents costly mistakes and opens collaborative opportunities. Orphan leaders often isolate decision-making, repeating errors that drain resources. Early church structures —elders, deacons, and communal oversight—created networks that multiplied care and preserved resources. Discipleship forms leaders who both receive counsel and steward networks responsibly. When counsel is practiced, prosperity is protected and multiplied.

Sons and daughters prosper differently because they steward time and rhythm—work, rest, and celebration —in ways that sustain endurance and joy, and Proverbs links steady labor with provision and rest with renewal (Proverbs 6:6–8; 10:4). Sons and daughters who honor rhythm avoid burnout and preserve clarity for long-term stewardship. Orphan cultures valorize frantic productivity that sacrifices sustainability for short-term output. Historical Christian rhythms—work, prayer, rest, and communal care—preserved leaders and multiplied witness. Discipleship forms habits that balance diligence with rest. When rhythm is honored, prosperity carries no sorrow.

Sons and daughters prosper differently because they plan for seasons and steward margin, recognizing that preparation preserves life and that margin enables generosity and resilience, and Proverbs commends planning and foresight (Proverbs 21:5; 27:12). Sons and daughters who prepare for seasons avoid panic and waste, and they position resources for strategic deployment. Orphan approaches neglect margin and are vulnerable to shocks that erode capacity. Early church communities practiced mutual aid and preparation that sustained them through famine and persecution. Discipleship trains leaders to plan with prudence and generosity. When seasons are honored, prosperity is steady.

Sons and daughters prosper differently because they cultivate teachability and humility, remaining open to correction and formation, and Proverbs links teachability with life and favor (Proverbs 9:9; 12:1). Sons and daughters who remain learners adapt to change and preserve relevance, and their humility attracts counsel and partnership. Orphan pride resists correction and isolates leaders from the wisdom that would preserve influence. Historical Christian leaders emphasized lifelong formation and accountability as safeguards for stewardship. Discipleship creates environments where teachability flourishes. When humility governs leadership, prosperity is entrusted and multiplied.

Sons and daughters prosper differently because they steward legacy intentionally, investing in institutions, families, and discipleship that outlast them, and Proverbs honors those who leave inheritance for children's children (Proverbs 13:22). Sons who think generationally build structures that multiply blessing beyond a single lifetime. Orphan thinking seeks immediate reward and often sacrifices continuity for speed. Historical Christian institutions that planned for the long term left legacies that shaped societies for centuries. Discipleship forms leaders who build beyond themselves. When legacy is stewarded, the hidden covenant continues to bless.

CHAPTER FOUR — RIGHTEOUSNESS AND JUSTICE: THE GOVERNMENT OF INCREASE

Righteousness as Structural Integrity

Righteousness in Proverbs functions as structural integrity for life and stewardship, establishing a moral architecture that preserves increase and influence (Proverbs 11:3; 21:3). When sons live righteously, their decisions create stable systems that resist corrosion from greed, envy, and short-term thinking. Righteousness is not merely private piety but public competence: it governs transactions, relationships, and institutional life so that trust becomes a reliable currency. The early church fathers taught that moral formation was the foundation for any lasting ministry, insisting that character precedes capacity and that integrity opens doors of responsibility. Discipleship forms the habits that make righteousness practical—daily choices, accountability, and correction that shape consistent behavior.

When righteousness becomes the norm, increase is protected by a framework that honors covenant order.

Righteousness protects reputation, and reputation functions as relational capital in the economy of covenant, because a good name opens doors and invites partnership (Proverbs 22:1). Sons and daughters who steward reputation with honesty and transparency attract counsel, favor, and delegated authority that multiply stewardship capacity. Righteousness therefore has an economic dimension: it preserves trust so that others will entrust resources and influence. Historical witnesses in the church show that communities known for integrity were entrusted with care for the vulnerable and with leadership in times of crisis. Discipleship trains leaders to value reputation over applause and to accept correction that preserves trust. When reputation is guarded by righteousness, relational capital grows.

Righteousness also functions as a preventative system against corruption, because Proverbs links honest scales and truthful lips with blessing and stability (Proverbs 11:1; 12:22). Sons who refuse dishonest shortcuts protect their communities from the hidden rot that eventually destroys influence and legacy. This preventative quality is practical: it reduces legal entanglements, relational fractures, and the long-term costs of compromised decisions. Early Christian leaders insisted that visible holiness was not mere show but a safeguard for communal life and stewardship. Discipleship cultivates the courage to refuse expedient compromise and to choose long-term fidelity. When corruption is resisted, increase remains sustainable.

Righteousness shapes governance and institutional

design by insisting that systems serve people and purposes rather than idols of profit, and Proverbs commends justice as the foundation of stable communities (Proverbs 29:4; 16:11). Sons and daughters who design structures with justice in view create organizations that endure because they honor human dignity and covenant responsibility. This governance ethic prevents exploitation and ensures that resources are deployed for flourishing rather than extraction. Historical church practice demonstrates that institutions grounded in justice outlast those built on expedience. Discipleship forms leaders who prioritize just structures and who steward authority with accountability. When governance is righteous, the economy of covenant flourishes.

Righteousness produces a climate of predictability that invites investment and partnership, because people and institutions prefer to entrust resources where integrity is evident (Proverbs 10:9). Sons who live transparently and keep their word create environments where others can plan, give, and collaborate without fear of betrayal. This predictability is an economic advantage: it lowers transaction costs and multiplies cooperative ventures. Early church communities that practiced mutual accountability attracted support and multiplied care across neighborhoods. Discipleship disciplines—confession, counsel, and mutual oversight—create the predictability that sustains networks. When predictability is rooted in righteousness, covenant increase becomes communal.

Righteousness is cultivated through disciplines that shape both private character and public action: Scripture, silence, confession, and communal accountability form the habits that produce consistent integrity. Proverbs calls for instruction and correction as means of life, and discipleship is the environment where correction becomes formation rather than shame (Proverbs 9:8; 12:1). The early fathers emphasized the role of spiritual disciplines in forming leaders who could steward resources without compromise. These practices are practical and repeatable, producing leaders who can be trusted with influence. When disciplines form righteousness, the structures of increase remain sound.

JUSTICE AS ECONOMIC ORDER

Justice in Proverbs is not merely legal fairness but the ordering principle that ensures resources flow to sustain life and community, and it is repeatedly linked with blessing and stability (Proverbs 14:31; 21:15). When justice governs commerce, care, and governance, the vulnerable are protected and social capital is preserved. Justice therefore functions as an economic regulator: it prevents exploitation, reduces social friction, and sustains long-term prosperity. Early Christian communities practiced justice through mutual aid, care for widows and orphans, and equitable distribution that preserved communal resilience. Discipleship forms hearts to see stewardship as communal responsibility rather than private accumulation. When justice is institutionalized, the covenant economy demonstrates its life.

Justice creates trust across social boundaries because it signals that systems are fair and that promises will be honored, and Proverbs links fair scales with divine favor (Proverbs 11:1). Sons who insist on just practices in business and community life attract partners who value reliability and honor. This trust becomes a multiplier for stewardship because it enables larger collaborations and shared risk. Historical witnesses show that communities known for justice were often the hubs of trade, care, and influence in their regions. Discipleship trains leaders to design systems that protect the weak and reward faithful stewardship. When justice governs exchange, covenant access expands.

Justice prevents the hidden costs of exploitation —resentment, rebellion, and reputational loss—that eventually erode capacity, and Proverbs warns that oppression leads to ruin (Proverbs 22:16; 28:3). Sons who steward with justice avoid the long-term liabilities that come from short-term gain at others' expense. This preventative dimension of justice is practical: it preserves human capital and reduces the need for costly remediation. Early church practice of communal care and equitable distribution preserved unity and multiplied witness in times of scarcity. Discipleship forms leaders who see justice as both moral imperative and strategic necessity. When exploitation is refused, covenant increase is preserved.

Justice also shapes taxation, giving, and communal provision by ensuring that resources are allocated to sustain life and mission rather than to feed greed, and Proverbs commends generosity as a stabilizing force (Proverbs 11:25; 19:17). Sons who design systems of giving and care that prioritize the vulnerable create resilient communities that can weather shocks. This design is economic because it preserves labor, morale, and social cohesion that are essential for sustained productivity. Historical Christian institutions—hospitals, schools, relief networks—were expressions of justice that multiplied societal flourishing. Discipleship trains communities to steward resources for common good. When allocation is just, the covenant economy thrives.

Justice requires discernment and wise counsel to implement fairly, because Proverbs links many counselors with safety and success (Proverbs 11:14; 15:22). Sons and daughters who build advisory structures and transparent processes reduce bias and ensure equitable outcomes. This procedural justice increases confidence among stakeholders and invites broader participation. Early church governance models included elders and deacons to provide oversight and to protect the vulnerable, demonstrating practical mechanisms for justice. Discipleship forms leaders who can both hear counsel and implement fair systems. When processes are just, covenant access is widened.

Justice is sustained by cultural practices that honor dignity—honor, hospitality, and mutual responsibility—and Proverbs repeatedly ties honor to favor and influence (Proverbs 3:9–10; 18:16). Sons and daughters who cultivate cultures of honor create environments where generosity and trust are normative. This cultural justice becomes self-reinforcing: honor begets honor and multiplies relational capital. Historical Christian communities that practiced hospitality and mutual care became centers of stability and blessing. Discipleship forms the habits that make cultural justice habitual rather than exceptional. When culture honors dignity, the government of increase is healthy.

INTEGRITY, SCALES, AND THE MECHANICS OF BLESSING

Integrity in speech and measurement is a recurring theme in Proverbs because honest scales and truthful lips preserve commerce and community, and these mechanics are essential to covenant blessing (Proverbs 11:1; 20:10). Sons and daughters who refuse deceptive practices maintain channels of trust that allow resources to circulate without friction. Integrity therefore is not merely moralism but an economic technology: it reduces transaction costs, prevents litigation, and preserves reputation. Early church leaders insisted that visible integrity was necessary for public trust and for the safe stewardship of communal resources. Discipleship forms the inner life that produces consistent outward honesty. When integrity governs exchange, blessing flows with fewer obstacles.

Honest measurement protects both buyer and seller and preserves the social fabric that enables markets and ministries to function, and Proverbs condemns dishonest weights as destructive (Proverbs 20:10; 11:1). Sons and daughters who insist on fairness in trade create environments where commerce can be trusted and where partnerships can scale. This fairness is practical: it sustains repeat transactions and long-term relationships that multiply capacity. Historical Christian practice included standards of care and oversight to prevent exploitation and to maintain trust in communal systems. Discipleship trains leaders to implement transparent practices that protect all parties. When measurement is honest, covenant increase is reliable.

Integrity in speech prevents the erosion of trust that comes from gossip, slander, and falsehood, and Proverbs links the tongue with life and death (Proverbs 18:21). Sons and daughters who guard their speech preserve relationships and avoid the costly fallout of broken trust. This verbal integrity is economic because it maintains networks and prevents the need for costly reconciliation. Early church fathers taught that disciplined speech was a mark of maturity and a safeguard for communal life. Discipleship disciplines—silence, confession, and accountability—shape speech into a tool for building rather than destroying. When speech is governed by integrity, blessing is multiplied.

Integrity in leadership creates predictable stewardship that invites delegation and entrustment, because those who are faithful in small things are given greater responsibility (Proverbs 28:20; 27:23–27). Sons and daughters who demonstrate consistent honesty are more likely to be entrusted with larger spheres of influence and resources. This pattern of entrustment is the covenantal mechanism by which stewardship scales across generations. Historical Christian structures of oversight and mentorship ensured that leaders were tested and proven before being given greater trust. Discipleship provides the context for proving faithfulness through small responsibilities. When leaders are proven, blessing expands responsibly.

Integrity in financial practice—transparent accounting, fair wages, and honest reporting—preserves communal trust and prevents the hidden drains that collapse organizations, and Proverbs commends fair treatment of workers and honest gain (Proverbs 3:27; 22:16). Sons and daughters who steward finances with transparency attract donors, partners, and volunteers who value accountability. This financial integrity is practical: it sustains funding streams and reduces the risk of scandal. Early church communities developed practices of stewardship and oversight to protect communal resources and to ensure care for the vulnerable. Discipleship trains stewards to manage resources with both competence and conscience. When finances are governed by integrity, covenant provision is sustained.

Integrity in covenant relationships—keeping promises, honoring agreements, and restoring trust when broken—creates a social environment where long-term partnerships can flourish, and Proverbs links faithfulness with favor (Proverbs 20:6; 28:6). Sons and daughters who practice covenant fidelity build networks that multiply stewardship capacity through mutual trust. This relational integrity is economic because it enables cooperative ventures and shared risk. Historical Christian practice emphasized reconciliation and restoration as means of preserving communal trust and capacity. Discipleship forms the habits that make covenant fidelity the norm. When relationships are kept, blessing becomes communal.

JUSTICE, MERCY, AND THE LONG VIEW OF INCREASE

Justice and mercy together form the long view of covenant increase because Proverbs balances righteous action with compassionate care, showing that both are necessary for sustainable flourishing (Proverbs 21:21; 14:31). Sons who practice justice without mercy create cold systems that lack life, while mercy without justice can enable dysfunction; the covenant requires both. This balance produces communities that are both orderly and compassionate, capable of sustaining productivity while caring for the vulnerable. Early church communities embodied this balance through institutions that combined care with accountability—hospitals that healed and schools that trained, relief that restored and structures that preserved. Discipleship forms leaders who can hold both truth and grace in tension. When justice and mercy are integrated, the covenant economy matures.

Mercy protects against the hardening that can accompany institutional success, because Proverbs warns that the proud and unmerciful lose favor and influence (Proverbs 16:5; 21:13). Sons who temper justice with mercy preserve relational capital and create environments where restoration is possible. This restorative posture is economic because it retains human capital and prevents the loss of gifted people through exclusion. Historical Christian practice of restoration and reconciliation preserved leaders and communities through seasons of failure. Discipleship provides the context for restoration that both corrects and heals. When mercy accompanies justice, increase carries life.

The long view of increase requires planning for seasons, and Proverbs repeatedly commends foresight and preparation as means of sustaining provision (Proverbs 6:6–8; 21:5). Sons who plan for droughts, transitions, and generational transfer preserve capacity and avoid panic. This seasonal planning is economic because it smooths volatility and enables strategic generosity even in lean times. Early church institutions that prepared for future needs—endowments, communal stores, training systems—survived crises and multiplied witness. Discipleship trains leaders to think generationally and to steward for continuity. When planning governs stewardship, covenant increase endures.

The long view also requires investment in formation —education, discipleship, and institutional capacity— because Proverbs links instruction with life and favor (Proverbs 4:1–9; 9:9). Sons who invest in formation multiply their impact by equipping others to steward well. This investment is economic because it converts present resources into future capacity and leadership. Historical Christian practice of catechesis, mentoring, and institutional training created leaders who could sustain mission across generations. Discipleship is the primary vehicle for this investment. When formation is prioritized, the covenant multiplies its fruit.

The long view of increase includes legacy thinking that secures inheritance for future generations, and Proverbs honors those who leave an inheritance for their children's children (Proverbs 13:22). Sons who steward with legacy in mind build institutions, habits, and relationships that outlast them. This legacy orientation is economic because it compounds stewardship across time rather than consuming it in a single season. Early Christian institutions—schools, hospitals, charitable trusts—were expressions of legacy thinking that multiplied blessing for centuries. Discipleship forms leaders who build beyond themselves. When legacy is stewarded, the hidden covenant continues to bless.

Finally, the long view requires humility and teachability, because Proverbs links the fear of the Lord and a teachable heart with life and favor (Proverbs 1:7; 9:10). Sons who remain learners adapt to change, receive correction, and preserve relevance across seasons. This humility is economic because it prevents the pride that destroys influence and because it invites counsel that refines strategy. Historical Christian leaders modeled lifelong formation and accountability as safeguards for stewardship. Discipleship creates environments where humility is practiced and where leaders are formed for endurance. When humility governs the long view, covenant increase is both steady and generational.

CHAPTER FIVE — DILIGENCE, DISCIPLINE, AND THE PATHWAY OF INCREASE

Diligence as Wisdom in Motion

The wisdom of Proverbs presents diligence as wisdom expressed through consistent, faithful action rather than frantic effort, and it frames steady work as a covenantal posture rather than a performance metric (Proverbs 10:4; 12:24). Sons and daughters who practice diligence move with intention, stewarding time and energy as entrusted resources rather than reacting to cultural urgency. This posture produces a rhythm of life where small, faithful choices compound into capacity and influence over seasons. Early church teachers observed that spiritual formation shows itself in daily habits, and figures like John Chrysostom commended steady faithfulness as the mark of mature discipleship. Diligence therefore is both spiritual formation and practical competence, shaping character and producing reliable fruit. When diligence governs action, increase becomes sustainable rather than sporadic.

Diligence is not the same as frantic busyness; Proverbs contrasts the diligent with the slothful and shows that steady labor yields provision without the weariness of anxious striving (Proverbs 6:6–8; 20:4). Sons and daughters who embrace disciplined work avoid the extremes of overwork and passivity because their labor is ordered by wisdom and rest. This balance preserves joy and prevents the erosion of soul that comes from frantic performance. Early Christian communities practiced rhythms of work and prayer that protected leaders from burnout and preserved communal capacity. Discipleship trains the heart to value faithful presence over frantic visibility. When diligence is practiced with wisdom, labor becomes life-giving.

Diligence shapes decision-making by prioritizing long-term fruit over immediate applause, and Proverbs warns that quick gain often leads to loss while steady increase endures (Proverbs 13:11; 21:5). Sons and daughters who choose the long view steward resources with foresight, resisting schemes that promise rapid wealth at the cost of integrity. This posture protects legacy and preserves relational capital that opens future doors. Historical witnesses in the church show that communities which built slowly and wisely left institutions and practices that multiplied blessing across generations. Discipleship forms patience and discernment that enable leaders to steward for continuity. When the long view governs choices, increase matures.

Diligence is an expression of trust in covenant order because it assumes that faithful stewardship will be recognized and multiplied by the Father, and Proverbs links faithfulness in small things with greater entrustment (Proverbs 28:20; 27:23–27). Sons and daughters who labor faithfully do not measure success by speed but by obedience and stewardship. Their confidence rests in the Father's oversight rather than in immediate results. Early fathers taught that faithful service, even in obscurity, prepares leaders for public responsibility and multiplies influence over time. Discipleship cultivates the humility to serve faithfully without immediate reward. When diligence is rooted in trust, blessing follows steadily.

Diligence refines character through repetition and endurance, and Proverbs shows that steady effort forms patience, resilience, and practical wisdom (Proverbs 4:5–7). Sons and daughters who persist through seasons of hidden growth develop discernment that protects them from impulsive choices when opportunity arrives. This formation produces leaders who can steward larger trusts without being overwhelmed by pressure. Historical Christian formation emphasized the slow work of character development as the foundation for sustainable ministry and stewardship. Discipleship provides the context where repetition becomes formation rather than mere routine. When diligence shapes character, stewardship expands responsibly.

Diligence also functions as a witness to others, attracting trust and opening relational doors because reliability becomes visible over time, and Proverbs links steady labor with honor before leaders (Proverbs 22:29). Sons and daughters who demonstrate consistent competence are more likely to be entrusted with responsibility and influence. This relational trust becomes a practical currency in the economy of covenant, enabling collaborative ventures and delegated stewardship. Early church leaders noted that communities known for faithful labor were often entrusted with care for the vulnerable and with leadership in times of crisis. Discipleship forms reputational trust through accountability and proven faithfulness. When diligence is visible, opportunity follows.

Diligence protects against fear-driven decisions by creating margin and preparedness, and Proverbs teaches that the diligent prepare while others panic (Proverbs 21:5; 6:6–8). Sons and daughters who steward time and resources prudently avoid the desperation that leads to compromise. This preparedness preserves clarity and prevents the erosion of influence through reactive choices. Historical examples show that communities with disciplined preparation weathered famine and persecution with resilience. Discipleship trains leaders to plan with prudence and to steward margin for seasons of need. When diligence prepares the way, stewardship remains steady.

Diligence is expressed in the stewardship of small things because Proverbs repeatedly links faithfulness in little with greater trust, and this principle is the coven antal logic of increase (Proverbs 28:20; 27:23–27). Sons and daughters who honor small responsibilities demonstrate character that invites entrustment with larger spheres. This incremental entrustment is the mechanism by which stewardship scales across time. Early church practice of entrusting small tasks to emerging leaders provided the testing ground for future responsibility. Discipleship creates opportunities to prove faithfulness in manageable steps. When small faithfulness is honored, greater stewardship follows.

Diligence shapes how seasons are navigated because it trains the soul to recognize sowing and reaping cycles, and Proverbs commends those who prepare in advance for harvest and hardship (Proverbs 6:6–8; 20:4). Sons and daughters who understand seasons avoid panic and waste, positioning resources for strategic deployment. This seasonal wisdom prevents the depletion of capacity and enables generosity even in lean times. Historical Christian communities practiced communal stores and mutual aid as practical expressions of seasonal preparation. Discipleship forms the foresight to steward across cycles rather than reacting to them. When seasons are honored, increase matures.

Diligence is sustained by disciplines—daily prayer, Scripture, silence, and accountable community—that shape the inner life and prevent drift, and Proverbs links instruction and correction with life (Proverbs 1:8–9; 9:9). Sons and daughters who embrace spiritual disciplines align their motives and actions with covenant priorities, making diligence sustainable rather than burdensome. These disciplines protect against the pride and isolation that often accompany success. Early fathers emphasized the role of spiritual rhythms in forming leaders who could steward resources without compromise. Discipleship provides the relational context where disciplines are practiced and reinforced. When disciplines sustain diligence, stewardship becomes a lifestyle.

Diligence ultimately becomes a testimony of covenant

faithfulness because steady labor that honors God and others produces rest rather than sorrow, and Proverbs teaches that the blessing of the Lord brings wealth without painful toil (Proverbs 10:22). Sons and daughters who labor in wisdom experience provision that carries peace and preserves joy. Their lives testify that Heaven's economy rewards faithful stewardship rather than frantic striving. Historical witnesses in the church affirmed that faithful communities enjoyed multiplied provision because they practiced steady, covenantal diligence. Discipleship forms the character that makes such testimony possible. When diligence is lived, increase becomes a witness to God's faithfulness.

DISCIPLINE, ORDER, AND THE PROTECTION OF GROWTH

Discipline in Proverbs is presented as the structure that protects growth from collapse, and it is described as correction that preserves life rather than punishment that destroys (Proverbs 12:1; 3:11–12). Sons and daughters who love discipline love knowledge, and they welcome correction as a means of formation rather than a threat to status. This posture creates ordered lives that can steward increase without confusion or waste. Early church teachers insisted that correction and formation were essential for leaders entrusted with resources and people. Discipleship provides the environment where discipline becomes habit and not merely a rule. When discipline governs life, growth is protected.

Order is the practical expression of discipline because it creates systems—budgets, rhythms, teams, and accountability—that prevent chaos during seasons of expansion, and Proverbs links wisdom with building and establishing the house (Proverbs 24:3–4). Sons and daughters who establish order before increase arrives create capacity to steward growth without being overwhelmed. This foresight prevents the common collapse that follows rapid expansion. Historical Christian communities developed structures of oversight and care that preserved unity and multiplied witness. Discipleship trains leaders to design systems that serve people and purposes rather than becoming idols. When order is established, growth becomes sustainable.

Discipline governs attention and priorities, and Proverbs teaches that the wise guard their hearts and watch their ways, prioritizing what aligns with covenant purposes (Proverbs 4:23; 21:5). Sons and daughters who discipline their attention avoid distraction and preserve momentum for long-term projects. This clarity protects against the fragmentation that wastes resources and energy. Early fathers counseled that disciplined focus was essential for leaders who would steward communities through trials. Discipleship forms habits of attention that translate vision into consistent action. When priorities are disciplined, stewardship deepens.

Discipline protects against emotional decision-making by cultivating restraint and discernment, and Proverbs warns that unchecked desire leads to loss (Proverbs 21:17; 25:28). Sons and daughters who practice discipline pause before acting and listen for counsel, resisting impulsive shortcuts that compromise integrity. This restraint preserves both resources and relationships. Historical Christian practice emphasized the role of fasting, silence, and counsel in forming leaders who could resist temptation and make sober choices. Discipleship provides the relational checks that prevent impulsive ruin. When discipline governs desire, growth remains secure.

Discipline refines discernment over time because instruction and correction sharpen understanding, and Proverbs links teachability with life and favor (Proverbs 9:9; 12:1). Sons and daughters who welcome correction grow in the capacity to steward larger trusts without being deceived by flattering counsel or quick schemes. This refined discernment prevents costly mistakes that erode influence. Early church structures of mentorship and oversight ensured that leaders were tested and formed before being given greater responsibility. Discipleship creates the context where discernment is practiced and proven. When discernment is refined, stewardship is protected.

Discipline establishes boundaries that preserve peace within stewardship, and Proverbs teaches that boundaries bring life and protect what is entrusted (Proverbs 25:28; 4:23). Sons and daughters who honor rhythms of work and rest prevent burnout and maintain clarity for long-term service. These boundaries also protect relationships from the corrosive effects of unchecked ambition. Historical Christian rhythms—work, prayer, rest, and communal care—sustained leaders and multiplied witness across seasons. Discipleship forms the habits that make boundaries practical rather than punitive. When boundaries are honored, growth carries no sorrow.

Discipline produces confidence rather than pressure because preparation and steady formation create a secure footing for leadership, and Proverbs links the disciplined walk with honor before leaders (Proverbs 22:29). Sons and daughters who are disciplined do not need to manufacture influence; their competence invites trust and responsibility. This confidence attracts opportunities that multiply stewardship capacity. Early church leaders who were formed through discipline were often entrusted with larger spheres of care and influence. Discipleship provides the testing ground where confidence is proven rather than assumed. When discipline produces confidence, stewardship expands responsibly.

Discipline protects against comparison and envy by anchoring identity in covenant rather than in external measures, and Proverbs warns that envy rots the bones (Proverbs 14:30; 23:4–5). Sons and daughters who are disciplined in their inner life resist the temptation to measure themselves by others' success and instead steward what they have been given. This inner stability preserves joy and prevents destructive competition. Historical Christian communities that emphasized formation over status avoided the rivalries that fracture movements. Discipleship cultivates contentment and focus on assignment rather than applause. When discipline guards the heart, growth remains aligned.

Discipline links correction with life because it refines character and prepares leaders for responsibility, and Proverbs teaches that correction leads to wisdom and long-term fruit (Proverbs 3:11–12; 12:1). Sons and daughters who welcome correction become more reliable stewards and are entrusted with greater influence. This pattern of formation is the covenantal pathway to sustained increase. Early fathers emphasized the necessity of correction for leaders who would shepherd communities faithfully. Discipleship provides the relational context where correction is restorative rather than punitive. When correction is embraced, stewardship matures.

Discipline governs how success is managed as increase arrives, and Proverbs warns against pride that follows sudden gain, revealing the danger of self-exaltation (Proverbs 16:18; 11:2). Sons and daughters who remain disciplined during seasons of blessing preserve teachability and accountability, preventing the corruption that often accompanies unchecked influence. This posture protects legacy and ensures that blessing multiplies rather than collapses. Historical Christian practice included accountability structures for leaders to prevent the abuses of power that destroy movements. Discipleship forms humility that sustains stewardship through success. When discipline governs success, growth remains pure.

Discipline sustains growth across seasons because preparation and steady formation create resilience, and Proverbs teaches that readiness preserves life (Proverbs 6:6–8; 21:5). Sons and daughters who anticipate change and prepare accordingly avoid panic and waste when transitions occur. This foresight preserves resources and relationships that are essential for continuity. Early church communities that planned for future needs—training leaders, storing resources, and building institutions—survived crises and multiplied witness. Discipleship trains leaders to steward for continuity rather than immediate gratification. When discipline prepares the way, covenant increase endures.

Discipline ultimately reveals that sustainable increase is not accidental but formed, and Proverbs shows that correction, order, and steady formation produce leaders who can steward well across generations (Proverbs 4:1–9; 13:22). Sons and daughters who embrace discipline build lives and institutions that outlast them, converting present stewardship into generational capacity. This covenantal perspective transforms how resources are used and how influence is measured. Historical Christian legacies—schools, hospitals, care systems—are testimonies to disciplined stewardship across time. Discipleship is the means by which such legacies are formed and preserved. When discipline is embraced, the pathway of increase becomes enduring.

FAITHFUL LABOR AND THE BLESSING OF CONSISTENCY

Faithful labor in Proverbs is presented as the steady expression of trust rather than a pursuit of recognition, and it frames consistent work as a spiritual principle that produces abundance over time (Proverbs 10:4; 12:11). Sons and daughters who labor faithfully do not measure success by speed or visibility but by obedience and stewardship. Their confidence rests in the Father's oversight rather than in applause or affirmation. Early church teachers commended steady service as the mark of mature discipleship and the foundation for entrusted responsibility. Discipleship forms the heart to labor with faithfulness even when results are delayed. When consistency governs effort, blessing follows.

Faithful labor contrasts with restless striving and impatience, and Proverbs teaches that those who work steadily are satisfied while the restless chase wind (Proverbs 12:24; 19:2). Sons and daughters who resist the pressure to constantly shift direction preserve clarity and momentum for long-term projects. This steadiness protects them from burnout and the fragmentation that wastes resources. Historical Christian practice valued perseverance and endurance as essential for leaders who would shepherd communities through trials. Discipleship cultivates the patience necessary to sustain labor across seasons. When labor is faithful, provision remains stable.

Faithful labor shapes character through repetition and endurance, and Proverbs shows that diligence refines the soul and produces practical wisdom (Proverbs 4:7; 8:10–11). Sons and daughters who persist in steady work grow in patience, resilience, and competence that attract trust and responsibility. This formation opens doors that talent alone cannot unlock because character becomes the basis for entrustment. Early church communities multiplied leaders by entrusting them with consistent service and observing their faithfulness. Discipleship provides the context where repetition becomes formation rather than mere routine. When character is formed, stewardship expands.

Faithful labor guards against discouragement and despair by anchoring hope in covenant promises rather than immediate results, and Proverbs teaches that steady effort leads to reward (Proverbs 13:11; 20:4). Sons and daughters who labor faithfully remain anchored during slow or hidden seasons because their identity secures provision beyond visible outcomes. This endurance preserves joy and clarity of purpose. Historical Christian testimony shows that communities sustained by faithful labor often experienced multiplied provision when seasons turned. Discipleship forms the hope that endures through waiting. When perseverance governs labor, blessing matures.

Faithful labor invites favor without manipulation because consistent service demonstrates reliability and competence, and Proverbs links the diligent with standing before leaders (Proverbs 22:29). Sons and daughters who labor faithfully attract opportunities through reputation rather than through self-promotion. Their visibility is the result of steady competence rather than manufactured acclaim. Early church leaders who were known for faithful service were often entrusted with larger spheres of care and influence. Discipleship forms reputational trust through accountability and proven faithfulness. When favor flows from faithfulness, stewardship increases.

Faithful labor protects the heart from pride and entitlement by grounding success in obedience rather than in personal merit, and Proverbs warns that self-exaltation leads to loss (Proverbs 16:18; 11:2). Sons and daughters who labor consistently remain humble and teachable, preserving alignment with covenant priorities. This humility prevents the misuse of influence and guards against the corruption that often follows unchecked success. Historical Christian practice included accountability and mutual correction to preserve leaders' humility. Discipleship forms the posture that keeps labor pure and service-centered. When humility governs labor, blessing remains untainted.

Faithful labor produces peace within work because steady effort brings rest rather than exhaustion, and Proverbs teaches that the diligent enjoy the fruit of their hands (Proverbs 10:4; 12:14). Sons and daughters who labor faithfully avoid extremes of overwork and neglect because their rhythm is ordered by wisdom and rest. This balance sustains joy and endurance across seasons. Early church rhythms of work and prayer preserved leaders and multiplied witness by preventing burnout. Discipleship forms habits that balance diligence with renewal. When peace governs labor, provision carries no sorrow.

Faithful labor strengthens discernment through experience because repeated practice reveals patterns and refines judgment, and Proverbs links wisdom with practice (Proverbs 1:5; 2:2–6). Sons and daughters who labor consistently learn to recognize God's guidance and to make better decisions over time. This practical discernment protects resources and relationships from costly mistakes. Historical Christian leaders who combined practice with counsel multiplied their capacity to steward communities. Discipleship provides the environment where experience is interpreted and refined. When wisdom grows through labor, stewardship deepens.

Faithful labor links present effort with future entrustment because those who are faithful in small things are given greater responsibility, and Proverbs affirms this pattern of progressive trust (Proverbs 28:20; 27:23–27). Sons and daughters who demonstrate reliability are more likely to be entrusted with larger spheres of influence and resources. This progressive entrustment is the covenantal mechanism by which stewardship scales across generations. Early church practice of mentoring and progressive responsibility prepared leaders to receive and exercise authority wisely. Discipleship creates the testing ground for proven faithfulness. When trust is earned, prosperity expands responsibly.

Faithful labor shapes how seasons are navigated wisely

because consistent effort during times of abundance prepares for times of scarcity, and Proverbs commends foresight and preparation (Proverbs 6:6–8; 21:5). Sons and daughters who labor faithfully recognize seasons of sowing and reaping and steward accordingly. Their awareness prevents panic and waste and positions resources for strategic deployment. Historical Christian communities practiced mutual aid and preparation that sustained them through famine and persecution. Discipleship trains leaders to steward across cycles rather than react to them. When seasons are honored, provision remains steady.

Faithful labor produces confidence rather than pressure because steady competence invites trust and reduces the need for frantic performance, and Proverbs links the diligent with standing before kings (Proverbs 22:29). Sons and daughters who labor faithfully carry quiet assurance that attracts opportunity and partnership. Their confidence flows from obedience rather than comparison. Early church leaders formed through faithful service were often sought for counsel and entrusted with communal care. Discipleship forms the inner assurance that sustains leadership. When confidence grows, influence expands.

Faithful labor ultimately reveals that blessing is the fruit of steady obedience rather than frantic striving, and Proverbs teaches that the diligent reap reward while the slothful suffer want (Proverbs 10:4; 12:24). Sons and daughters who labor faithfully experience provision that is steady, sustainable, and generational. Their lives reflect order, peace, and clarity because their work is shaped by covenant priorities. Historical Christian witness confirms that communities formed by faithful labor multiplied provision and preserved legacy. Discipleship is the means by which such labor is cultivated and sustained. When faithfulness endures, blessing multiplies.

REST, RHYTHM, AND THE WISDOM OF KNOWING WHEN TO PAUSE

Rest in Proverbs is not the absence of diligence but the preservation of it, and wisdom understands proper timing so that labor produces fruit rather than exhaustion (Proverbs 3:24; 6:6–8). Sons and daughters who honor rhythm recognize that unbroken labor leads to depletion and that pause is a form of stewardship. This wisdom protects both soul and stewardship capacity, enabling long-term service without collapse. Early church rhythms—work, prayer, rest, and communal care—modeled sustainable patterns that preserved leaders and multiplied witness. Discipleship forms the habits that make rest a discipline rather than an indulgence. When rest is honored, diligence remains effective.

Rhythm links seasons of sowing and reaping with times of pause and reflection, and Proverbs commends those who prepare and who understand cycles (Proverbs 20:4; 21:5). Sons and daughters who observe seasons avoid panic and waste, positioning resources for strategic deployment when opportunity arrives. This seasonal wisdom enables generosity even in lean times because margin has been preserved. Historical Christian communities practiced communal stores and mutual aid as practical expressions of seasonal preparation. Discipleship trains leaders to steward across cycles rather than react to them. When rhythm governs life, increase becomes sustainable.

Rest guards the heart from striving and anxiety because Proverbs warns that anxious toil produces little, and a calm soul preserves clarity for wise decisions (Proverbs 12:25; 14:30). Sons and daughters who practice rest resist the cultural pressure to perform and instead trust covenant provision. This trust preserves discernment and prevents the compromises that come from fear-driven choices. Early fathers counseled that a tranquil heart is better positioned to hear God's voice and to steward well. Discipleship cultivates the inner peace that sustains long-term service. When rest replaces striving, provision remains secure.

Rest sharpens discernment rather than dulling it because reflection produces understanding, and Proverbs links stillness with insight (Proverbs 17:27; 18:13). Sons and daughters who pause intentionally gain perspective that prevents misaligned decisions and wasted resources. This clarity protects both reputation and stewardship capacity. Historical Christian practice of retreat, silence, and communal reflection preserved leaders from impulsive errors. Discipleship provides the rhythms that make reflection habitual rather than occasional. When rest is practiced, wisdom deepens.

Rest restores strength for future labor because renewal precedes fruitfulness, and Proverbs teaches that preparation and rest preserve life (Proverbs 6:6–8; 24:30–34). Sons and daughters who honor rest return to labor with renewed clarity and endurance rather than depleted energy. This renewal sustains consistency across seasons and prevents the collapse that follows prolonged strain. Early church communities modeled sabbath rhythms that preserved leaders and multiplied witness across generations. Discipleship forms the practices that make renewal regular and reliable. When rest restores strength, stewardship endures.

Rest establishes humility within stewardship because pausing acknowledges dependence on the Father rather than self-reliance, and Proverbs warns against self-exaltation (Proverbs 3:5–6; 16:18). Sons and daughters who pause recognize that provision is ultimately relational and not solely the product of human effort. This humility preserves alignment and prevents the pride that corrupts influence. Historical Christian formation emphasized dependence and communal reliance as safeguards for leaders. Discipleship cultivates the posture of dependence that keeps stewardship pure. When humility governs rest, covenant access remains intact.

Rest protects joy within work because ordered living produces satisfaction rather than pressure, and Proverbs links contentment with life (Proverbs 15:16; 17:22). Sons and daughters who honor rhythm experience work as vocation rather than as burden, and this joy sustains endurance across seasons. This contentment preserves clarity and gratitude that multiply relational capital. Early church communities practiced celebration and rest as integral to communal life, preserving morale and witness. Discipleship forms the habits that keep joy central to stewardship. When joy is protected, increase carries no sorrow.

Rest strengthens trust in God's timing because patience is wisdom, and Proverbs teaches that waiting often precedes reward (Proverbs 20:22; 21:5). Sons and daughters who pause resist the urge to force outcomes and instead steward what is entrusted with faith. This patience preserves resources and prevents the compromises that come from hurried decisions. Historical Christian testimony shows that patient communities often saw multiplied provision when seasons turned. Discipleship forms the patience necessary to steward across cycles. When timing is honored, provision unfolds naturally.

Rest guards against comparison and competition by creating space for contentment and focus on assignment, and Proverbs warns that envy disrupts peace (Proverbs 14:30; 23:4–5). Sons and daughters who pause remain centered on their calling rather than measuring themselves by others' success. This focus preserves clarity and prevents destructive striving. Early church communities that emphasized formation over status avoided the rivalries that fracture movements. Discipleship cultivates contentment and a focus on vocation rather than applause. When rest guards the heart, alignment remains intact.

Rest prepares the heart for obedience because a quiet spirit receives instruction, and Proverbs links teachability with life and favor (Proverbs 1:7; 9:10). Sons and daughters who pause become attentive to God's direction and more responsive to correction. This readiness sharpens discernment and protects future decisions.

Historical Christian practice of retreat and communal reflection created leaders who could hear and obey with clarity. Discipleship provides the environment where stillness becomes receptivity. When rest prepares the heart, obedience flows easily.

Rest is essential to sustainable increase because it preserves capacity, cultivates wisdom, and protects joy, and Proverbs teaches that endurance requires renewal (Proverbs 6:6–8; 24:30–34). Sons and daughters who honor rhythm experience steady growth without exhaustion, and their stewardship becomes generational rather than seasonal. This covenantal perspective transforms how resources are used and how influence is measured. Historical Christian legacies testify that rhythms of work and rest preserved leaders and multiplied witness across centuries. Discipleship is the means by which such rhythms are formed and sustained. When rest is honored, Heaven's economy endures.

CHAPTER SIX — GENEROSITY: THE COVENANT FLOW OF RESOURCES

Generosity as a Covenant Law

Generosity in Proverbs is presented not as optional charity but as a covenantal principle that governs the flow of Heaven's resources, and it functions like a law that produces predictable returns when practiced from identity rather than obligation (Proverbs 11:24–25). Sons and daughters who give from belonging and stewardship release a current that invites relational returns and divine partnership, because covenant exchange is relational rather than transactional. This covenant law reframes giving as an act of alignment: it declares trust in the Father's provision and participates in the economy He governs. Early church teachers observed that communal sharing was not merely benevolence but the practical expression of family identity, and writers like Chrysostom commended the church's generosity as a sign of covenant life. Discipleship forms the heart to give without calculation, teaching that generosity is a habit of the formed soul rather than a response to guilt. When generosity is practiced as covenant law, resources circulate in ways that sustain life and multiply influence.

Generosity as covenant law requires a posture of trust because it assumes that the Father's provision is sufficient and that stewardship is an entrusted responsibility rather than personal ownership, and Proverbs links giving with blessing rather than loss (Proverbs 3:9–10). Sons and daughters who give from trust do not clutch resources out of fear but steward them for Kingdom purposes, knowing that honor and firstfruits invite overflow. This posture protects against the scarcity thinking that drives hoarding and short-term manipulation. Augustine and other early fathers taught that true charity flows from a heart formed by reverence and dependence, and they saw communal generosity as evidence of spiritual maturity. Discipleship trains the soul to trust through repeated acts of obedience that rewire imagination from scarcity to stewardship. When trust governs giving, covenant channels open and provision follows.

Generosity as covenant law is practiced with wisdom because Proverbs warns against reckless giving that leads to ruin, and it commends discernment in how resources are deployed (Proverbs 21:20; 11:24). Sons and daughters who steward generously also steward prudently, balancing immediate compassion with long-term sustainability so that generosity becomes enduring rather than episodic. This wisdom protects both giver and recipient and ensures that resources are multiplied rather than exhausted. Early church communities combined radical sharing with practical systems of care—oversight, accountability, and planning—to preserve capacity across seasons. Discipleship forms the discernment to give strategically and to build structures that sustain generosity. When generosity is wise, the covenant flow becomes sustainable.

Generosity as covenant law is communal by design because Proverbs links blessing with the care of the vulnerable and with equitable exchange, and covenant life multiplies when resources are shared within a formed community (Proverbs 14:31; 19:17). Sons and daughters who practice generosity in community create networks of mutual aid that preserve dignity and multiply provision across seasons. This communal generosity prevents isolation and creates resilience in times of scarcity. Early Christian practice of shared resources and mutual care demonstrated how covenant generosity could sustain entire neighborhoods and preserve witness under pressure. Discipleship cultivates communal habits—regular giving, shared counsel, and mutual accountability—that make generosity habitual rather than exceptional. When generosity is communal, the covenant flow strengthens the whole body.

Generosity as covenant law is an expression of identity because giving from sonship reveals that resources are entrusted rather than owned, and Proverbs links faithful stewardship with increased responsibility (Proverbs 28:20). Sons and daughters who give from identity demonstrate that their security rests in relationship rather than in accumulation, and this posture invites greater entrustment. This identity-driven generosity protects against the pride and entitlement that often accompany wealth. Early fathers taught that the truly wealthy are those who give freely and that generosity is the visible sign of a heart aligned with Heaven. Discipleship forms identity through repeated practice so that giving becomes natural and not performative. When generosity flows from identity, covenant access is evident.

Generosity as covenant law transforms motives by replacing transactional calculation with sacrificial love, and Proverbs commends the generous soul that refreshes others and is refreshed in return (Proverbs 11:25). Sons and daughters who give sacrificially reflect the Father's heart and participate in a flow that blesses both giver and receiver. This sacrificial posture resists the temptation to measure return and instead trusts the relational economy of covenant reciprocity. Early church writings celebrated martyr generosity and communal sharing as the highest expression of discipleship, showing that sacrifice often precedes multiplied provision. Discipleship forms sacrificial habits through communal practice and teaching that values people over profit. When generosity is sacrificial, the covenant flow becomes a testimony of God's provision.

SCATTERING AND INCREASING

Proverbs teaches a paradox: scattering often precedes increase, and the act of giving widely can produce multiplication rather than depletion (Proverbs 11:24; 11:25). Sons and daughters who scatter resources into people, mission, and formation often find that what they release returns in unexpected forms—favor, opportunity, and multiplied provision. This pattern is not magical but covenantal: generosity opens relational channels that invite reciprocal blessing and partnership. Early Christian communities practiced wide distribution of resources—care for widows, hospitality, and mission—and observed that scattering multiplied witness and provision. Discipleship trains the heart to scatter with wisdom, trusting that the Father multiplies what is released for Kingdom purposes. When scattering is practiced, increase often follows.

Scattering and increasing requires faith to release what seems scarce, because the visible ledger may show loss even as unseen relational returns are being established, and Proverbs links faithfulness in giving with eventual blessing (Proverbs 3:9–10). Sons and daughters who step out in faith to scatter resources participate in a covenant dynamic that values trust over immediate accounting. This faith is formed through repeated obedience and through communal testimony of God's faithfulness. Early church narratives recount communities that gave sacrificially in famine and persecution and later experienced multiplied provision through networks of care. Discipleship forms the courage to scatter in faith rather than clutch in fear. When faith accompanies scattering, increase is often the result.

Scattering and increasing is strategic when it targets formation and multiplication—investing in people, training, and institutions that reproduce stewardship rather than merely consuming resources (Proverbs 13:22). Sons and daughters who scatter into discipleship, education, and community structures create leverage that multiplies impact across generations. This strategic scattering converts present sacrifice into future capacity. Early Christian institutions—schools, hospitals, and catechetical systems—were examples of strategic scattering that produced long-term fruit. Discipleship ensures that scattering is not random but intentional, aligning gifts with covenant priorities. When scattering is strategic, increase compounds.

Scattering and increasing requires discernment to avoid enabling dependency, because Proverbs warns against enabling laziness and calls for wise stewardship that empowers rather than enslaves (Proverbs 19:17; 20:13). Sons and daughters who scatter with wisdom design pathways for recipients to grow in dignity and capacity rather than creating long-term dependence. This discernment preserves resources and multiplies fruit by equipping others to steward. Early church care models combined relief with training and community integration to restore dignity and multiply resilience. Discipleship forms the discernment to give in ways that empower recipients toward stewardship. When scattering empowers, increase becomes generational.

Scattering and increasing is relational because it builds networks of reciprocity where trust and reputation circulate as forms of capital, and Proverbs links a good name with favor that opens doors (Proverbs 22:1; 18:16). Sons and daughters who scatter build reputational capital by honoring others and investing in relationships that later return as opportunities and support. This relational multiplication is practical: it creates partnerships, referrals, and collaborative ventures that expand capacity. Early Christian communities that practiced hospitality and mutual aid became hubs of influence and care. Discipleship forms the relational skills to scatter wisely and to steward networks responsibly. When scattering builds relationships, increase follows.

Scattering and increasing also reshapes imagination from scarcity to abundance because repeated acts of release train the soul to expect multiplication rather than depletion, and Proverbs teaches that generous giving often results in unexpected return (Proverbs 11:25). Sons and daughters who practice scattering reshape their expectations and begin to see resources as channels rather than endpoints. This shift in imagination changes decision-making and risk tolerance in ways that enable larger stewardship. Early church testimony shows that communities formed by generous practice often experienced multiplied provision through mutual care and external favor. Discipleship rewires imagination through repeated practice and testimony. When imagination is reshaped, scattering becomes a habit that produces increase.

Scattering and increasing requires patience because multiplication often unfolds over seasons rather than instantly, and Proverbs commends those who prepare and wait for harvest (Proverbs 6:6–8; 21:5). Sons and daughters who scatter with patience avoid the temptation to demand immediate return and instead steward for long-term fruit. This patience preserves resources and prevents the discouragement that can follow delayed results. Historical Christian practice of planting institutions and training leaders demonstrates that patient scattering yields generational impact. Discipleship forms the endurance to scatter faithfully across seasons. When patience accompanies scattering, increase matures.

Scattering and increasing is tested by seasons of scarcity, and the covenant proves itself when generosity persists under pressure, because Proverbs links steadfastness with eventual reward (Proverbs 11:25; 19:17). Sons and daughters who continue to scatter in lean times demonstrate that their giving is identity-driven rather than reactive, and this steadfastness often invites supernatural provision. Early church communities that shared during famine and persecution often found unexpected provision through networks and divine favor. Discipleship forms the resolve to give when it is hardest, revealing the depth of covenant trust. When generosity persists in scarcity, the covenant flow deepens.

Scattering and increasing requires communal structures to multiply effectively, because individual acts of generosity are amplified when coordinated through accountable systems that steward gifts for maximum impact (Proverbs 24:3–4). Sons and daughters who build transparent systems—teams, budgets, and oversight—ensure that scattered resources are multiplied rather than dissipated. This organizational wisdom preserves trust and enables scaling of generosity. Early Christian institutions developed governance and care systems that multiplied the effect of communal giving. Discipleship trains leaders to design structures that steward generosity responsibly. When systems support scattering, increase is optimized.

Scattering and increasing is a spiritual discipline that forms character as much as it distributes resources, because repeated release cultivates a heart of trust, humility, and dependence on the Father (Proverbs 11:24–25). Sons and daughters who practice scattering are shaped by the habit of giving, and their character becomes the primary asset that attracts further stewardship. This formation is the covenantal logic: character precedes capacity. Early church formation emphasized habitual generosity as a mark of maturity and a safeguard for communal life. Discipleship provides the rhythms that make scattering a formative practice rather than a sporadic act. When scattering forms character, increase becomes sustainable.

Scattering and increasing ultimately reveals that Heaven's economy multiplies what is released for Kingdom purposes, and Proverbs shows that generosity often results in unexpected blessing and multiplied capacity (Proverbs 11:25). Sons and daughters who scatter with wisdom, faith, and patience participate in a covenant flow that honors the Father and blesses communities. This pattern is both spiritual and practical: it produces relational returns, institutional capacity, and generational legacy. Early church witness confirms that communities formed by scattering multiplied provision and influence across seasons. Discipleship is the means by which scattering becomes habitual and fruitful. When scattering is embraced, the covenant multiplies its resources.

REFRESHING OTHERS AS ACCESS

Refreshing others is a form of access in the covenant because when sons and daughters refresh people—through generosity, encouragement, and practical care—they open relational channels that invite reciprocal blessing and responsibility (Proverbs 11:25; 19:17). This refreshing is not transactional but relational: it communicates value and creates trust that later becomes a platform for stewardship. The act of refreshing others often positions givers to receive opportunities and support that are not available to those who hoard. Early church practice of hospitality and care for the vulnerable demonstrated how refreshing others multiplied witness and provision. Discipleship forms the posture of refreshing as a daily habit rather than a sporadic charity. When others are refreshed, covenant access is often granted.

Refreshing others functions as spiritual hospitality that creates environments where gifts and callings can flourish, and Proverbs links hospitality with blessing and favor (Proverbs 3:27; 22:9). Sons and daughters who practice hospitality and practical care create spaces where people are empowered and where networks of mutual support form. This hospitality becomes a strategic avenue for stewardship because it cultivates relationships that later yield collaborative opportunities. Early Christian households that practiced radical hospitality became centers of mission and multiplication. Discipleship trains communities to welcome and to resource others in ways that multiply capacity. When hospitality refreshes, access expands.

Refreshing others is a form of investment in human capital because it strengthens people's capacity to contribute and to steward, and Proverbs commends the one who gives to the poor as lending to the Lord (Proverbs 19:17). Sons and daughters who refresh others invest in skills, dignity, and relational trust that later return as multiplied fruit. This investment perspective prevents paternalism and focuses on empowerment and capacity building. Early church care models combined relief with training and integration so that recipients became contributors rather than perpetual dependents. Discipleship forms the discernment to refresh in ways that equip others for stewardship. When investment accompanies refreshing, access multiplies.

Refreshing others creates reputational capital because those who are known for renewing others attract trust and partnership, and Proverbs links a good name with favor (Proverbs 22:1). Sons and daughters who consistently refresh others build reputations for reliability and compassion that open doors for collaboration and stewardship. This reputational capital is practical: it invites leaders to entrust resources and responsibilities to those who have demonstrated care. Early Christian leaders who were known for hospitality and care were often sought for counsel and entrusted with communal oversight. Discipleship forms reputational trust through consistent practice and accountability. When reputation is built by refreshing others, covenant access increases.

Refreshing others is a spiritual practice that cultivates humility because it requires seeing need and responding without seeking credit, and Proverbs warns against self-exaltation while commending humility (Proverbs 16:18; 22:4). Sons and daughters who refresh others do so from identity rather than for applause, and this humility preserves integrity and invites divine favor. This posture prevents the corruption that often follows public recognition and keeps stewardship pure. Early church writings praised anonymous generosity and humble service as marks of true discipleship. Discipleship forms the inner motive that sustains refreshing as a humble practice. When humility governs refreshing, access is granted without cost to character.

Refreshing others is a means of spiritual warfare because it counters the isolating effects of scarcity and fear, and Proverbs links generosity with the breaking of oppression and the restoration of life (Proverbs 14:31; 22:9). Sons and daughters who refresh others weaken the cultural narratives of scarcity and build communities of abundance and mutual care. This restorative work protects social and spiritual capital that sustains mission. Early Christian communities that practiced mutual aid resisted the corrosive effects of poverty and persecution by creating networks of care. Discipleship equips believers to see refreshing as strategic resistance to scarcity culture. When refreshing counters fear, covenant access is preserved.

Refreshing others requires discernment to ensure that help leads to dignity and capacity rather than dependency, and Proverbs calls for wise counsel and planning in stewardship (Proverbs 15:22; 21:5). Sons and daughters who refresh with strategy design pathways for recipients to grow in competence and contribution. This discernment preserves resources and multiplies fruit by equipping others to steward. Early church practice combined relief with training and community integration to restore dignity and multiply resilience. Discipleship forms the wisdom to refresh in ways that empower recipients toward stewardship. When refreshing is strategic, access becomes generational.

Refreshing others multiplies spiritual fruit because acts of care open hearts to instruction and formation, and Proverbs links hospitality and care with the spread of wisdom and influence (Proverbs 3:27; 11:30). Sons and daughters who refresh others often find that those they serve become carriers of wisdom and partners in stewardship. This multiplication is both spiritual and practical: it expands the pool of competent stewards and multiplies influence. Early church hospitality often accompanied teaching and formation, producing leaders who carried the faith into new contexts. Discipleship integrates refreshing with instruction so that care and formation advance together. When refreshing is paired with formation, covenant access deepens.

Refreshing others builds reciprocal networks that function as practical insurance in seasons of need, because those who have been refreshed are often the first to respond when others face crisis, and Proverbs commends mutual aid and counsel (Proverbs 17:17; 11:14). Sons and daughters who cultivate reciprocal relationships create resilient communities that can weather shocks without collapse. This reciprocal network is economic because it preserves labor, morale, and resources that sustain productivity. Early Christian communities relied on mutual aid networks that multiplied provision during famine and persecution. Discipleship forms the relational habits that make reciprocity reliable rather than accidental. When networks are reciprocal, covenant access is secure.

Refreshing others opens doors of influence because those who are known for renewing people are often invited into broader spheres of responsibility, and Proverbs links generosity with standing before leaders (Proverbs 22:29; 18:16). Sons and daughters who refresh others gain credibility and are more likely to be entrusted with opportunities that multiply stewardship. This influence is practical: it enables collaborative ventures and delegated authority that expand capacity. Early church leaders who practiced hospitality and care were often sought for counsel and entrusted with communal oversight. Discipleship forms the character that makes such entrustment wise. When refreshing builds influence, covenant access expands.

Refreshing others is a spiritual discipline that forms the giver as much as the recipient, because repeated acts of care cultivate compassion, humility, and dependence on the Father, and Proverbs links the generous heart with life and favor (Proverbs 11:25; 19:17). Sons and daughters who make refreshing habitual are shaped into reliable stewards whose character attracts further responsibility. This formation is the covenantal logic: the giver is prepared to steward greater trusts through the practice of care. Early church formation emphasized habitual service as a mark of maturity and a safeguard for communal life. Discipleship provides the rhythms that make refreshing a formative practice. When refreshing forms the giver, covenant access is multiplied.

Refreshing others ultimately reveals that access in Heaven's economy is relational: those who bless and renew people participate in a flow that opens doors of provision, partnership, and responsibility, and Proverbs shows that generosity refreshes both giver and receiver (Proverbs 11:25). Sons and daughters who refresh others live in the covenant rhythm where blessing circulates and multiplies. This relational access is both spiritual and practical, producing networks, reputation, and institutional capacity. Early church witness confirms that communities formed by refreshing multiplied provision and influence across seasons. Discipleship is the means by which refreshing becomes habitual and fruitful. When others are refreshed, the covenant flow of resources is activated.

THE GENEROUS SOUL MADE RICH AND HOW GENEROSITY REVEALS SONSHIP

The generous soul is described in Proverbs as being made rich, not merely in material terms but in relational capital, spiritual depth, and lasting influence, and this richness often exceeds what mere accumulation can produce (Proverbs 11:25; 19:17). Sons and daughters who give from identity discover that their lives are enriched by community, favor, and opportunities that arise from faithful stewardship. This richness is a composite of reputation, networks, and formed character that opens doors for further stewardship. Early church writers celebrated the generous soul as truly wealthy because such persons multiplied blessing across communities and seasons. Discipleship forms the generous soul through repeated practice and communal reinforcement. When generosity shapes life, true richness follows.

Generosity reveals sonship because giving from belonging demonstrates that security is relational rather than material, and Proverbs links the fear of the Lord with life and honor that surpasses wealth (Proverbs 1:7; 22:4). Sons and daughters who give sacrificially show that their identity is rooted in covenant and not in accumulation, and this posture attracts both divine favor and human trust. Generosity therefore becomes a visible sign of inheritance rather than a performance to earn favor. Early Christian communities saw generosity as the hallmark of family identity, and fathers like Augustine taught that charity is the evidence of a heart aligned with God. Discipleship forms the inner conviction that enables generosity to be authentic rather than performative. When generosity reveals sonship, covenant access is unmistakable.

The generous soul is enriched by reciprocal blessing because Proverbs teaches that giving often results in unexpected returns—favor, opportunity, and multiplied provision—and these returns compound relationally rather than merely financially (Proverbs 11:25). Sons and daughters who give strategically and sacrificially often find doors opening that were previously closed, and these openings multiply stewardship capacity. This reciprocal blessing is relational and practical: it creates partnerships, referrals, and collaborative ventures that expand influence. Early church testimony shows that communities known for generosity attracted support and multiplied witness. Discipleship forms the humility to receive and the wisdom to steward returned blessing. When reciprocity accompanies generosity, richness increases.

Generosity reveals sonship through the posture of stewardship because heirs treat resources as entrusted rather than owned, and Proverbs links faithful stewardship with increased responsibility (Proverbs 28:20; 27:23–27). Sons and daughters who steward generously demonstrate that they understand accountability and that they are prepared for delegated authority. This stewardship posture protects against entitlement and prepares heirs for larger trusts. Early church practice of entrusting responsibilities to proven servants ensured that inheritance included competence and character. Discipleship provides the testing ground where stewardship is proven through small responsibilities. When stewardship accompanies generosity, sonship is evident.

The generous soul is rich in influence because generosity builds reputational capital that invites trust and partnership, and Proverbs links a good name with favor that opens doors (Proverbs 22:1; 18:16). Sons and daughters who give consistently build reputations for reliability and compassion that attract collaborative opportunities and delegated authority. This influence is practical: it enables scaling of mission and stewardship through trusted networks. Early Christian leaders known for generosity were often sought for counsel and entrusted with communal oversight. Discipleship forms reputational trust through consistent practice and accountability. When generosity builds influence, the covenant entrusts more.

Generosity reveals sonship by shaping motives away from self-exaltation toward communal flourishing, because Proverbs warns that pride precedes ruin while humility precedes honor (Proverbs 16:18; 22:4). Sons and daughters who give from identity resist the temptation to use generosity for status and instead invest in people and institutions that multiply blessing. This motive preserves integrity and ensures that generosity produces lasting fruit rather than temporary acclaim. Early church writings condemned ostentatious giving and praised humble charity as the truest expression of discipleship. Discipleship forms motives through accountability and communal correction. When motives are pure, generosity reveals true sonship.

The generous soul is rich in spiritual depth because repeated acts of giving cultivate dependence on the Father and humility before others, and Proverbs links the fear of the Lord with wisdom and life (Proverbs 1:7; 9:10). Sons and daughters who practice generosity grow in trust, teachability, and spiritual maturity that prepare them for greater stewardship. This depth is the primary asset that attracts further responsibility and multiplies influence. Early church formation emphasized habitual charity as a means of spiritual growth and communal preservation. Discipleship provides the rhythms that make generosity formative rather than episodic. When generosity forms depth, the covenant entrusts treasures.

Generosity reveals sonship through the practice of honor because giving often accompanies honoring others—leaders, elders, and the vulnerable—and Proverbs links honor with favor and influence (Proverbs 3:9–10; 18:16). Sons and daughters who give while honoring relationships create environments of trust that invite delegated responsibility and partnership. This honor protects against exploitation and preserves relational capital that multiplies stewardship. Early Christian communities practiced honor through submission to elders and mutual respect, which preserved unity and multiplied witness. Discipleship forms the habit of honoring others as a practical expression of sonship. When honor accompanies generosity, covenant access is amplified.

The generous soul is rich in legacy because generosity invested in formation, institutions, and families compounds across generations, and Proverbs commends leaving an inheritance for children's children (Proverbs 13:22). Sons and daughters who give strategically to training, structures, and discipleship create multiplying effects that outlast a single lifetime. This legacy orientation converts present sacrifice into future capacity and influence. Historical Christian institutions—schools, hospitals, and charitable trusts—are testimonies to generosity that produced generational blessing. Discipleship ensures that generosity is paired with formation so that legacy is preserved. When generosity builds legacy, the hidden covenant continues to bless.

Generosity reveals sonship by producing joy and contentment rather than anxiety, because Proverbs links a generous heart with life and satisfaction (Proverbs 11:25; 15:16). Sons and daughters who give from identity experience a freedom that resists the clutch of scarcity and finds joy in blessing others. This joy sustains endurance and prevents the corrosive effects of envy and comparison. Early church communities that practiced joyful generosity preserved morale and multiplied witness even under hardship. Discipleship forms the inner contentment that makes generosity sustainable. When generosity produces joy, covenant increase carries no sorrow.

The generous soul is rich because generosity aligns motives with Heaven's priorities and invites supernatural partnership, and Proverbs teaches that the blessing of the Lord brings wealth without painful toil (Proverbs 10:22). Sons and daughters who give in alignment with covenant values often find doors opening that are not explained by human effort alone. This supernatural partnership is relational and practical: it multiplies resources and influence through favor and opportunity. Early church testimony records instances where sacrificial giving preceded multiplied provision through networks and divine favor. Discipleship forms the posture that invites such partnership. When generosity aligns with covenant, the Father's economy flows.

Generosity reveals sonship finally because it is the visible fruit of an inward reality: a heart formed by reverence, dependence, and teachability, and Proverbs links the fear of the Lord with life, honor, and wisdom (Proverbs 1:7; 22:4). Sons and daughters who give from this inward reality demonstrate that their identity is rooted in covenant and that their stewardship is trustworthy. This visible fruit invites entrustment, multiplies influence, and secures legacy for future generations. Early church formation practiced generosity as a mark of family identity and a test of character.

CHAPTER SEVEN — HONOR: THE RELATIONAL CURRENCY OF HEAVEN

Honor Opens Doors

Honor functions in Proverbs as a relational key that opens doors of favor and opportunity, and it is presented as a practical currency that multiplies stewardship when practiced with humility (Proverbs 3:9; 18:16). Sons and daughters who honor others—leaders, neighbors, and institutions—create environments of trust where resources and responsibility flow more freely than through coercion or manipulation. Honor is not flattery but a posture of recognition that affirms dignity and invites reciprocal trust, and Proverbs links honor with favor that precedes increase. Early church teachers like John Chrysostom taught that honor toward elders and the poor preserved communal unity and attracted divine blessing, showing that honor has both spiritual and social consequences. Discipleship forms the habit of honoring others through repeated practice, teaching the heart to esteem rather than to exploit. When honor is practiced, doors that were closed by suspicion and rivalry begin to open through relationships of trust.

Honor opens doors because it signals reliability and character to those who must entrust resources and influence, and Proverbs repeatedly ties a good name to access and opportunity (Proverbs 22:1; 11:3). Sons and daughters who protect reputation through consistent honor are more likely to be recommended, partnered with, and delegated responsibility by leaders and communities. This reputational currency reduces friction in transactions and multiplies cooperative ventures because others can predict integrity. Early Christian communities that honored one another became hubs of hospitality and mission, and writers like Augustine observed that honor among believers attracted civic trust and opened avenues for service. Discipleship disciplines —accountability, confession, and mutual correction— preserve reputation so that honor continues to open doors. When reputation is stewarded, relational access expands.

Honor opens doors by creating bridges across social and cultural divides, because honoring the other disarms suspicion and invites collaboration, and Proverbs commends the peacemaker and the one who seeks wise counsel (Proverbs 11:14; 16:7). Sons and daughters who practice honor intentionally cross barriers of class, ethnicity, and status to build networks that multiply capacity and care. This bridge-building is economic as well as spiritual: it enlarges the pool of partners, donors, and stewards who can be mobilized for common purposes. Early church practice of hospitality and honoring strangers turned households into centers of care and mission, demonstrating how honor expands influence beyond immediate circles. Discipleship trains believers to honor across difference, creating durable networks that open doors in unexpected places. When bridges are built by honor, opportunities multiply.

Honor opens doors because it cultivates favor in leadership circles where decisions about entrustment are made, and Proverbs links honor with standing before rulers and leaders (Proverbs 22:29; 18:16). Sons and daughters who honor those in authority without sycophancy gain access to mentorship, recommendation, and delegated responsibility that accelerate stewardship capacity. This access is practical: it creates pathways for institutional influence and for the scaling of mission. Early church leaders who honored civic and ecclesial authorities while maintaining integrity often found doors opened for ministry and care. Discipleship forms the posture that honors authority while preserving conscience, enabling wise access to leadership spheres. When honor is practiced toward leaders, institutional doors open for stewardship.

Honor opens doors by preserving relational capital in times of crisis, because those who have honored others are more likely to receive support when seasons turn difficult, and Proverbs links faithful relationships with mutual aid (Proverbs 17:17; 27:10). Sons and daughters who have invested honor into networks find that those networks respond in times of need, providing counsel, resources, and shelter. This reciprocal protection is economic because it functions as practical insurance against shocks that would otherwise collapse stewardship capacity. Early Christian communities that honored one another sustained each other through famine and persecution, showing how honor becomes a lifeline. Discipleship forms the long-term investments of honor that yield support when trials come. When honor is stored relationally, doors of refuge and provision open.

Honor opens doors because it aligns with Heaven's order, and Proverbs teaches that humility and honor precede blessing while pride precedes ruin (Proverbs 22:4; 16:18). Sons and daughters who practice honor reflect covenant priorities and therefore attract both human favor and divine partnership. This alignment is not manipulative but obedient: honor is a fruit of reverence that positions people under covenant promises. Early fathers taught that honor toward God and neighbor was the outward sign of an inwardly ordered heart, and that such hearts were entrusted with greater stewardship. Discipleship forms the inner posture that naturally expresses honor, making access a byproduct of alignment rather than a tactic. When honor aligns life with Heaven, doors open as part of covenant flow.

Honor opens doors because it creates a culture where gifts and callings are recognized and released, and Proverbs commends the one who gives honor to the worthy (Proverbs 31:31). Sons and daughters who honor emerging leaders and faithful servants create pathways for delegation and multiplication, enabling stewardship to scale through others. This culture of recognition prevents bottlenecks of control and invites distributed responsibility. Early church practice of ordaining and honoring elders and deacons multiplied care and preserved unity across growing communities. Discipleship trains communities to spot and honor faithful service so that stewardship is multiplied through many hands. When honor releases gifts, doors open for broader stewardship.

Honor opens doors because it protects against the corrosive effects of envy and rivalry, and Proverbs warns that envy rots the bones while honor preserves peace (Proverbs 14:30; 15:18). Sons and daughters who choose to honor rather than to compare create environments where collaboration is possible and where resources are pooled for common good. This cooperative culture reduces wasteful competition and multiplies collective capacity. Early Christian communities that practiced mutual honor avoided the factionalism that destroyed other movements, preserving witness and influence. Discipleship forms the humility to celebrate others and to steward communal resources rather than hoard them. When honor displaces envy, doors open for shared increase.

Honor opens doors because it models a posture that invites mentorship and formation, and Proverbs links instruction with life and favor (Proverbs 4:1–9; 9:9). Sons and daughters who honor mentors and elders receive guidance that refines judgment and prepares them for greater responsibility. This mentorship is a practical pathway to access because it transmits wisdom, reputation, and relational networks. Early church structures of catechesis and mentoring ensured that honor toward teachers resulted in formation and entrustment. Discipleship creates the reciprocal dynamic where honor begets instruction and instruction begets access. When honor invites mentorship, doors open for competent stewardship.

Honor opens doors because it creates a moral climate that attracts investment and partnership, and Proverbs teaches that fair dealing and honor invite favor (Proverbs 11:1; 16:8). Sons and daughters who steward with honor attract partners who value integrity and who are willing to invest time and resources into shared projects. This attraction is practical: it lowers the barriers to collaboration and increases the pool of available capital for Kingdom work. Early Christian communities known for honorable practice often became centers of philanthropy and care. Discipleship forms the practices that make communities trustworthy partners. When honor attracts investment, doors open for expanded stewardship.

Honor opens doors because it preserves the dignity of those served, and Proverbs links care for the vulnerable with blessing and stability (Proverbs 14:31; 19:17). Sons and daughters who honor the poor, the widow, and the stranger create social systems that sustain life and invite communal flourishing. This preservation of dignity is economic because it maintains human capital and prevents the social breakdown that undermines prosperity. Early church care for the vulnerable demonstrated how honor toward the least multiplied communal resilience and witness. Discipleship trains hearts to honor the vulnerable as a practical expression of covenant. When dignity is preserved, doors open for communal flourishing.

Honor opens doors because it is contagious: when one person models honor, others are encouraged to follow, and Proverbs links righteous example with influence (Proverbs 11:30). Sons and daughters who live honorably inspire imitation and create cultures where honor becomes normative, multiplying relational capital across networks. This contagion accelerates the opening of doors because trust spreads and partnerships form more readily. Early Christian leaders who embodied honor catalyzed movements of care and formation that multiplied across regions. Discipleship amplifies honorable example through communal practice and testimony. When honor becomes contagious, doors open widely for the covenant economy.

HONOR AND AUTHORITY

Honor and authority are intertwined in Proverbs because authority is most safely exercised where honor is given and received, and honor legitimizes delegated power within covenant structures (Proverbs 16:12; 20:28). Sons and daughters who honor those in authority create a climate where leadership can function without coercion, and where authority is exercised for stewardship rather than self-exaltation. This relational legitimacy preserves institutions from the abuses that arise when authority is disconnected from honor. Early church structures—elders, presbyters, and deacons—relied on mutual honor to maintain order and to multiply care across communities. Discipleship forms the posture that honors authority while preserving accountability, enabling healthy delegation and growth. When honor and authority align, stewardship scales responsibly.

Honor grants moral authority because those who are honored are more likely to be heard and followed, and Proverbs links honor with influence and standing before leaders (Proverbs 22:29; 18:16). Sons and daughters who honor wise leaders gain access to counsel and mentorship that refine judgment and prepare them for delegated roles. This moral authority is practical: it creates channels for instruction, recommendation, and entrustment that expand stewardship capacity. Early church fathers taught that moral authority derived from character and honor rather than from coercive power, and they modeled leadership that attracted trust. Discipleship cultivates the character that earns honor and thus moral authority. When honor grants authority, stewardship is entrusted.

Honor stabilizes authority by creating reciprocal obligations: leaders who are honored feel responsible to steward well, and those who honor expect accountability and care, and Proverbs links faithful leadership with blessing (Proverbs 29:2; 11:14). Sons and daughters who honor leaders create a covenantal dynamic where authority is exercised for the common good and where leaders are held to standards of justice and mercy. This reciprocal structure prevents tyranny and preserves institutional integrity. Early Christian governance included mutual oversight precisely to maintain this balance between honor and accountability. Discipleship trains both leaders and followers in the practices that sustain reciprocal authority. When honor stabilizes authority, institutions endure.

Honor protects authority from corruption because leaders who are honored are less likely to resort to coercion and more likely to seek counsel and correction, and Proverbs warns that pride corrupts while humility preserves (Proverbs 16:18; 11:2). Sons and daughters who honor leaders encourage a culture of humility that resists the seduction of power and preserves stewardship purity. This protective effect is practical: it reduces abuses that destroy trust and capacity. Early church communities that honored elders while maintaining accountability avoided the scandals that fractured other movements. Discipleship forms the checks and balances—confession, counsel, and mutual oversight—that keep authority healthy. When honor protects authority, stewardship remains trustworthy.

Honor enables delegated authority to multiply stewardship because leaders who are honored are more willing to entrust responsibilities to proven servants, and Proverbs links faithfulness in small things with greater trust (Proverbs 28:20; 27:23–27). Sons and daughters who honor leaders and demonstrate reliability are often given increasing spheres of influence that expand communal capacity. This ladder of entrustment is the covenantal mechanism by which stewardship scales across generations. Early church practice of progressive responsibility prepared leaders to receive and exercise authority wisely. Discipleship provides the testing ground where honor and faithfulness are proven. When honor enables delegation, stewardship multiplies.

Honor clarifies the use of authority by orienting leaders toward service rather than self-exaltation, and Proverbs teaches that the greatest leaders are those who serve with humility (Proverbs 11:14; 16:12). Sons and daughters who honor servant leadership model an ethic where authority is measured by care for the vulnerable and by justice in governance. This servant posture preserves the moral purpose of authority and prevents its conversion into domination. Early Christian leaders modeled servant authority in ministry and care, showing that honor and service are inseparable. Discipleship forms leaders to exercise authority as stewardship rather than privilege. When honor shapes authority, institutions serve life.

Honor creates a climate where prophetic correction can be received without fracturing authority, because honored leaders are more likely to listen and to be corrected for the sake of the common good, and Proverbs links correction with life and wisdom (Proverbs 3:11–12; 9:8). Sons and daughters who honor leaders while speaking truth in love preserve both authority and accountability, enabling institutions to adapt and to remain healthy. This capacity for correction prevents stagnation and preserves trust. Early church structures included elders and councils precisely to provide channels for correction that honored both office and conscience. Discipleship trains communities to balance honor with courageous truth-telling. When honor allows correction, authority matures.

Honor and authority together create a predictable environment for stewardship because people can plan and invest where leadership is stable and trustworthy, and Proverbs links faithful governance with prosperity (Proverbs 29:2; 11:3). Sons and daughters who honor leaders contribute to institutional predictability that attracts partners and donors willing to invest in long-term projects. This predictability is economic: it lowers risk and multiplies cooperative ventures. Early Christian institutions that combined honorable leadership with transparent governance became centers of education, care, and mission. Discipleship forms the practices that make leadership predictable and trustworthy. When honor and authority produce predictability, stewardship scales.

Honor disciplines authority by reminding leaders of their accountability to God and community, and Proverbs teaches that those who rule must do so with justice and humility (Proverbs 16:12; 20:28). Sons and daughters who honor leaders also call them to righteousness, creating a covenantal pressure that preserves integrity. This disciplining function prevents the drift toward self-interest that undermines stewardship. Early church councils and communal oversight served to discipline authority and to protect the vulnerable. Discipleship forms the courage to honor while holding leaders accountable. When honor disciplines authority, stewardship remains aligned with covenant.

Honor and authority together shape legacy because leaders who are honored and who steward well leave institutions that outlast them, and Proverbs commends those who build for future generations (Proverbs 13:22; 21:5). Sons and daughters who honor leaders and who are formed under wise authority inherit structures and practices that enable generational stewardship. This legacy orientation converts present stewardship into future capacity. Historical Christian institutions—schools, hospitals, and charitable trusts—were often the fruit of honorable leadership and disciplined authority. Discipleship ensures that legacy is transmitted through formation and entrustment. When honor and authority build legacy, the covenant continues to bless.

Honor and authority together guard against factionalism because mutual respect and accountable leadership reduce the rivalries that fracture movements, and Proverbs warns against the strife that destroys unity (Proverbs 6:16–19; 16:28). Sons and daughters who honor leaders and who practice humility contribute to unity that preserves capacity and witness. This unity is economic because it enables coordinated action and pooled resources for common purposes. Early church communities that prioritized honor and accountable authority avoided the schisms that weakened other groups. Discipleship forms the relational habits that sustain unity under honorable leadership. When honor and authority prevent faction, stewardship is multiplied.

Honor and authority together invite divine partnership because leaders who are honored and who lead with justice align institutions with Heaven's priorities, and Proverbs links righteous governance with blessing (Proverbs 29:2; 16:12). Sons and daughters who honor such leadership participate in an economy where divine favor accompanies faithful stewardship. This partnership is both spiritual and practical: it opens doors, multiplies resources, and preserves legacy. Early church testimony records instances where honorable leadership attracted unexpected provision and influence. Discipleship forms the character that invites such partnership. When honor and authority align with Heaven, stewardship becomes a conduit of blessing.

HONOR AND ALIGNMENT

Honor and alignment are inseparable because honoring God and neighbor reorders motives and practices toward covenant priorities, and Proverbs teaches that alignment with the Lord brings direction and blessing (Proverbs 3:5–6; 8:20). Sons and daughters who honor God in their decisions align their stewardship with Heaven's economy rather than with worldly measures of success. This alignment produces clarity in planning, generosity in giving, and integrity in transactions that invite both human and divine favor. Early church fathers emphasized that honoring God first shaped all other relationships and that such alignment produced sustainable communities. Discipleship forms the inner orientation that keeps honor and alignment consistent rather than episodic. When honor aligns life with Heaven, stewardship becomes faithful.

Honor aligns communities by creating shared values that guide decision-making and resource allocation, and Proverbs links counsel and many advisors with safety and success (Proverbs 11:14; 15:22). Sons and daughters who honor one another cultivate common priorities—care for the vulnerable, investment in formation, and justice in commerce—that direct communal stewardship. This shared alignment prevents fragmentation and ensures that resources are deployed for covenant purposes rather than personal gain. Early Christian communities that practiced mutual honor developed coherent practices that multiplied care and witness. Discipleship forms the conversations and disciplines that keep communities aligned. When honor creates shared values, stewardship is coordinated.

Honor aligns leadership and membership by establishing expectations of service, accountability, and mutual care, and Proverbs teaches that those who lead must do so with justice and humility (Proverbs 16:12; 20:28). Sons and daughters who honor leaders while expecting righteous governance create a covenantal balance that preserves trust and prevents abuse. This alignment enables delegated stewardship because both leaders and followers share a common ethic. Early church governance models balanced honor with oversight to maintain this alignment. Discipleship trains both leaders and members in the practices that sustain mutual responsibility. When honor aligns leadership and membership, stewardship is entrusted wisely.

Honor aligns motives by shifting the heart from self-promotion to communal flourishing, and Proverbs warns that pride leads to ruin while humility precedes honor (Proverbs 16:18; 22:4). Sons and daughters who honor others cultivate motives that prioritize legacy, formation, and care rather than personal acclaim. This motive alignment protects institutions from the corrosive effects of ambition and preserves resources for long-term purposes. Early Christian writers counseled that honor reorients desire toward service and that such reorientation preserved witness. Discipleship forms motives through accountability and example so that honor becomes the default posture. When motives are aligned by honor, stewardship serves the common good.

Honor aligns practice by embedding rituals and disciplines that reinforce covenant priorities—regular giving, communal counsel, hospitality, and training—and Proverbs links instruction with life and favor (Proverbs 4:1–9; 9:9). Sons and daughters who honor these practices create predictable rhythms that sustain stewardship across seasons. This practical alignment prevents drift and ensures that resources are used for formation and care rather than consumption. Early church rhythms—catechesis, communal meals, and mutual aid—kept communities aligned with their calling. Discipleship institutionalizes practices that make honor habitual. When practice is aligned by honor, stewardship endures.

Honor aligns reputation with responsibility because those who are honored are expected to steward well, and Proverbs links faithfulness with increased trust (Proverbs 28:20; 27:23–27). Sons and daughters who accept the responsibilities that accompany honor demonstrate competence and preserve communal trust. This alignment of reputation and responsibility prevents the hollowing out of honor into mere status. Early church structures ensured that honor came with accountability and training to preserve its integrity. Discipleship forms the pathways by which honored persons are prepared for entrusted roles. When reputation aligns with responsibility, stewardship is sustainable.

Honor aligns generosity with justice by ensuring that giving is both compassionate and wise, and Proverbs commends generosity that refreshes others while warning against enabling dependency (Proverbs 11:24–25; 19:17). Sons and daughters who honor recipients design giving that empowers and restores dignity, aligning mercy with prudence. This alignment preserves resources and multiplies fruit by equipping others to steward. Early Christian care models combined relief with training to produce lasting restoration. Discipleship forms the discernment to give in ways that honor recipients and preserve stewardship. When generosity aligns with justice, covenant flow is healthy.

Honor aligns speech with truth because honoring others requires truthful, edifying words rather than gossip or slander, and Proverbs links the tongue with life and death (Proverbs 18:21; 15:4). Sons and daughters who honor through speech build trust and avoid the costly fallout of broken relationships. This verbal alignment preserves networks and prevents the erosion of relational capital that sustains stewardship. Early church fathers taught disciplined speech as essential for communal life and for the safe exercise of influence. Discipleship forms the habits of speech that honor and build. When speech aligns with honor, stewardship networks remain intact.

Honor aligns planning with legacy because honoring future generations shapes decisions about institutions, training, and resource allocation, and Proverbs commends leaving an inheritance for children's children (Proverbs 13:22). Sons and daughters who honor posterity invest in formation and structures that multiply blessing beyond their lifetime. This legacy alignment converts present stewardship into generational capacity. Historical Christian institutions are evidence that honor toward future generations produces enduring impact. Discipleship forms the foresight and disciplines necessary for legacy planning. When planning aligns with honor, the covenant continues to bless.

Honor aligns correction with restoration because honoring the person does not preclude calling them to repentance and formation, and Proverbs teaches that correction, when received, leads to life (Proverbs 3:11–12; 9:8). Sons and daughters who honor while correcting preserve dignity and enable restoration rather than exclusion. This restorative alignment protects human capital and prevents the loss of gifted people through shame. Early church practice emphasized restoration and reconciliation as means of preserving community and stewardship. Discipleship provides the relational context where correction becomes formation. When correction aligns with honor, stewardship is renewed.

Honor aligns authority with service because honoring leaders shapes their exercise of power toward care and justice rather than domination, and Proverbs links righteous rule with blessing (Proverbs 29:2; 16:12). Sons and daughters who honor leaders while expecting servant governance create institutions that serve life and multiply influence. This alignment prevents the conversion of authority into exploitation. Early Christian governance models balanced honor with accountability to preserve the servant nature of leadership. Discipleship forms leaders to exercise authority as stewardship. When authority aligns with honor, stewardship becomes a blessing.

Honor aligns the heart with Heaven because honoring God and neighbor reorders desire toward covenant priorities, and Proverbs teaches that the fear of the Lord is the beginning of wisdom and life (Proverbs 1:7; 9:10). Sons and daughters who practice honor cultivate an inner orientation that naturally aligns decisions with Heaven's economy rather than with worldly measures. This heart alignment produces consistent stewardship that invites both human and divine partnership. Early fathers taught that honor toward God shaped all other relationships and produced sustainable communities. Discipleship forms the heart so that honor is not merely external but the fruit of inward alignment. When the heart aligns by honor, stewardship participates in Heaven's flow.

HONOR AND LEGACY; HONOR AS ECONOMIC PROTECTION

Honor secures legacy because institutions and families that practice honor transmit reputation, practice, and relational capital across generations, and Proverbs commends leaving an inheritance for children's children (Proverbs 13:22). Sons and daughters who honor predecessors preserve practices and structures that enable future stewardship and care. This transmission is economic because it converts present stewardship into future capacity rather than immediate consumption. Early Christian legacies—schools, hospitals, and charitable trusts—were often the fruit of communities that honored formation and succession. Discipleship ensures that legacy is not accidental but intentional through training and entrustment. When honor builds legacy, the covenant continues to bless beyond a single lifetime.

Honor protects legacy by preserving institutional memory and by ensuring that values are passed on through example and instruction, and Proverbs links instruction with life and favor (Proverbs 4:1–9). Sons and daughters who honor the past while adapting wisely for the future maintain continuity that prevents destructive reinvention. This protection is practical: it preserves systems that care for the vulnerable and that sustain mission across seasons. Historical Christian institutions that honored their founders and their formation practices preserved capacity through upheaval. Discipleship forms the rituals and curricula that transmit legacy faithfully. When honor protects memory, stewardship endures.

Honor as economic protection functions because it reduces the hidden costs of mistrust—litigation, faction, and reputational loss—that erode capacity, and Proverbs warns that strife and deceit destroy wealth (Proverbs 6:16–19; 11:1). Sons and daughters who practice honor lower transaction costs and preserve relational capital that enables cooperative ventures and pooled resources. This protective effect is measurable: trustworthy communities attract investment and sustain partnerships more readily than fractured ones. Early church communities that prioritized honor avoided the costly divisions that drained other movements. Discipleship forms the habits that prevent the erosion of trust. When honor protects against mistrust, stewardship is secure.

Honor as economic protection also guards against predatory practices by creating norms and expectations that deter exploitation, and Proverbs condemns dishonest scales and deceitful gain (Proverbs 11:1; 20:10). Sons and daughters who institutionalize honor in commerce and governance make exploitation socially costly and reduce the incidence of predatory behavior. This normative protection preserves human capital and prevents the social breakdown that undermines prosperity. Historical Christian care systems included standards and oversight to prevent abuse and to protect the vulnerable. Discipleship forms the ethical frameworks that make honor enforceable in practice. When honor deters exploitation, covenant increase is preserved.

Honor protects legacy by ensuring that wealth is stewarded for communal flourishing rather than personal aggrandizement, and Proverbs links righteous use of resources with blessing and stability (Proverbs 21:3; 14:31). Sons and daughters who honor the trust placed in them allocate resources toward formation, care, and institutions that multiply blessing across generations. This protective allocation prevents the squandering of inheritance and secures continuity. Early Christian legacies survived because stewards honored the communal purpose of resources. Discipleship trains heirs to steward with prudence and generosity. When honor governs allocation, legacy is protected.

Honor protects communities from the corrosive effects of envy and rivalry by cultivating gratitude and mutual esteem, and Proverbs warns that envy destroys while honor preserves peace (Proverbs 14:30; 15:18). Sons and daughters who practice honor reduce internal competition and create cooperative cultures that multiply capacity. This cultural protection is economic because it enables coordinated action and shared investment rather than destructive fragmentation. Early church communities that emphasized honor avoided the rivalries that fractured other groups. Discipleship forms the practices that cultivate gratitude and mutual esteem. When honor prevents envy, stewardship is multiplied.

Honor protects institutions by creating accountability structures that preserve integrity, and Proverbs links correction with life and wisdom (Proverbs 3:11–12; 9:8). Sons and daughters who honor one another also create mechanisms for mutual oversight that prevent abuse and ensure faithful stewardship. This institutional protection reduces the risk of scandal and preserves donor and partner confidence. Historical Christian governance models included elders, deacons, and councils to provide such accountability. Discipleship forms the relational networks that make accountability relational rather than merely bureaucratic. When honor institutionalizes accountability, stewardship is safeguarded.

Honor protects families by modeling intergenerational respect and by ensuring that inheritance includes formation as well as resources, and Proverbs commends leaving an inheritance for children's children (Proverbs 13:22). Sons and daughters who honor family responsibilities invest in training, character, and structures that preserve legacy beyond material transfer. This familial protection prevents the collapse of wealth through mismanagement and preserves relational continuity. Early Christian households practiced formation and mutual care that sustained families across hardship. Discipleship equips families to pass on both character and capacity. When honor protects family formation, legacy endures.

Honor protects reputation in public life because communities known for honorable practice attract civic trust and partnership, and Proverbs links a good name with favor (Proverbs 22:1; 11:3). Sons and daughters who steward reputation through honor create opportunities for institutional collaboration with civic and philanthropic partners. This public trust is economic because it opens access to broader networks of support and influence. Early Christian communities that maintained honorable witness often became centers of education and care in their cities. Discipleship forms the public habits that preserve reputation. When honor secures public trust, stewardship expands.

Honor protects the vulnerable by making their care a normative expectation rather than an optional charity, and Proverbs repeatedly ties justice for the poor with blessing and stability (Proverbs 14:31; 22:9). Sons and daughters who honor the weak institutionalize care that preserves social cohesion and prevents the long-term costs of neglect. This protective care is economic because it maintains labor, morale, and social capital essential for flourishing. Early church institutions—hospitals, orphanages, and relief systems—were expressions of honor toward the vulnerable that multiplied communal resilience. Discipleship forms the practices that make care habitual. When honor protects the vulnerable, covenant increase is sustained.

Honor protects against short-term thinking by embedding long-term values into decision-making, and Proverbs commends foresight and preparation as means of sustaining provision (Proverbs 6:6–8; 21:5). Sons and daughters who honor future generations plan and invest in formation, institutions, and stewardship practices that outlast immediate cycles. This long-term protection converts present resources into generational capacity. Historical Christian legacies testify that honor toward the future produced institutions that served societies for centuries. Discipleship forms the foresight and disciplines necessary for such planning. When honor protects the long view, the covenant continues to bless.

Honor protects spiritual health by cultivating humility and teachability, and Proverbs links the fear of the Lord and a teachable heart with life and favor (Proverbs 1:7; 9:10). Sons and daughters who honor God and neighbor remain open to correction and formation, preventing the pride that destroys influence. This spiritual protection preserves the inner life that sustains outward stewardship. Early church formation emphasized humility as the safeguard for leaders and communities. Discipleship creates environments where teachability is practiced and honored. When honor protects spiritual health, stewardship remains faithful.

Honor protects the flow of Heaven's economy because it creates the relational conditions—trust, accountability, generosity, and justice—under which covenant resources circulate without collapse, and Proverbs teaches that blessing follows righteous practice (Proverbs 10:22; 11:25). Sons and daughters who institutionalize honor produce communities where provision is both practical and supernatural, where resources are multiplied and preserved for future generations. This protective effect is the essence of covenant stewardship: honor makes the economy of Heaven accessible and sustainable. Early church witness confirms that honorable communities multiplied provision and influence across seasons. Discipleship remains the primary means by which honor is formed, transmitted, and protected. When honor governs life, the relational currency of Heaven secures increase.

CHAPTER EIGHT — COUNSEL, ALIGNMENT, AND THE PATH OF THE WISE

The Safety of Many Counselors

The wisdom of Proverbs insists that many counselors bring safety because collective discernment reduces error and multiplies perspective (Proverbs 11:14). Sons and daughters who seek counsel avoid the blind spots of solitary decision-making and gain access to tested insight that protects resources and reputation. Counsel is not a substitute for responsibility but a safeguard that refines plans and exposes hidden risks before they become crises. Early church teachers affirmed this communal wisdom; Clement of Alexandria and later Chrysostom urged believers to surround themselves with elders and mentors who could temper zeal with prudence. Discipleship communities historically provided the relational context for counsel—places where correction was given in love and where plans were sharpened by experience. When many counselors are consulted, decisions are more resilient and covenant access is preserved.

Wise counsel functions as a filter for impulse because it forces a proposal to be tested against multiple perspectives before action is taken, and Proverbs commends the one who listens to advice (Proverbs 12:15; 15:22). Sons and daughters who submit plans to counsel discover assumptions they missed and alternatives they had not considered, and this testing prevents costly mistakes. Counsel also disciplines imagination by requiring concrete steps and accountability rather than vague optimism. Early Christian communities used councils and elders to vet initiatives, recognizing that spiritual fervor without tested strategy often led to fragmentation. Discipleship trains the heart to receive correction without offense so that counsel becomes formation rather than mere opinion. When counsel filters impulse, stewardship is protected.

Counsel creates redundancy in decision-making, which is a practical risk-management strategy: multiple voices reduce the chance that a single error will cascade into collapse (Proverbs 24:6). Sons and daughters who build advisory networks create layers of oversight that preserve institutional capacity and prevent the isolation that invites deception. This redundancy is not bureaucratic inertia but relational insurance—trusted voices who will speak truth when convenience tempts compromise. Early fathers recommended councils precisely because they observed how solitary leaders could be swayed by flattery or fear. Discipleship forms the humility to invite redundancy and the courage to heed it.

When redundancy through counsel exists, covenant resources are less vulnerable.

Counsel protects against charismatic error because it subjects prophetic or visionary impulses to communal discernment, and Proverbs warns that the way of the fool is right in his own eyes (Proverbs 12:15). Sons and daughters who welcome counsel allow prophetic insight to be tested by wisdom and experience, preserving both zeal and prudence. This balance prevents the misuse of influence and the collapse that follows unchecked initiative. Early church history records movements that splintered when charismatic leaders were not held accountable; conversely, communities that combined prophetic gifting with elder oversight endured. Discipleship creates the relational structures that hold vision and test it. When counsel tempers charisma, covenant flow remains steady.

Counsel multiplies creativity because diverse perspectives often produce solutions that a single mind would not conceive, and Proverbs commends many advisors for safety and success (Proverbs 15:22; 11:14). Sons and daughters who invite varied counsel benefit from complementary strengths—strategic, relational, financial, and spiritual—that together form a robust plan. This collaborative creativity turns constraints into leverage and scarcity into strategic allocation. Early Christian councils combined theological insight with practical governance to solve complex problems facing growing communities. Discipleship cultivates the humility to listen and the discernment to synthesize counsel into coherent action. When counsel multiplies creativity, stewardship becomes adaptive and fruitful.

Counsel preserves reputation because decisions vetted by trusted advisors are less likely to produce scandal or unintended harm, and Proverbs links wise counsel with honor (Proverbs 11:3; 22:1). Sons and daughters who consult broadly reduce the risk of reputational damage that can close doors and drain resources. This reputational protection is economic: trust is a currency that opens opportunities and invites partnership. Early church leaders guarded reputation through councils and public accountability, understanding that trust once lost is difficult to restore. Discipleship forms the practices of transparency and mutual oversight that preserve reputation. When counsel protects reputation, covenant access remains open.

Counsel builds institutional memory because repeated consultation creates records of tested decisions and the reasoning behind them, and Proverbs values instruction and remembrance (Proverbs 4:1–5). Sons and daughters who institutionalize counsel create archives of wisdom that future leaders can consult, preventing repeated mistakes and preserving learned lessons. This memory is a strategic asset that compounds over generations. Early Christian communities preserved teaching and practice through councils, letters, and catechesis so that formation continued beyond a single leader's tenure. Discipleship ensures that counsel is not ephemeral but recorded and transmitted. When counsel builds memory, stewardship matures.

Counsel protects against isolation by creating relational accountability that prevents leaders from drifting into self-reliance, and Proverbs warns that pride isolates while humility invites counsel (Proverbs 16:18; 11:2).

Sons and daughters who cultivate advisory relationships remain connected to reality and to the needs of those they serve. This connection prevents the distortions that come from echo chambers and preserves empathy in governance. Early fathers emphasized communal oversight as a remedy for isolation and as a means of preserving pastoral sensitivity. Discipleship forms the relational habits that keep leaders connected and accountable. When counsel prevents isolation, covenant stewardship remains compassionate.

Counsel clarifies priorities because advisors help distinguish urgent from important, and Proverbs teaches the value of ordered living and wise planning (Proverbs 21:5). Sons and daughters who bring plans to counsel receive help in prioritizing tasks that align with covenant purposes rather than reactive demands. This clarity preserves energy and resources for what truly matters. Early church councils often helped communities focus on core mission rather than peripheral controversies. Discipleship trains leaders to present clear proposals and to receive prioritized feedback. When counsel clarifies priorities, stewardship becomes focused and effective.

Counsel protects against deception by exposing proposals to scrutiny that can reveal hidden motives or faulty assumptions, and Proverbs links discernment with life (Proverbs 2:6–8; 14:15). Sons and daughters who welcome probing questions reduce the chance that flattering counsel or false promises will mislead them. This protective scrutiny is practical: it prevents entanglement with schemes that promise rapid gain at the cost of integrity. Early Christian communities used councils to test teachers and to protect the flock from false doctrine and exploitative practices. Discipleship forms the capacity to ask hard questions and to receive correction. When counsel exposes deception, covenant resources are safeguarded.

Counsel fosters humility because seeking advice acknowledges limits and invites formation, and Proverbs links teachability with life and favor (Proverbs 9:9; 12:1). Sons and daughters who habitually consult others cultivate a posture of learning that keeps them open to correction and growth. This humility is the soil in which sustainable stewardship grows. Early church formation prized humility as the prerequisite for wisdom and for responsible leadership. Discipleship creates the relational contexts where humility is practiced and reinforced. When counsel fosters humility, covenant access is preserved and expanded.

Counsel creates a culture of mutual care because advisors who speak truth in love form a network that both protects and equips, and Proverbs commends faithful friends and many counselors (Proverbs 17:17; 11:14). Sons and daughters who participate in such networks receive both correction and encouragement, enabling endurance through trials. This culture multiplies resilience and preserves communal capacity. Early Christian communities embodied this mutual care through shared life and accountability. Discipleship forms the practices that make counsel both corrective and restorative. When counsel creates mutual care, the path of the wise is communal and strong.

ALIGNMENT WITH THE WISE

Alignment with the wise means intentionally placing oneself within communities and relationships that reflect covenant priorities, because proximity shapes practice and imagination (Proverbs 13:20). Sons and daughters who align with the prudent absorb patterns of speech, decision, and stewardship that form their capacity over time. This proximity is not passive mimicry but active participation in rhythms that produce competence and character. Early church fathers taught that spiritual formation occurs in community—through mentors, elders, and peers who model faithful living. Discipleship provides the structure for alignment, creating apprenticeships of the heart where wisdom is transmitted. When alignment with the wise is pursued, stewardship becomes competent and trustworthy.

Alignment with the wise protects against cultural drift because communities of wisdom maintain standards that resist the fashions of the moment, and Proverbs warns against the path of the fool (Proverbs 1:7; 4:14–15). Sons and daughters who embed themselves in wise communities are less likely to adopt destructive practices that erode legacy. This protective alignment preserves identity and purpose across changing seasons. Early Christian communities that prioritized formation maintained coherence despite external pressures. Discipleship forms the disciplines that keep communities anchored in covenant priorities. When alignment resists drift, stewardship remains faithful.

Alignment with the wise accelerates learning because proximity to experienced counselors compresses the time it takes to gain discernment, and Proverbs values instruction and the company of the prudent (Proverbs 4:1–9; 13:20). Sons and daughters who intentionally seek wise company shortcut costly errors and inherit tested strategies for stewardship. This acceleration is practical: it converts years of trial into seasons of guided growth. Early church mentoring relationships functioned precisely to accelerate formation for younger leaders. Discipleship creates the apprenticeship pathways that make alignment intentional and fruitful. When alignment accelerates learning, covenant capacity grows faster.

Alignment with the wise clarifies vocation because mentors and peers help discern calling and fit, and Proverbs links counsel with established plans (Proverbs 16:3; 15:22). Sons and daughters who align with wise communities receive feedback that refines calling and prevents misapplied energy. This vocational clarity preserves resources and directs influence toward covenant ends. Early Christian mentors helped disciples discover gifts and place them in service for the common good. Discipleship forms the processes by which calling is tested and confirmed. When alignment clarifies vocation, stewardship is both effective and joyful.

Alignment with the wise strengthens resilience because shared wisdom provides models for enduring hardship, and Proverbs teaches that instruction prepares the heart for trials (Proverbs 2:1–5; 3:11–12). Sons and daughters who stand with seasoned counselors learn how to navigate setbacks without losing integrity. This resilience is communal: it is sustained by stories, counsel, and shared practices that have weathered storms. Early church elders who had endured persecution offered invaluable perspective to younger leaders. Discipleship transmits those survival patterns so that new generations do not repeat avoidable mistakes. When alignment builds resilience, covenant stewardship endures.

Alignment with the wise multiplies influence because networks of trusted leaders amplify reputation and open collaborative opportunities, and Proverbs links a good name with favor (Proverbs 22:1; 18:16). Sons and daughters who are known within wise circles are more likely to be recommended, partnered with, and entrusted with responsibility. This network effect is practical: it increases access to resources and to platforms for stewardship. Early Christian networks of bishops, presbyters, and house churches multiplied care and mission across regions. Discipleship forms the relational capital that enables such multiplication. When alignment multiplies influence, covenant flow expands.

Alignment with the wise disciplines ambition by orienting desire toward communal flourishing rather than personal acclaim, and Proverbs warns that pride precedes ruin while humility precedes honor (Proverbs 16:18; 22:4). Sons and daughters who align with wise mentors learn to measure success by legacy and stewardship rather than by applause. This disciplining of ambition preserves character and prevents the corruption that often follows unchecked drive. Early Christian formation emphasized service and legacy over personal glory. Discipleship forms motives through example and accountability. When alignment disciplines ambition, stewardship remains pure.

Alignment with the wise improves decision quality because counsel provides tested heuristics and frameworks for evaluating opportunities, and Proverbs commends the prudent who consider the path of their feet (Proverbs 4:26–27; 21:5). Sons and daughters who align with wise advisors gain access to mental models that simplify complex choices and reduce costly experimentation. This improvement is practical: it increases the hit rate of strategic initiatives and preserves capital. Early church leaders developed governance practices that guided communal decisions wisely. Discipleship transmits those heuristics so that new leaders can act with confidence. When alignment improves decisions, covenant resources are used well.

Alignment with the wise fosters generational continuity because mentors intentionally pass on practices, rituals, and institutional memory, and Proverbs values leaving an inheritance for children's children (Proverbs 13:22). Sons and daughters who align with elders inherit not only resources but also the habits that preserve them. This continuity is economic: it converts present stewardship into future capacity. Early Christian catechesis and mentoring ensured that formation continued across generations. Discipleship institutionalizes transmission so that legacy is not accidental. When alignment secures continuity, the covenant endures.

Alignment with the wise cultivates discernment in speech because wise communities model edifying communication and restraint, and Proverbs links the tongue with life and death (Proverbs 18:21; 15:4). Sons and daughters who practice speech within wise circles learn to build rather than to destroy, preserving networks and reputation. This verbal discipline is practical: it prevents costly conflicts and preserves relational capital. Early church fathers taught disciplined speech as essential for communal life and for the safe exercise of influence. Discipleship forms the habits of speech that honor and build. When alignment shapes speech, stewardship networks remain intact.

Alignment with the wise encourages strategic generosity because mentors model how to give in ways that empower and multiply, and Proverbs commends generosity that refreshes others (Proverbs 11:24–25; 19:17). Sons and daughters who align with wise givers learn to scatter strategically—investing in formation, institutions, and people who reproduce stewardship. This strategic generosity converts present sacrifice into future capacity. Early Christian institutions grew through coordinated generosity guided by elders. Discipleship teaches the discernment to give in ways that honor recipients and multiply fruit. When alignment guides generosity, covenant flow is optimized.

Alignment with the wise deepens spiritual formation because proximity to mature believers accelerates inward change, and Proverbs links instruction with life and favor (Proverbs 4:1–9; 9:9). Sons and daughters who align with wise communities are shaped in character, not merely in technique, and this inward formation is the primary asset for stewardship. Early church formation prioritized the heart as the locus of sustainable ministry. Discipleship provides the relational context where inward change is practiced and reinforced. When alignment deepens formation, covenant access is entrusted to formed hearts.

AVOIDING THE PATH OF FOOLS

Proverbs repeatedly warns that the path of fools is attractive but destructive, and avoiding it requires intentional separation from patterns that erode character and capacity (Proverbs 14:7; 1:7). Sons and daughters who recognize the signs of folly—quick schemes, flattery, and isolation—can choose alternative paths that preserve reputation and resources. Foolish paths often promise speed and visibility but deliver instability and loss. Early church writers cataloged common follies—pride, greed, and divisiveness—and counseled communities to guard against them through discipline and counsel. Discipleship trains the eye to spot folly early and the will to refuse it. When the path of fools is avoided, stewardship remains intact.

Fools are often seduced by shortcuts that compromise integrity, and Proverbs warns that dishonest gain is fleeting while honest increase endures (Proverbs 13:11; 20:17). Sons and daughters who resist shortcuts protect both reputation and legacy by choosing steady, covenantal increase. This resistance is practical: it prevents legal entanglements, relational fractures, and the long-term costs of compromised decisions. Early Christian communities that refused expedient compromise preserved witness and multiplied provision across hardship. Discipleship forms the discipline to choose integrity over quick gain. When shortcuts are refused, covenant resources are preserved.

Fools often surround themselves with flatterers rather than counselors, and Proverbs cautions that flattering speech conceals danger (Proverbs 29:5; 26:28). Sons and daughters who cultivate honest counsel avoid the echo chambers that amplify error and invite collapse. This avoidance requires humility to welcome correction and the courage to remove toxic influences. Early church elders warned against sycophancy and modeled accountability structures to prevent it. Discipleship forms the relational courage to speak truth in love and to receive it. When flatterers are displaced by counselors, stewardship is safer.

Fools confuse confidence with competence, acting boldly without tested judgment, and Proverbs contrasts the proud fool with the prudent planner (Proverbs 12:15; 21:5). Sons and daughters who value tested competence over performative confidence build institutions that endure rather than spectacles that fade. This preference is practical: it reduces costly experimentation and preserves capital for strategic deployment. Early Christian leaders prized proven character and competence when entrusting responsibility. Discipleship provides the testing ground where competence is demonstrated through faithful service. When competence is chosen over bravado, covenant stewardship scales.

Fools neglect formation and assume inheritance without preparation, and Proverbs links faithfulness in small things with greater trust (Proverbs 28:20; 27:23–27). Sons and daughters who skip formation risk squandering resources and fracturing legacy. This neglect is costly because resources without stewardship skills often lead to ruin. Early church practice emphasized catechesis and progressive responsibility to prevent such collapse. Discipleship ensures that heirs are formed in character and competence before being entrusted with larger trusts. When formation is prioritized, inheritance becomes stewardship rather than entitlement.

Fools are often impatient with seasons and force outcomes prematurely, and Proverbs commends those who prepare and wait for harvest (Proverbs 6:6–8; 21:5). Sons and daughters who respect seasons avoid panic and waste, positioning resources for strategic deployment when opportunity arrives. This patience preserves capacity and enables generosity even in lean times. Early Christian communities practiced seasonal preparation and mutual aid to survive famine and persecution. Discipleship forms the endurance to steward across cycles rather than react to them. When seasons are honored, covenant increase matures.

Fools ignore counsel and rely on their own understanding, and Proverbs warns that such reliance leads to ruin (Proverbs 3:5–6; 12:15). Sons and daughters who refuse counsel are vulnerable to deception and to decisions that erode trust. This isolation is practical: it increases the likelihood of costly mistakes and reduces the chance of recovery. Early church history records leaders who fell when they refused correction and communities that thrived when they embraced counsel. Discipleship forms the humility to seek and to heed wise advice. When counsel is embraced, the path of fools is avoided.

Fools prioritize appearance over substance, seeking applause rather than faithful stewardship, and Proverbs condemns the pursuit of vain glory (Proverbs 25:27; 27:2). Sons and daughters who chase visibility often sacrifice long-term fruit for short-term acclaim. This posture corrodes character and invites scandal. Early Christian writers warned against ostentation and praised humble service as the mark of true maturity. Discipleship forms motives that prize legacy and formation over applause. When substance is chosen over show, stewardship remains pure.

Fools neglect justice and exploit the vulnerable, and Proverbs repeatedly links oppression with ruin (Proverbs 22:16; 28:3). Sons and daughters who ignore justice create instability that eventually undermines prosperity and witness. This neglect is economic as well as moral: it destroys social capital and invites backlash. Early church institutions that cared for the poor preserved social cohesion and multiplied witness. Discipleship forms hearts to see stewardship as communal responsibility rather than private accumulation. When justice is chosen, the path of fools is avoided.

Fools fail to build systems and assume charisma will carry them, and Proverbs values planning and counsel as the architecture of life (Proverbs 24:3–4; 21:5). Sons and daughters who neglect systems are vulnerable to collapse when circumstances change. This failure is practical: it leaves organizations brittle and dependent on personalities rather than practices. Early Christian communities that built governance, training, and care systems endured beyond the lifespan of any single leader. Discipleship institutionalizes practices so that stewardship is not person-dependent. When systems are built, folly is mitigated.

Fools hoard rather than scatter, confusing security with possession, and Proverbs teaches that scattering often precedes increase (Proverbs 11:24–25). Sons and daughters who clutch resources out of fear cut off relational flows that could multiply provision. This hoarding is shortsighted because it sacrifices relational capital for perceived safety. Early church generosity multiplied provision through networks of mutual aid and hospitality. Discipleship forms the courage to scatter wisely and to trust covenant reciprocity. When scattering replaces hoarding, the path of fools is avoided.

Fools refuse restoration and exile those who stumble, and Proverbs calls for correction that leads to life rather than exclusion that destroys (Proverbs 3:11–12; 9:8). Sons and daughters who refuse restorative practices lose human capital and fracture communities. This refusal is costly because gifted people are discarded rather than formed. Early church practice emphasized restoration and reconciliation as means of preserving leaders and communities. Discipleship creates the relational pathways for correction that heals and prepares. When restoration is practiced, folly is transformed into formation.

HOW COUNSEL PROTECTS INCREASE AND WISDOM COMMUNITIES AND COVENANT FLOW

Counsel protects increase by converting individual plans into communal strategies that have been stress-tested and refined, and Proverbs links many counselors with safety and success (Proverbs 15:22; 11:14). Sons and daughters who bring proposals to wise advisors reduce the probability of catastrophic error and increase the likelihood of sustainable growth. This protection is practical: vetted plans attract partners, donors, and volunteers who trust the process. Early church councils and advisory networks preserved communal resources by ensuring that initiatives were both spiritually aligned and practically feasible. Discipleship forms the relational channels through which counsel is given and received. When counsel protects plans, covenant increase is preserved.

Counsel protects increase by exposing hidden liabilities—legal, relational, and reputational—that a single planner might miss, and Proverbs values the prudent who considers the path of his feet (Proverbs 4:26–27). Sons and daughters who welcome probing questions identify contingencies and build mitigations before commitments are made. This foresight prevents costly remediation and preserves momentum. Early Christian governance included oversight mechanisms precisely to surface such liabilities and to protect communal trust. Discipleship trains leaders to anticipate risks and to design resilient responses. When counsel reveals liabilities early, stewardship remains intact.

Counsel protects increase by creating shared ownership of decisions, which distributes responsibility and reduces the chance of unilateral failure, and Proverbs links many counselors with safety (Proverbs 11:14). Sons and daughters who involve trusted advisors create buy-in that mobilizes networks for implementation and support. This shared ownership is economic: it multiplies capacity and reduces the burden on any single steward. Early church structures of elders and deacons distributed responsibility so that care could scale without collapse. Discipleship forms the practices that enable shared stewardship rather than centralized control. When counsel creates shared ownership, covenant flow scales.

Counsel protects increase by refining strategy through iterative feedback, turning initial ideas into executable plans with measurable milestones, and Proverbs commends instruction and correction as life (Proverbs 4:1–9; 3:11–12). Sons and daughters who submit to iterative counsel convert vision into sustainable programs rather than one-off initiatives. This iterative refinement increases the probability of long-term impact. Early Christian leaders used councils and mentoring to refine mission strategy across contexts. Discipleship institutionalizes feedback loops so that learning is continuous. When counsel refines strategy, stewardship becomes adaptive and enduring.

Counsel protects increase by preserving relational capital through mediated conflict resolution, because advisors can help negotiate disputes before they escalate, and Proverbs warns against the strife that destroys (Proverbs 6:16–19; 16:28). Sons and daughters who use counsel to resolve tensions prevent fractures that would otherwise drain resources and morale. This mediation is practical: it keeps teams functional and donors confident. Early church councils often served as forums for reconciliation and for preserving unity. Discipleship forms the skills of peacemaking and mediated restoration. When counsel mediates conflict, covenant capacity is preserved.

Counsel protects increase by ensuring ethical clarity, because advisors help test motives and methods against covenant priorities, and Proverbs links righteousness with blessing (Proverbs 21:3; 11:1). Sons and daughters who seek counsel avoid rationalizations that compromise justice and integrity. This ethical clarity preserves reputation and invites long-term partnership. Early Christian oversight guarded against exploitative practices and ensured that care remained just. Discipleship forms moral discernment so that counsel is not merely strategic but also righteous. When counsel enforces ethics, covenant increase is trustworthy.

Counsel protects increase by enabling strategic partnerships, because advisors often introduce networks and resources that accelerate implementation, and Proverbs links a good name with favor (Proverbs 22:1; 18:16). Sons and daughters who consult widely gain access to collaborators who can scale initiatives beyond what a single leader could achieve. This network effect is practical: it multiplies reach and resource pools. Early church networks of house churches and elders enabled rapid multiplication of care and mission. Discipleship forms the relational capital that makes partnerships reliable. When counsel unlocks networks, covenant flow expands.

Counsel protects increase by institutionalizing learning—capturing what worked and what failed—so that future leaders inherit tested practices, and Proverbs values instruction and remembrance (Proverbs 4:1–5). Sons and daughters who document counsel and outcomes create a living library of wisdom that prevents repeated mistakes. This institutional memory compounds stewardship capacity across generations. Early Christian writings, letters, and councils preserved lessons that guided later communities. Discipleship ensures that counsel is recorded, taught, and practiced. When counsel institutionalizes learning, covenant stewardship deepens.

Counsel protects increase by aligning resources with mission through prioritized feedback, ensuring that budgets, teams, and time are directed toward covenant ends, and Proverbs commends wise planning (Proverbs 21:5; 24:3–4). Sons and daughters who use counsel to prioritize avoid mission drift and ensure that resources are leveraged for maximum Kingdom impact. This alignment is practical: it prevents dilution of effort and preserves donor confidence. Early church governance used councils to align communal resources with core mission. Discipleship forms the discipline of strategic allocation. When counsel aligns resources, covenant increase is focused.

Counsel protects increase by creating accountability that deters misuse and encourages faithful reporting, and Proverbs links faithfulness with entrustment (Proverbs 28:20; 27:23–27). Sons and daughters who accept counsel also accept accountability structures that preserve trust and enable scaling. This accountability is economic: it sustains funding and partnership by demonstrating stewardship competence. Early Christian communities developed oversight roles—deacons, elders—to ensure transparent care. Discipleship trains stewards to report faithfully and to receive correction. When counsel enforces accountability, covenant resources are entrusted more widely.

Counsel protects increase by forming wisdom communities that become engines of covenant flow—places where generosity, training, and governance intersect to multiply provision—and Proverbs celebrates the company of the prudent (Proverbs 13:20; 11:14). Sons and daughters who invest in wisdom communities create ecosystems where counsel, formation, and generosity circulate in healthy patterns. These communities function like living banks of relational capital, distributing resources, training leaders, and preserving legacy. Early church households and monastic communities exemplified such ecosystems, sustaining mission across centuries. Discipleship is the mechanism that builds and renews these communities. When wisdom communities form, the covenant economy flows robustly.

Counsel protects increase by making stewardship replicable: tested counsel becomes curriculum for discipleship, enabling new leaders to step into responsibility with competence, and Proverbs links instruction with life and favor (Proverbs 4:1–9; 9:9). Sons and daughters who translate counsel into formation pathways multiply stewardship capacity across generations. This replication is practical: it scales care without diluting quality. Early Christian catechesis and mentoring turned counsel into reproducible formation. Discipleship institutionalizes counsel so that it becomes the engine of multiplication. When counsel is translated into formation, covenant flow becomes generational and enduring.

CHAPTER NINE — SPEECH, DECREES, AND THE POWER TO BUILD WEALTH

Words as Builders

The Scriptures present speech as a formative force that constructs reality, and Proverbs repeatedly affirms that life and death are in the power of the tongue (Proverbs 18:21). Sons and daughters who learn to speak with wisdom build environments where trust, opportunity, and stewardship can flourish rather than collapse under careless words. Words shape reputation, and reputation functions as relational capital that opens doors for partnership and provision; a good name is more desirable than great riches (Proverbs 22:1). Early church teachers observed that disciplined speech was a mark of maturity; Chrysostom counseled believers to let their words be measured and life-giving, recognizing that public witness depends on private restraint. Discipleship forms the tongue through repeated practice—listening, confession, correction, and the habit of speaking truth in love—so that speech becomes a reliable instrument of construction. When sons and daughters speak to build, their words become scaffolding for covenant increase.

Speech builds because it clarifies vision and mobilizes people toward shared purposes, and Proverbs links counsel and many advisors with safety and success (Proverbs 15:22). Sons and daughters who articulate clear, covenantal aims invite others to invest time, talent, and treasure into those aims rather than scattering resources across competing priorities. This clarity reduces friction and aligns networks around measurable steps, turning abstract calling into executable plans. Early Christian communities multiplied when leaders could name a vision plainly and gather others to it, and elders provided the counsel that refined and protected those plans. Discipleship trains leaders to translate revelation into language that others can steward, converting prophetic insight into practical action. When speech builds vision, stewardship becomes coordinated and fruitful.

Words build trust because consistent, truthful speech creates predictability in relationships, and Proverbs links truthful lips with enduring favor (Proverbs 12:22; 11:3). Sons and daughters who guard their words avoid the reputational erosion that closes doors and drains influence, and they become reliable partners in both human and divine economies. This trust is economic because it lowers transaction costs and invites larger collaborations that require mutual confidence. Early fathers taught that a disciplined tongue preserved communal unity and made leaders safe to follow. Discipleship forms the habit of speaking truth with humility so that trust is earned rather than assumed. When speech builds trust, covenant resources circulate more freely.

Speech builds authority when words are matched by character, because moral credibility amplifies the effect of decrees and declarations, and Proverbs links honor with influence (Proverbs 22:29; 18:16). Sons and daughters who live what they declare gain moral authority that opens doors for delegated responsibility and stewardship. This authority is not coercive but relational: people follow those whose words are proven by life. Early church leaders who combined integrity with clear teaching were entrusted with communal oversight and resources. Discipleship forms the congruence between speech and life so that declarations carry weight without manipulation. When speech builds authority, stewardship is entrusted responsibly.

Words build culture because repeated language and ritual shape communal norms, and Proverbs emphasizes the power of instruction and repeated teaching to form life (Proverbs 4:1–9). Sons and daughters who steward language—prayers, liturgies, public declarations, and everyday speech—shape the habits that determine how resources are used and how people relate. This cultural shaping is practical: it determines whether generosity, honor, and justice become default behaviors or occasional exceptions. Early Christian households used repeated prayers and catechesis to form communal character that sustained institutions across generations. Discipleship institutionalizes formative language so that culture is transmitted rather than accidental. When speech builds culture, covenant practices endure.

Words build legacy because the stories we tell about stewardship, sacrifice, and faithfulness become the inheritance passed to the next generation, and Proverbs commends leaving an inheritance for children's children (Proverbs 13:22). Sons and daughters who narrate covenant faithfulness create memory that orients future stewards toward the same priorities. This narrative legacy is economic because it preserves practices that multiply blessing beyond a single lifetime. Early church writings and letters preserved testimonies that guided later communities in times of trial. Discipleship embeds story into formation so that language becomes a vehicle for generational transfer. When speech builds legacy, the covenant continues to bless.

Words build protection because clear, truthful speech exposes deception and prevents the slow corrosion of trust, and Proverbs warns that deceit destroys while honesty preserves (Proverbs 11:1; 20:17). Sons and daughters who speak plainly about values, expectations, and boundaries reduce the hidden costs of ambiguity and the risk of exploitation. This protective clarity is practical: it prevents legal entanglements, relational fractures, and the erosion of donor confidence. Early church councils used public statements and letters to clarify doctrine and practice, protecting communities from destructive error. Discipleship trains leaders to communicate boundaries and expectations with both firmness and grace. When speech builds protection, stewardship is safeguarded.

Words build opportunity because declarations of blessing, invitation, and endorsement often open doors in human networks, and Proverbs links a good name with favor that precedes increase (Proverbs 18:16; 22:1). Sons and daughters who speak blessing over others and who endorse faithful workers create pathways for those people to be recommended and entrusted with responsibility. This endorsement functions as social capital that multiplies access to resources. Early Christian leaders who publicly commended faithful servants often catalyzed wider networks of support for mission. Discipleship forms the discernment to bless rightly and to recommend with integrity. When speech builds opportunity, covenant flow accelerates.

Words build restoration when they are used to reconcile, forgive, and restore dignity, and Proverbs teaches that correction given in love leads to life (Proverbs 3:11–12; 9:8). Sons and daughters who use speech to restore rather than to shame preserve human capital and prevent the loss of gifted people through exclusion. This restorative speech is economic because it retains talent and preserves relational networks that sustain mission. Early church practice emphasized reconciliation as a means of preserving leaders and communities. Discipleship creates the relational pathways for restorative speech to be practiced and received. When speech builds restoration, stewardship remains whole.

Words build discernment when they are used to test spirits, to ask hard questions, and to expose false counsel, and Proverbs links discernment with life and favor (Proverbs 2:6–8; 14:15). Sons and daughters who cultivate speech that probes motives and assumptions protect their communities from schemes that promise rapid gain at the cost of integrity. This discerning speech is practical: it prevents entanglement with deceptive offers and preserves long-term capacity. Early church elders used questioning and testing to protect flocks from false teachers. Discipleship forms the courage to ask hard questions and the humility to receive correction. When speech builds discernment, covenant resources are preserved.

Words build worship because language shapes the posture of the heart and aligns communities with Heaven's priorities, and Proverbs links the fear of the Lord with the beginning of wisdom (Proverbs 1:7). Sons and daughters who cultivate liturgies, prayers, and declarations that honor the Father create spiritual atmospheres where provision is stewarded as covenant rather than as commodity. This worshipful speech invites divine partnership and frames stewardship as sacred trust. Early Christian liturgies formed communities to live sacrificially and to steward resources for care and mission. Discipleship embeds worshipful language into daily practice so that stewardship is an act of devotion. When speech builds worship, Heaven's economy is honored.

THE TONGUE AS A CREATIVE FORCE

The biblical witness portrays the tongue as creative because God spoke the world into being and human speech participates in that creative pattern when aligned with Heaven, and Proverbs affirms the generative power of words (Genesis 1; Proverbs 18:21). Sons and daughters who learn to decree in alignment with covenant principles participate in a creative economy where words release favor, open doors, and mobilize resources. This creativity is not magical but relational: words that align with God's character and with tested counsel invite partnership rather than coercion. Early church writers reflected on the power of blessing and benediction as instruments that released grace and favor in communities. Discipleship forms the capacity to speak creatively by grounding speech in Scripture, counsel, and character. When the tongue is used creatively, covenant realities are advanced.

The tongue creates because it names reality and thereby focuses attention and resources, and Proverbs teaches that naming and wisdom precede increase (Proverbs 8:10–11). Sons and daughters who name priorities—schools to be built, leaders to be trained, neighborhoods to be served—direct communal energy and attract partners who can steward those priorities. This naming is practical: it converts vague longing into concrete projects that can be resourced and measured. Early Christian leaders used public naming of needs and commitments to mobilize communities for care and mission. Discipleship trains leaders to name with precision and humility so that creative speech becomes executable. When the tongue names rightly, stewardship becomes actionable.

The tongue creates because decrees can align human action with divine timing, and Scripture shows moments when spoken words opened doors of provision and favor (Esther 4–5; 1 Kings 17). Sons and daughters who decree in alignment with counsel and justice often find that human systems respond—networks open, legal barriers shift, and opportunities arise. This alignment requires discernment and communal confirmation to avoid presumption. Early church testimony recounts instances where spoken blessing preceded practical openings for mission and care. Discipleship forms the rhythms of testing and confirmation that make decrees responsible rather than impulsive. When the tongue decrees with wisdom, covenant timing is honored.

The tongue creates because it shapes identity through repeated declarations, and Proverbs links the heart with the mouth so that inner orientation is expressed outwardly (Proverbs 4:23; 18:21). Sons and daughters who declare covenant identity—belonging, stewardship, generosity—rehearse a reality that their actions begin to embody. This performative speech rewires imagination and behavior over time, producing habits that attract provision. Early Christian catechesis used repeated confession and creedal language to form identity across generations. Discipleship embeds declarative practices that align speech with lived formation. When the tongue shapes identity, stewardship becomes natural.

The tongue creates because it can dismantle fear and replace it with faith, and Proverbs contrasts the anxious heart with the one that trusts the Lord (Proverbs 3:5–6; 10:22). Sons and daughters who speak faith over scarcity reframe decisions and free themselves from scarcity-driven compromises that erode legacy. This spoken faith is not denial of reality but a covenantal posture that trusts the Father while acting prudently. Early church prayers often named trust in God's provision as a means of sustaining communities through famine and persecution. Discipleship forms the habit of speaking faith that is matched by wise stewardship. When the tongue dismantles fear, covenant creativity flourishes.

The tongue creates because it can bless and thereby release favor, and Proverbs links blessing with the opening of doors and the multiplication of resources (Proverbs 11:25; 18:16). Sons and daughters who bless leaders, donors, and workers create relational momentum that invites reciprocal support and partnership. This blessing is practical: it builds networks of goodwill that translate into tangible opportunities. Early Christian benedictions functioned as public endorsements that mobilized support for mission. Discipleship forms the discernment to bless in ways that are authentic and strategic. When the tongue blesses, covenant favor is released.

The tongue creates because it can name injustice and call for restoration, and Scripture models prophetic speech that reorders corrupt systems toward justice (Isaiah 1; Amos 5). Sons and daughters who speak against exploitation and who call for restitution participate in the prophetic work of rebalancing economies toward covenant care. This prophetic naming must be paired with practical mechanisms for restoration to avoid mere rhetoric. Early prophets and later church leaders insisted that prophetic speech be matched by action to restore the vulnerable. Discipleship forms the courage to speak truth to power and the wisdom to implement restorative measures. When the tongue names injustice, covenant restoration follows.

The tongue creates because it can commission and release leaders, and Proverbs links the recognition of the worthy with the opening of influence (Proverbs 31:31; 18:16). Sons and daughters who use speech to commission faithful servants multiply stewardship by delegating responsibility and releasing authority. This commissioning is practical: it creates new centers of care and multiplies capacity through trusted hands. Early church ordination and commissioning prayers functioned to release leaders into service with communal endorsement. Discipleship forms the criteria and practices for wise commissioning. When the tongue commissions, stewardship multiplies.

The tongue creates because it can declare boundaries that protect communities from exploitation, and Proverbs teaches the value of wise planning and guarded speech (Proverbs 21:5; 4:23). Sons and daughters who speak clear policies, covenants, and expectations reduce ambiguity and prevent the slow erosion of trust. This boundary language is economic because it preserves donor confidence and prevents mission drift. Early church councils issued canons and guidelines to protect communal life and to preserve resources for care. Discipleship forms the practices of covenant language that make boundaries both clear and compassionate. When the tongue declares boundaries, stewardship is preserved.

The tongue creates because it can teach and transmit wisdom, and Proverbs emphasizes instruction as the pathway to life and favor (Proverbs 4:1–9; 9:9). Sons and daughters who use speech to teach stewardship practices—budgeting, governance, generosity—multiply competent leaders who can steward resources faithfully. This teaching is practical: it converts experience into reproducible formation. Early Christian catechesis and mentoring turned counsel into curricula that equipped new generations. Discipleship institutionalizes teaching so that wisdom is not lost with a single leader. When the tongue teaches, covenant capacity is multiplied.

The tongue creates because it can declare thanksgiving and thereby reframe scarcity into gratitude, and Proverbs links a thankful heart with life and favor (Proverbs 15:13; 17:22). Sons and daughters who cultivate speech of gratitude shift communal imagination from lack to stewardship, enabling generosity and resilience. This thankful language sustains morale and invites further blessing. Early Christian liturgies embedded thanksgiving as a formative practice that preserved joy under pressure. Discipleship forms the habit of gratitude so that speech becomes a conduit of hope. When the tongue gives thanks, covenant provision is reinforced.

DECREES THAT ALIGN WITH HEAVEN

Decrees function in Scripture as authoritative speech that aligns human action with divine intent when they are rooted in covenant and tested by counsel, and Jesus taught about binding and loosing within the community of faith (Matthew 16:19; 18:18). Sons and daughters who decree in alignment with Scripture, justice, and wise counsel participate in a relational authority that opens doors rather than coercing outcomes. This alignment requires humility, testing, and communal confirmation to avoid presumption and to ensure that decrees serve Kingdom ends. Early church practice emphasized the need for communal discernment before public declarations were acted upon, and councils served to confirm or correct prophetic words. Discipleship forms the protocols for decreeing responsibly so that spoken authority becomes a channel of blessing rather than a source of division. When decrees align with Heaven, covenant increase is released.

Decrees align with Heaven when they are grounded in the fear of the Lord, because reverence orders motives and prevents the misuse of prophetic speech, and Proverbs teaches that the fear of the Lord is the beginning of wisdom (Proverbs 1:7; 9:10). Sons and daughters who approach decreeing from a posture of reverence seek to reflect God's character—justice, mercy, and humility—rather than to secure personal advantage. This posture protects communities from manipulative or self-serving declarations. Early fathers counseled that prophetic speech must be tested by character and fruit, not merely by eloquence. Discipleship forms the inner life that makes decrees trustworthy. When decrees are reverent, they align with Heaven's heart.

Decrees align with Heaven when they are tested by many counselors, because communal confirmation reduces error and multiplies perspective, and Proverbs commends many counselors for safety (Proverbs 11:14; 15:22). Sons and daughters who bring prophetic words into advisory contexts allow elders and peers to weigh motives, methods, and likely consequences before implementation. This testing prevents rash pronouncements and ensures that decrees serve justice and restoration. Early church councils modeled this practice by vetting prophetic claims and by providing corrective guidance. Discipleship institutionalizes testing so that decrees are not idiosyncratic but communal. When decrees are tested, covenant flow is protected.

Decrees align with Heaven when they prioritize restoration and justice, because prophetic speech that catalyzes transfer must be tethered to ethical obligations to restore what was taken unjustly and to care for the vulnerable, and Scripture repeatedly links justice with blessing (Proverbs 14:31; Isaiah 58). Sons and daughters who decree for transfer without plans for restitution and care risk perpetuating injustice under the guise of blessing. This ethical tethering is practical: it ensures that transferred resources build institutions of care rather than fueling personal aggrandizement. Early prophetic practice in Scripture often accompanied calls for justice and restoration, and the early church echoed that prophetic ethic. Discipleship forms the moral imagination that pairs decrees with restorative action. When decrees prioritize justice, covenant transfer becomes redemptive.

Decrees align with Heaven when they are accompanied by practical stewardship plans, because prophetic words that release resources must be matched by governance, accountability, and training to preserve legacy, and Proverbs links planning with stability (Proverbs 21:5; 24:3–4). Sons and daughters who receive prophetic transfer without structures for stewardship risk rapid dissipation of blessing. This practical pairing is essential: it converts prophetic momentum into sustainable institutions. Early church communities that received resources for mission established oversight and training to ensure continuity. Discipleship provides the frameworks for converting prophetic release into durable stewardship. When decrees are paired with plans, covenant increase endures.

Decrees align with Heaven when they are humble in posture, acknowledging dependence on God and on communal wisdom, because pride corrupts prophetic speech and invites error, and Proverbs warns that pride precedes ruin (Proverbs 16:18). Sons and daughters who decree with humility invite correction and preserve relational trust, making their words more likely to be received and acted upon responsibly. This humility is practical: it prevents the elevation of personality over covenant practice. Early church leaders who combined prophetic insight with humble service were more often heeded and entrusted with responsibility. Discipleship forms the humility that keeps decrees accountable. When decrees are humble, covenant access is preserved.

Decrees align with Heaven when they are consistent with Scripture, because the Word is the measuring rod for prophetic speech and the safeguard against error, and Proverbs links instruction with life (Proverbs 4:1–9). Sons and daughters who test decrees against Scripture avoid declarations that contradict covenant character and priorities. This scriptural tether ensures that prophetic words serve Kingdom ends rather than personal agendas. Early church councils appealed to Scripture as the final arbiter in disputes and prophetic claims. Discipleship forms the habit of Scripture-testing so that decrees remain faithful. When decrees align with Scripture, covenant flow is trustworthy.

Decrees align with Heaven when they invite participation rather than coercion, because prophetic speech that mobilizes communities for shared stewardship multiplies capacity, and Proverbs commends many counselors and shared responsibility (Proverbs 11:14; 27:17). Sons and daughters who decree in ways that invite collaboration create networks that can implement and sustain the declared vision. This participatory approach prevents the concentration of power and preserves communal ownership. Early church practice of communal discernment and shared mission ensured that prophetic initiatives were implemented by many hands. Discipleship forms the practices that translate decrees into mobilized communities. When decrees invite participation, covenant increase is multiplied.

Decrees align with Heaven when they are patient with timing, recognizing that prophetic words often require seasons to manifest and that premature enforcement can produce harm, and Proverbs teaches the value of seasons and preparation (Proverbs 6:6–8; 21:5). Sons and daughters who wait for confirmation and for the right season avoid forcing outcomes that would compromise integrity. This patience is practical: it preserves resources and prevents the waste of premature action. Early prophetic narratives often show seasons of preparation before provision arrived. Discipleship forms the endurance to steward prophetic words across time. When decrees respect timing, covenant promises unfold rightly.

Decrees align with Heaven when they are transparent about motives and methods, because openness builds trust and prevents suspicion that prophetic words are being used for private gain, and Proverbs links honesty with favor (Proverbs 11:3; 22:1). Sons and daughters who declare both the word and the stewardship plan invite communal oversight and reduce the risk of scandal. This transparency is practical: it sustains donor confidence and preserves relational capital. Early church letters often accompanied prophetic encouragement with clear instructions for care and accountability. Discipleship forms the discipline of transparent reporting and communal review. When decrees are transparent, covenant transfer is stewarded well.

Decrees align with Heaven when they include mechanisms for restoration and redress, because prophetic transfer must not perpetuate injustice, and Scripture calls for restitution where wrong has been done (Exodus 22; Luke 19:8). Sons and daughters who build restoration into prophetic outcomes ensure that transferred wealth repairs harm and builds communal resilience. This restorative mechanism is practical: it prevents the perpetuation of systems that once exploited others. Early prophetic and apostolic practice emphasized restitution and care for the vulnerable as signs of true blessing. Discipleship forms the ethical frameworks that make restoration integral to prophetic action. When decrees include restoration, covenant transfer becomes healing.

Decrees align with Heaven when they are accompanied by ongoing discipleship, because prophetic release without formation often leads to misuse, and Proverbs links instruction with life and favor (Proverbs 4:1–9). Sons and daughters who pair prophetic words with training, mentoring, and accountability convert sudden openings into long-term stewardship capacity. This pairing is practical: it equips new stewards to manage resources with wisdom and integrity. Early church structures of catechesis and mentorship ensured that new leaders were formed to steward entrusted resources. Discipleship institutionalizes the follow-through that makes prophetic release sustainable. When decrees are matched with discipleship, covenant increase is preserved.

SPEECH THAT ATTRACTS FAVOR

Speech attracts favor when it honors God and neighbor, because honor opens doors and creates relational momentum, and Proverbs links honor with favor and influence (Proverbs 3:9–10; 18:16). Sons and daughters who speak honor into relationships—publicly affirming faithful service, blessing donors, and recognizing the dignity of the vulnerable—invite reciprocal trust and partnership. This honoring speech is practical: it builds reputational capital that translates into opportunities for stewardship. Early church leaders who publicly honored faithful servants often catalyzed wider networks of support for mission. Discipleship forms the discernment to honor rightly and to avoid flattery. When speech attracts favor, covenant access widens.

Speech attracts favor when it is truthful and winsome, because honesty combined with grace preserves relationships and invites cooperation, and Proverbs links truthful lips with enduring favor (Proverbs 12:22). Sons and daughters who speak truth with humility avoid the alienation that closes doors and instead cultivate allies who will stand with them in seasons of need. This combination of candor and kindness is practical: it sustains long-term partnerships rather than transactional exchanges. Early Christian rhetoric prized winsome truth as the means of persuasion and communal cohesion. Discipleship forms the skill of speaking truth in love so that favor is earned rather than demanded. When speech is truthful and winsome, covenant networks expand.

Speech attracts favor when it blesses rather than curses, because spoken blessing releases goodwill and opens relational channels, and Proverbs teaches that a generous spirit is made rich (Proverbs 11:25). Sons and daughters who bless leaders, workers, and neighbors create a culture of reciprocity that invites support and partnership. This blessing is practical: it mobilizes volunteers, donors, and collaborators who want to be associated with life-giving communities. Early church benedictions functioned as public endorsements that mobilized resources for care and mission. Discipleship forms the habit of blessing so that favor becomes a natural byproduct of communal life. When speech blesses, covenant favor flows.

Speech attracts favor when it is strategic in timing and tone, because well-timed words delivered with discernment open doors that blunt force cannot, and Proverbs links discretion with honor and success (Proverbs 19:11; 25:11). Sons and daughters who learn when to speak and when to be silent preserve relationships and create opportunities for influence. This strategic speech is practical: it prevents unnecessary conflict and positions leaders to be heard when it matters most. Early church elders counseled restraint and timing as marks of wise leadership. Discipleship forms the sensitivity to timing that makes speech effective. When speech is strategic, covenant favor is gained.

Speech attracts favor when it testifies to faithfulness under pressure, because consistent testimony builds credibility and invites trust, and Proverbs links faithful reputation with honor (Proverbs 22:1; 27:2). Sons and daughters who speak of tested faith and proven stewardship attract partners who value reliability over novelty. This testimony is practical: it reassures donors and collaborators that resources will be stewarded well. Early Christian testimonies of endurance under persecution often drew support and opened new fields for mission. Discipleship forms the character that makes such testimony believable. When speech testifies to faithfulness, covenant favor increases.

Speech attracts favor when it is accompanied by visible acts of care, because words that match deeds create credibility and invite reciprocal investment, and Proverbs links action with reputation (Proverbs 20:7; 11:3). Sons and daughters who speak of care while practicing it demonstrate integrity that attracts long-term partners. This congruence is practical: it builds donor confidence and mobilizes volunteers who see authenticity. Early church communities that combined proclamation with practical care multiplied witness and provision. Discipleship forms the disciplines that align speech with action. When words and deeds align, covenant favor deepens.

Speech attracts favor when it advocates for justice and the vulnerable, because communities that protect the weak gain moral credibility and civic trust, and Proverbs repeatedly ties justice to blessing (Proverbs 14:31; 21:15). Sons and daughters who use speech to defend the oppressed create reputational capital that opens doors for institutional partnerships and public support. This advocacy is practical: it positions communities as trustworthy stewards of resources for common good. Early Christian institutions that cared for widows and orphans gained civic respect and support. Discipleship forms the courage to speak for the voiceless and the wisdom to do so effectively. When speech advocates justice, covenant favor follows.

Speech attracts favor when it invites collaboration rather than competition, because cooperative language builds networks that multiply capacity, and Proverbs commends many counselors for safety and success (Proverbs 11:14; 15:22). Sons and daughters who frame initiatives as shared endeavors attract partners who bring complementary gifts and resources. This collaborative speech is practical: it reduces duplication and increases impact. Early church networks of house churches and elders multiplied care through cooperative structures. Discipleship forms the relational skills to invite and manage collaboration. When speech invites partnership, covenant flow expands.

Speech attracts favor when it is humble about success, giving credit to God and to others, because humility preserves relationships and prevents envy, and Proverbs warns that pride precedes ruin (Proverbs 16:18; 11:2). Sons and daughters who attribute success to covenant faithfulness rather than personal merit invite continued support and avoid the rivalries that fracture movements. This humility is practical: it sustains donor confidence and preserves team morale. Early Christian leaders who modeled humility were often entrusted with greater responsibility. Discipleship forms the habit of shared credit and communal celebration. When speech is humble, covenant favor endures.

Speech attracts favor when it is consistent with institutional values, because predictable language that reflects practiced priorities builds trust among stakeholders, and Proverbs links instruction with life (Proverbs 4:1–9). Sons and daughters who communicate consistently about mission, stewardship, and care reassure partners that resources will be used according to agreed principles. This consistency is practical: it reduces uncertainty and increases willingness to invest. Early church letters and creeds provided such consistency across dispersed communities. Discipleship institutionalizes language so that values are communicated clearly and repeatedly. When speech is consistent, covenant favor is sustained.

Speech attracts favor when it is generous in recognition, celebrating contributors publicly and privately, because recognition multiplies goodwill and invites further investment, and Proverbs links honor with influence (Proverbs 18:16; 3:9–10). Sons and daughters who publicly affirm donors, volunteers, and leaders create a culture of appreciation that fuels continued engagement. This recognition is practical: it strengthens networks and increases retention. Early Christian communities practiced mutual commendation as a means of sustaining care. Discipleship forms the discipline of gratitude and public affirmation. When speech recognizes others, covenant favor multiplies.

Speech attracts favor when it is disciplined by truth and mercy, balancing correction with restoration, because communities that practice both preserve human capital and invite trust, and Proverbs teaches that correction given in love leads to life (Proverbs 3:11–12). Sons and daughters who speak truth with mercy maintain credibility while enabling restoration and growth. This balanced speech is practical: it prevents the loss of gifted people and preserves institutional capacity. Early church practice emphasized restorative correction as a means of preserving leaders and communities. Discipleship forms the skills to correct without destroying and to restore without enabling. When speech balances truth and mercy, covenant favor is both deep and durable.

HOW SONS AND DAUGHTERS SPEAK DIFFERENTLY

Sons and daughters speak differently because their words flow from identity rather than from insecurity, and Proverbs links the heart with the mouth so that inner orientation shapes outward speech (Proverbs 4:23; 18:21). Those formed in covenant speak with confidence that is humble, not boastful, and their declarations reflect stewardship rather than entitlement. This identity-driven speech produces decisions that prioritize legacy, justice, and communal flourishing over personal gain. Early church formation emphasized identity in Christ as the source of speech that blesses rather than curses. Discipleship cultivates this identity so that speech becomes an expression of belonging and responsibility. When sons and daughters speak, their words carry covenant weight.

Sons and daughters speak differently because they practice reverence that orders motives, and Proverbs teaches that the fear of the Lord is the beginning of wisdom (Proverbs 1:7). Their speech honors God and neighbor, and it resists the temptation to manipulate language for personal advantage. This reverent speech invites divine partnership and human trust. Early fathers counseled that reverent speech was the hallmark of mature discipleship and public witness. Discipleship forms reverence through prayer, Scripture, and communal practice so that speech remains aligned with Heaven's priorities. When sons and daughters speak reverently, covenant access is honored.

Sons and daughters speak differently because they submit words to counsel, testing prophetic impressions against many advisors, and Proverbs commends many counselors for safety (Proverbs 11:14; 15:22). Their decrees are not impulsive but communal, and they carry the weight of tested confirmation. This communal speech reduces error and preserves relational trust. Early church councils modeled the practice of communal discernment for prophetic claims. Discipleship institutionalizes testing so that prophetic speech is accountable. When sons and daughters speak with counsel, their words are both bold and wise.

Sons and daughters speak differently because they prioritize restoration and justice in their declarations, ensuring that prophetic release is tethered to ethical obligations, and Scripture repeatedly links justice with blessing (Proverbs 14:31; Isaiah 58). Their speech calls for restitution where needed and for structures that protect the vulnerable. This justice-centered speech prevents the misuse of transferred resources. Early prophetic practice and apostolic teaching emphasized the inseparability of blessing and justice. Discipleship forms the moral imagination that pairs prophetic words with restorative action. When sons and daughters speak for justice, covenant transfer becomes redemptive.

Sons and daughters speak differently because they pair decrees with practical stewardship plans, recognizing that prophetic words must be matched by governance and training to preserve legacy, and Proverbs links planning with stability (Proverbs 21:5; 24:3–4). Their speech includes the how as well as the what, inviting implementation rather than mere proclamation. This practical pairing converts prophetic momentum into sustainable institutions. Early church communities that received resources for mission established oversight and training to ensure continuity. Discipleship provides the frameworks for converting prophetic release into durable stewardship. When sons and daughters speak with plans, covenant increase endures.

Sons and daughters speak differently because they bless others publicly and privately, creating reputational capital that opens doors for stewardship, and Proverbs links honor with favor (Proverbs 3:9–10; 18:16). Their speech of blessing is strategic and sincere, inviting reciprocal trust and partnership. This honoring language mobilizes networks and multiplies access. Early Christian benedictions functioned as public endorsements that catalyzed support. Discipleship forms the discernment to bless rightly and to recommend with integrity. When sons and daughters bless, covenant favor flows.

Sons and daughters speak differently because they steward speech as a tool for formation, teaching stewardship practices through repeated instruction and example, and Proverbs emphasizes instruction as the pathway to life (Proverbs 4:1–9; 9:9). Their words transmit habits—generosity, honor, counsel—that become institutionalized through discipleship. This formative speech converts knowledge into character and competence. Early church catechesis and mentoring turned counsel into curricula that equipped new generations. Discipleship institutionalizes teaching so that wisdom is reproducible. When sons and daughters teach, covenant capacity multiplies.

Sons and daughters speak differently because they use speech to commission and release others into responsibility, delegating authority to multiply stewardship, and Proverbs links faithfulness in small things with greater trust (Proverbs 28:20; 27:23–27). Their commissioning language is accompanied by training and accountability so that released leaders are prepared. This delegation multiplies care and prevents bottlenecks of control. Early church ordination and commissioning prayers released leaders into service with communal endorsement. Discipleship forms the criteria and practices for wise commissioning. When sons and daughters commission, stewardship scales.

Sons and daughters speak differently because they practice restorative speech that heals and reintegrates, preferring correction that leads to life rather than exclusion that destroys, and Proverbs teaches that correction given in love produces wisdom (Proverbs 3:11–12; 9:8). Their words restore dignity and retain human capital for the common good. This restorative posture preserves gifted people and prevents the loss of institutional capacity. Early church practice emphasized reconciliation as a means of preserving leaders and communities. Discipleship creates the relational pathways for correction that heals and prepares. When sons and daughters speak restoratively, stewardship remains whole.

Sons and daughters speak differently because they balance prophetic boldness with tested humility, declaring what they believe God has said while inviting correction and confirmation, and Scripture models prophetic speech that is both courageous and accountable (1 Kings 17; Acts 11). Their declarations are courageous but not reckless, and they are always submitted to communal testing. This balance prevents presumption and preserves relational trust. Early prophetic figures were often accountable to elders and councils, and the early church continued that practice. Discipleship forms the rhythms of courage and submission that make prophetic speech wise. When sons and daughters speak with both boldness and humility, covenant access is honored.

Sons and daughters speak differently because they steward speech for legacy, telling stories of faithfulness that orient future generations toward covenant priorities, and Proverbs commends leaving an inheritance for children's children (Proverbs 13:22). Their narratives preserve practices and values that convert present stewardship into generational capacity. This storytelling is economic because it transmits habits that multiply blessing beyond a single lifetime. Early church testimonies guided later communities in times of trial and transition. Discipleship embeds story into formation so that language becomes a vehicle for generational transfer. When sons and daughters speak legacy, the covenant continues to bless.

Sons and daughters speak differently because they root their words in worship, aligning speech with the fear of the Lord so that declarations invite divine partnership rather than human manipulation, and Proverbs links reverence with wisdom (Proverbs 1:7; 9:10). Their liturgies, prayers, and public declarations frame stewardship as sacred trust and invite Heaven's economy to move in ways that honor the Father. This worshipful speech transforms provision into covenant blessing rather than commodity. Early Christian liturgies formed communities to live sacrificially and to steward resources for care and mission. Discipleship embeds worshipful language into daily practice so that stewardship is an act of devotion. When sons and daughters speak in worship, Heaven's economy is honored and accessed.

CHAPTER TEN — STEWARDSHIP, PLANNING, AND THE ARCHITECTURE OF INCREASE

Planning as Spiritual Discipline

The discipline of planning is presented in Proverbs as a spiritual practice that orders the heart and prepares the household for seasons of harvest and drought, and Proverbs repeatedly links careful planning with stability and success (Proverbs 21:5; 24:3–4). Sons and daughters who treat planning as a spiritual discipline recognize that foresight is an expression of reverence: it trusts God enough to steward what He entrusts rather than reacting in panic when seasons change. Planning disciplines the imagination to think generationally, converting short-term impulses into long-term structures that preserve legacy and multiply blessing. Early Christian leaders taught that prudent preparation was a mark of wisdom; Augustine counseled that prudence in ordering life is a fruit of formed character and a safeguard for communities. Discipleship forms planners by teaching rhythms of prayerful foresight, communal counsel, and practical steps that translate vision into executable plans. When planning is practiced as devotion, stewardship becomes an act of worship rather than mere management.

Planning as spiritual discipline requires humility because it begins with listening—listening to Scripture, to counsel, and to the seasons—and Proverbs commends the one who seeks counsel before acting (Proverbs 15:22). Sons and daughters who plan from humility invite correction and avoid the arrogance of unilateral schemes that collapse under pressure. This humble planning is practical: it builds contingency, margin, and accountability into projects so that blessing is preserved rather than squandered. Early fathers like Chrysostom urged leaders to surround themselves with wise counselors to temper zeal with prudence, recognizing that unchecked enthusiasm without planning often leads to waste. Discipleship trains the heart to receive feedback and to revise plans in light of tested wisdom. When planning is humble, covenant increase is protected.

Planning as spiritual discipline integrates prayer and strategy because Proverbs links committing plans to the Lord with established outcomes (Proverbs 16:3). Sons and daughters who pray over plans do not abdicate responsibility; they align their strategies with Heaven's priorities and invite divine partnership in execution. This integration prevents the false dichotomy between faith and work, showing that prayerful planning is both spiritual and practical. Early Christian practice combined prayerful discernment with administrative competence, modeling how devotion and governance can coexist. Discipleship forms the habit of praying through plans and then acting with diligence. When prayer and planning unite, stewardship becomes both faithful and fruitful.

Planning as spiritual discipline includes scenario thinking because Proverbs values the one who considers the path of his feet and watches his ways (Proverbs 4:26–27). Sons and daughters who anticipate contingencies—market shifts, leadership transitions, and social shocks—design systems that can adapt rather than collapse. This scenario planning is economic protection: it reduces the need for crisis responses that often compromise integrity. Early church communities that prepared for famine and persecution through communal stores and training preserved life and mission. Discipleship forms the foresight to plan for multiple seasons rather than assuming uninterrupted prosperity. When scenario planning is practiced, stewardship endures.

Planning as spiritual discipline requires measurable milestones because Proverbs commends the one who builds and establishes the house through wise counsel and ordered work (Proverbs 24:3–4). Sons and daughters who set clear benchmarks convert vision into accountable steps that can be evaluated and corrected. This measurement prevents drift and ensures that resources are deployed toward demonstrable fruit. Early Christian leaders used practical metrics—care delivered, catechumens trained, widows supported—to steward communal resources responsibly. Discipleship forms the discipline of reporting and reflection so that plans remain alive and accountable. When milestones guide planning, covenant increase is trackable and sustainable.

Planning as spiritual discipline includes succession thinking because Proverbs honors those who leave an inheritance for children's children (Proverbs 13:22). Sons and daughters who plan for leadership development, institutional continuity, and family formation convert present stewardship into generational capacity. This succession planning prevents the collapse that follows personality-dependent structures and secures legacy for future stewards. Early church institutions that trained elders and deacons ensured continuity of care across generations. Discipleship institutionalizes succession pathways so that stewardship is reproducible. When succession is planned, the covenant endures.

Planning as spiritual discipline embraces transparency because Proverbs links honest scales and truthful lips with blessing and trust (Proverbs 11:1; 12:22). Sons and daughters who plan with openness about budgets, goals, and risks invite communal confidence and reduce suspicion that can drain resources. This transparency is practical: it sustains donor trust and mobilizes wider participation. Early Christian communities practiced public accountability in resource distribution to preserve unity and witness. Discipleship forms the habit of transparent reporting and communal review. When planning is transparent, stewardship attracts partnership.

Planning as spiritual discipline includes ethical foresight because Proverbs ties righteousness and justice to stable increase (Proverbs 21:3; 16:8). Sons and daughters who plan with justice in view design systems that protect the vulnerable and prevent exploitation, ensuring that prosperity is redemptive rather than extractive. This ethical planning is economic protection: it prevents the social costs of injustice that eventually undermine prosperity. Early church leaders insisted that care for widows and orphans be integral to planning, not an afterthought. Discipleship forms the moral imagination to embed justice into strategy. When ethics guide planning, covenant increase blesses many.

Planning as spiritual discipline requires iterative learning because Proverbs values instruction and correction as life (Proverbs 4:1–5; 9:8). Sons and daughters who treat plans as living documents revise them in light of feedback, preserving agility and preventing repeated mistakes. This iterative approach institutionalizes learning and prevents the ossification of poor practices. Early Christian councils and letters preserved lessons that guided later communities through changing contexts. Discipleship creates the feedback loops that convert experience into wisdom for future planning. When planning is iterative, stewardship becomes adaptive and wise.

Planning as spiritual discipline includes resource mapping because Proverbs links wise provision with the prudent who prepare (Proverbs 6:6–8; 21:20). Sons and daughters who map assets—people, networks, finances, and time—allocate them strategically rather than scattering them across competing priorities. This mapping preserves margin and enables targeted investment in formation and mission. Early church communities inventoried communal resources to ensure equitable care and sustainable mission. Discipleship trains leaders to identify and deploy assets with discernment. When resources are mapped, stewardship is efficient and resilient.

Planning as spiritual discipline honors Sabbath rhythms because Proverbs and the wider biblical witness affirm rest as part of ordered life (Proverbs 3:24; Exodus 20:8–11). Sons and daughters who plan with built-in rhythms of rest protect leaders from burnout and preserve clarity for long-term stewardship. This rhythm is practical: it sustains creativity, prevents moral erosion, and models a covenantal pace for communities. Early Christian monastic and communal rhythms institutionalized rest as a safeguard for formation and mission. Discipleship forms the habit of Sabbath that sustains stewardship across seasons. When planning includes rest, increase carries no sorrow.

ORDER AS ECONOMIC PROTECTION

Order in Proverbs is presented as the architecture that preserves increase, and the book repeatedly links wise building and established houses with stability and flourishing (Proverbs 24:3–4). Sons and daughters who create ordered systems—governance, accounting, teams, and rhythms—protect resources from the entropy that follows growth without structure. Order reduces the hidden costs of chaos: litigation, relational fracture, and mission drift that erode capacity over time. Early church institutions that developed roles like elders and deacons created ordered care systems that multiplied witness and preserved unity. Discipleship forms the leaders who can design and maintain order without turning it into legalism. When order governs life, covenant increase is protected.

Order functions as economic protection because it creates predictable processes that lower transaction costs and invite investment, and Proverbs links predictability with favor (Proverbs 10:9; 11:3). Sons and daughters who institutionalize transparent procedures for stewardship attract partners who value reliability and accountability. This predictability is practical: it enables long-term partnerships and reduces the friction of ad hoc decision-making. Early Christian communities that documented practices and expectations were more likely to be trusted by civic and philanthropic partners. Discipleship trains stewards to implement processes that balance flexibility with accountability. When order creates predictability, covenant resources are more readily entrusted.

Order protects reputation because consistent practices demonstrate integrity over time, and Proverbs links a good name with favor that opens doors (Proverbs 22:1). Sons and daughters who maintain orderly reporting, fair wages, and honest accounting preserve reputational capital that multiplies influence. This reputational protection is economic: trust built over time becomes a currency that invites larger opportunities. Early church leaders guarded reputation through public accountability and transparent distribution of care. Discipleship forms the disciplines that make order habitual rather than bureaucratic. When order preserves reputation, stewardship scales responsibly.

Order protects relationships by clarifying roles and expectations, preventing the confusion that leads to conflict and fragmentation, and Proverbs values many counselors and clear governance (Proverbs 11:14; 24:6). Sons and daughters who define responsibilities and decision pathways reduce the relational strain that often accompanies growth. This relational protection preserves human capital and prevents the loss of gifted people through misunderstanding or resentment. Early church structures—elders, deacons, and house leaders

—created role clarity that enabled expansion without collapse. Discipleship forms the practices that make role clarity relational rather than rigid. When order protects relationships, covenant capacity endures.

Order protects against mission drift by embedding core values into procedures and rituals, and Proverbs emphasizes instruction and repeated teaching as formative (Proverbs 4:1–9). Sons and daughters who institutionalize practices—regular teaching, communal counsel, and transparent budgeting—ensure that mission remains coherent across seasons and leaders. This protection is practical: it prevents the dilution of purpose that wastes resources and confuses stakeholders. Early Christian catechesis and liturgical rhythms preserved identity across dispersed communities. Discipleship institutionalizes formative practices so that order sustains calling. When order prevents drift, stewardship remains focused.

Order protects legacy by creating systems for succession, record-keeping, and formation that transmit capacity to future generations, and Proverbs honors leaving an inheritance for children's children (Proverbs 13:22). Sons and daughters who design orderly succession pathways convert present stewardship into generational capacity rather than ephemeral success. This legacy protection is economic because it compounds stewardship across time. Early church institutions that trained leaders and preserved records ensured continuity of care and mission. Discipleship forms the curricula and mentorship that make legacy reproducible. When order secures legacy, the covenant continues to bless.

Order protects against fraud and abuse by establishing checks and balances—oversight committees, transparent reporting, and independent review—that deter predatory behavior, and Proverbs condemns dishonest scales and deceit (Proverbs 11:1; 20:10). Sons and daughters who institutionalize oversight reduce the risk of scandal that can collapse movements and drain resources. This protective architecture is practical: it preserves donor confidence and prevents the costly remediation of abuse. Early Christian governance included roles and councils to provide such oversight. Discipleship forms the ethical frameworks and relational networks that make oversight relational rather than merely bureaucratic. When order deters abuse, stewardship remains trustworthy.

Order protects against the tyranny of urgency by creating prioritized decision frameworks that distinguish urgent from important, and Proverbs commends the prudent planner (Proverbs 21:5). Sons and daughters who use ordered prioritization avoid reactive cycles that waste energy and compromise integrity. This prioritization preserves strategic focus and prevents the fragmentation of resources. Early church councils helped communities focus on core mission rather than peripheral controversies. Discipleship forms the discipline to prioritize covenant ends over immediate pressures. When order disciplines urgency, stewardship is strategic.

Order protects institutional memory by documenting decisions, lessons learned, and tested practices so that future leaders inherit wisdom rather than repeating mistakes, and Proverbs values instruction and remembrance (Proverbs 4:1–5). Sons and daughters who create archives of counsel, budgets, and outcomes build a living library that compounds stewardship capacity across generations. This memory is practical: it shortens learning curves and preserves tested strategies. Early Christian letters and councils preserved teaching that guided later communities through changing contexts. Discipleship institutionalizes memory so that counsel becomes curriculum. When order preserves memory, covenant stewardship deepens.

Order protects the vulnerable by embedding procedures for care—transparent criteria for aid, accountable distribution, and restorative pathways—that prevent favoritism and ensure justice, and Proverbs links care for the poor with blessing (Proverbs 14:31; 19:17). Sons and daughters who design ordered care systems ensure that resources reach those in need and that dignity is preserved. This protective ordering prevents the ad hoc responses that often miss the most vulnerable or create dependency. Early church institutions developed standards for care that preserved fairness and multiplied resilience. Discipleship forms the practices that make care both compassionate and accountable. When order protects the vulnerable, covenant increase is redemptive.

Order protects creativity by providing safe containers for experimentation—pilot projects, accountable risk, and review—so that innovation can occur without endangering core capacity, and Proverbs values counsel and testing (Proverbs 15:22; 24:6). Sons and daughters who balance order with controlled experimentation enable adaptive growth while preserving core functions. This protective balance allows new initiatives to be trialed and scaled responsibly. Early church communities experimented with new forms of care within accountable structures that preserved unity. Discipleship forms the governance that allows creativity to flourish without chaos. When order contains innovation, stewardship becomes both stable and inventive.

Order protects financial health by enforcing budgeting, reserves, and transparent accounting that prevent overspending and ensure margin, and Proverbs commends the prudent who prepare (Proverbs 21:20; 6:6–8). Sons and daughters who institutionalize financial order create the conditions for sustainable generosity and long-term investment. This fiscal protection is practical: it prevents the boom-and-bust cycles that erode trust and capacity. Early Christian communities practiced communal stores and prudent distribution to survive lean seasons. Discipleship forms the financial disciplines that make stewardship sustainable. When order secures finances, covenant increase is steady.

Order protects reputation in public life by ensuring consistent ethical practice and transparent governance that attract civic trust and partnership, and Proverbs links a good name with favor (Proverbs 22:1). Sons and daughters who steward public reputation through ordered practice open doors for institutional collaboration and broader impact. This public trust is economic because it multiplies access to networks and resources beyond the immediate community. Early Christian institutions that maintained honorable witness often became centers of education and care in their cities. Discipleship forms the public habits that preserve reputation. When order secures public trust, stewardship expands.

MARGIN AS WISDOM

Margin is presented in Proverbs as a wise buffer that preserves life and enables generosity, and the text commends the prudent who prepare and the diligent who avoid scarcity (Proverbs 6:6–8; 21:20). Sons and daughters who build margin into budgets, time, and relationships create capacity to respond to opportunity and crisis without panic. Margin is not waste but wisdom: it prevents forced compromises and preserves the ability to give generously when need arises. Early Christian communities practiced margin through communal stores and mutual aid, demonstrating that prepared generosity multiplies provision. Discipleship forms the habit of margin by teaching restraint, foresight, and the discipline of saving. When margin is honored, stewardship becomes resilient.

Margin as wisdom protects against the tyranny of scarcity because it prevents decisions made under pressure that often sacrifice integrity for immediate relief, and Proverbs warns that anxious toil produces little (Proverbs 10:22; 12:25). Sons and daughters who maintain margin avoid the shortcuts that erode reputation and legacy. This protective margin preserves clarity and prevents the erosion of influence through reactive choices.

Early church examples show that communities with reserves and mutual support weathered famine and persecution with resilience. Discipleship trains leaders to steward margin so that generosity can be sustained. When margin guards decisions, covenant increase endures.

Margin as wisdom enables strategic generosity because reserves allow for sacrificial giving without collapsing core functions, and Proverbs commends the generous soul that refreshes others (Proverbs 11:24–25). Sons and daughters who steward margin can scatter resources into formation, mission, and care, trusting that reserves will sustain core operations. This strategic generosity multiplies influence and opens doors for partnership. Early Christian practice of communal stores enabled radical sharing that multiplied witness. Discipleship forms the discipline to allocate margin for Kingdom priorities. When margin enables generosity, covenant flow deepens.

Margin as wisdom preserves leadership health because time margin—rest, retreat, and reflection—prevents burnout and sustains clarity for long-term stewardship, and Proverbs links rest with renewal (Proverbs 3:24; 6:6–8). Sons and daughters who protect time margin return to labor with renewed vision rather than depleted energy. This temporal margin sustains endurance and prevents the moral erosion that accompanies chronic overwork. Early Christian rhythms of prayer and rest preserved leaders and multiplied witness across seasons. Discipleship forms the practices that make rest a discipline rather than an indulgence. When time margin is honored, stewardship carries joy.

Margin as wisdom enables risk management because financial and relational buffers allow for prudent experimentation without endangering core capacity, and Proverbs values the prudent planner (Proverbs 21:5). Sons and daughters who maintain margin can pilot new initiatives, learn, and scale without risking collapse. This risk margin is practical: it converts failure into learning rather than catastrophe. Early church communities used reserves to support mission experiments that later multiplied care. Discipleship forms the governance that allows for safe risk and iterative growth. When margin supports experimentation, stewardship becomes adaptive.

Margin as wisdom protects families and future generations because reserves and planned giving prevent the sudden depletion of inheritance, and Proverbs honors leaving an inheritance for children's children (Proverbs 13:22). Sons and daughters who steward margin for legacy ensure that resources are available for formation and care beyond their lifetime. This intergenerational margin converts present stewardship into generational capacity. Early Christian households practiced planned care and formation to preserve continuity. Discipleship forms the disciplines of saving and planned generosity that secure legacy. When margin secures future generations, the covenant continues to bless.

Margin as wisdom preserves institutional credibility because transparent reserves and contingency plans reassure partners and donors that stewardship is prudent, and Proverbs links prudent planning with stability (Proverbs 21:20). Sons and daughters who demonstrate margin attract long-term investment because partners see stewardship competence. This credibility is practical: it lowers perceived risk and increases willingness to commit resources. Early church institutions that maintained prudent reserves were trusted by civic authorities and benefactors. Discipleship forms the financial disciplines that build credibility. When margin builds trust, covenant partnerships expand.

Margin as wisdom enables rapid response to opportunity because available resources and relational bandwidth allow swift, faithful action when doors open, and Proverbs links preparedness with harvest (Proverbs 6:6–8). Sons and daughters who maintain margin can seize strategic openings without compromising core functions. This responsiveness is practical: it turns readiness into multiplied impact. Early Christian networks that had reserves and trained leaders could mobilize care quickly in crises. Discipleship forms the readiness to act faithfully when opportunity arises. When margin enables response, stewardship multiplies fruit.

Margin as wisdom reduces stress and preserves discernment because buffers prevent panic decisions that cloud judgment, and Proverbs warns that anxious hearts make poor choices (Proverbs 12:25; 14:30). Sons and daughters who steward margin maintain clarity and resist fear-driven compromises. This preserved discernment protects both resources and reputation. Early church leaders who practiced margin were better positioned to hear counsel and to make sober choices under pressure. Discipleship forms the inner calm that margin supports. When margin preserves discernment, covenant increase is wise.

Margin as wisdom supports equitable care because reserves allow for consistent support of the vulnerable rather than sporadic relief, and Proverbs ties justice for the poor to communal stability (Proverbs 14:31; 19:17). Sons and daughters who allocate margin for ongoing care prevent the cycles of crisis that deepen poverty and erode social capital. This equitable margin is practical: it sustains dignity and multiplies communal resilience. Early Christian institutions used planned resources to provide steady care for widows and orphans. Discipleship forms the commitment to consistent care rather than episodic charity. When margin supports equity, covenant blessing is communal.

Margin as wisdom enables disciplined investment in formation because reserves fund training, discipleship, and institutional capacity that multiply stewardship over time, and Proverbs values instruction and the passing of wisdom (Proverbs 4:1–9). Sons and daughters who allocate margin to formation convert present resources into future leaders and multiplied care. This investment margin is economic: it compounds stewardship across generations. Early church catechesis and training were sustained by planned resources that ensured continuity. Discipleship institutionalizes formation funding so that capacity grows. When margin invests in formation, covenant increase becomes generational.

Margin as wisdom protects against moral compromise because buffers reduce the pressure to accept unethical shortcuts in lean times, and Proverbs warns that dishonest gain is fleeting (Proverbs 13:11). Sons and daughters who maintain margin can refuse expedient compromises and preserve integrity. This moral margin is practical: it prevents the erosion of trust that destroys long-term capacity. Early Christian communities that prioritized prudent reserves resisted corrupting offers during persecution and scarcity. Discipleship forms the resolve to steward with integrity even under pressure. When margin guards morality, covenant increase remains pure.

Margin as wisdom fosters generosity because those who are not clutching can give freely, and Proverbs teaches that the generous soul is made rich (Proverbs 11:25). Sons and daughters who steward margin experience the freedom to scatter into mission and care without endangering core functions. This generous margin multiplies relational capital and invites reciprocal blessing. Early church generosity was sustainable because communities planned for giving even in lean seasons. Discipleship forms the habit of generous margin so that giving is steady rather than sporadic. When margin enables generosity, covenant flow deepens.

LONG TERM THINKING IN PROVERBS

Proverbs consistently privileges long-term thinking over short-term gain, teaching that steady increase and prudent planning produce durable wealth and legacy (Proverbs 13:11; 21:5). Sons and daughters who adopt long-term thinking prioritize formation, institutions, and relationships that outlast a single season rather than chasing immediate applause. This horizon shifts decision-making from consumption to investment, converting present resources into future capacity. Early Christian leaders modeled long-term thinking by founding schools, hospitals, and care systems that served societies for generations. Discipleship forms the patience and foresight necessary to steward across decades rather than quarters. When long-term thinking governs choices, covenant increase compounds.

Long-term thinking in Proverbs values character formation because moral maturity secures trust and entrustment over time, and the text links humility and righteousness with honor and legacy (Proverbs 22:4; 16:8). Sons and daughters who invest in character produce leaders who can be entrusted with greater responsibility and resources. This character investment is economic: trust built over years becomes a multiplier for stewardship. Early church formation prioritized catechesis and mentorship to ensure that leaders were formed for endurance. Discipleship institutionalizes character formation so that stewardship is sustainable. When character is prioritized, covenant increase is entrusted.

Long-term thinking in Proverbs plans for seasons and cycles, recognizing that harvests and famines alternate and that preparation preserves life (Proverbs 6:6–8; 21:20). Sons and daughters who plan for cycles avoid panic and waste, positioning resources for strategic deployment when opportunity arrives. This seasonal foresight prevents the depletion of capacity and enables generosity even in lean times. Early Christian communities practiced communal stores and mutual aid to survive hardship and to sustain mission. Discipleship forms the discipline to steward across cycles rather than react to them. When seasons are honored, covenant increase endures.

Long-term thinking in Proverbs invests in institutions because structures multiply care beyond individual lifespans, and the text commends building and establishing the house with wisdom (Proverbs 24:3–4). Sons and daughters who invest in schools, hospitals, and training centers convert present stewardship into generational capacity. This institutional investment is economic: it compounds impact across time and preserves legacy. Early Christian institutions that served the poor and educated children became enduring testimonies of covenant care. Discipleship forms the governance and curricula that make institutions sustainable. When institutions are built, covenant blessing multiplies.

Long-term thinking in Proverbs values generational transfer because leaving an inheritance for children's children secures continuity of care and formation (Proverbs 13:22). Sons and daughters who plan for intergenerational transfer ensure that resources are stewarded for formation and mission beyond their lifetime. This transfer thinking prevents the squandering of legacy and preserves relational continuity. Early Christian households practiced intentional formation to pass on faith and stewardship practices. Discipleship equips families and institutions to steward inheritance with prudence and generosity. When generational transfer is planned, the covenant continues to bless.

Long-term thinking in Proverbs protects against the seduction of quick gain by warning that ill-gotten wealth is fleeting, and the text contrasts steady increase with sudden riches that vanish (Proverbs 13:11). Sons and daughters who resist schemes that promise rapid wealth preserve reputation and legacy for future generations. This resistance is practical: it prevents legal entanglements and moral compromise that erode capacity. Early church leaders counseled prudence and warned against the temptations of expedient gain. Discipleship forms the discernment to choose continuity over speed. When quick gain is refused, covenant increase is durable.

Long-term thinking in Proverbs invests in people because training leaders multiplies stewardship capacity, and the text values instruction and the passing of wisdom (Proverbs 4:1–9). Sons and daughters who prioritize leadership development convert present resources into future stewards who can sustain mission. This human investment is economic: it compounds influence through trained hands. Early church catechesis and mentoring ensured that new leaders were equipped to steward entrusted resources. Discipleship institutionalizes formation so that capacity grows beyond a single generation. When people are invested in, covenant stewardship multiplies.

Long-term thinking in Proverbs embeds justice into planning because sustainable prosperity requires fair systems that protect the vulnerable, and the text links justice with blessing (Proverbs 14:31; 21:15). Sons and daughters who design just economic practices prevent social breakdown that undermines prosperity. This justice orientation secures social capital and preserves the moral foundation of stewardship. Early Christian institutions that integrated care for the poor into their planning sustained witness and attracted civic trust. Discipleship forms the moral frameworks that make justice integral to long-term strategy. When justice is embedded, covenant increase is redemptive.

Long-term thinking in Proverbs values margin and reserves because preparedness preserves capacity across seasons, and the text commends the prudent who prepare (Proverbs 6:6–8; 21:20). Sons and daughters who build reserves avoid panic decisions and maintain the ability to give generously even in lean times. This reserve thinking is practical: it smooths volatility and enables strategic generosity. Early Christian communities that maintained communal stores survived crises and multiplied care. Discipleship forms the discipline of saving and planned generosity. When reserves are maintained, covenant increase is steady.

Long-term thinking in Proverbs plans for accountability because sustained stewardship requires transparent governance and oversight, and the text links faithfulness with entrustment (Proverbs 28:20; 27:23–27). Sons and daughters who institutionalize accountability preserve donor confidence and prevent misuse that destroys legacy. This accountability is practical: it sustains funding and partnership by demonstrating stewardship competence. Early church governance included elders and deacons to ensure transparent care. Discipleship trains stewards to report faithfully and to receive correction. When accountability is institutionalized, covenant resources are entrusted more widely.

Long-term thinking in Proverbs cultivates patience because enduring projects require seasons of hidden growth, and the text honors those who wait for harvest (Proverbs 20:22; 21:5). Sons and daughters who practice patience avoid the compromises of hurried action and steward for continuity rather than immediate applause. This patience preserves relationships and prevents the erosion of trust that follows impulsive decisions. Early Christian leaders modeled patient formation and long-term institution building. Discipleship forms the endurance necessary to steward across decades. When patience governs planning, covenant increase matures.

Long-term thinking in Proverbs integrates worship and work because sustainable stewardship treats resources as sacred trust, and the text links the fear of the Lord with wisdom and life (Proverbs 1:7; 3:9–10). Sons and daughters who frame stewardship as worship align daily work with covenant priorities and invite divine partnership in long-term projects. This integration prevents the secularization of stewardship and preserves its sacred purpose. Early Christian liturgies and practices embedded stewardship within worship, shaping institutions that served both God and neighbor. Discipleship forms the habit of offering work as devotion. When worship informs planning, covenant increase is both practical and holy.

HOW SONS AND DAUGHTERS STEWARD DIFFERENTLY

Sons and daughters steward differently because their identity precedes their activity: belonging to the Father's household reframes resources as entrusted rather than owned, and Proverbs links the heart with the mouth so that inner orientation shapes outward stewardship (Proverbs 4:23; 28:20). Those formed in sonship and daughtership plan with legacy, justice, and generosity as primary metrics rather than mere accumulation. This identity-driven stewardship produces decisions that prioritize formation, care, and institutional continuity over personal aggrandizement. Early Christian households modeled familial stewardship that multiplied care through shared responsibility. Discipleship forms heirs who steward with humility and competence. When sons and daughters steward, covenant priorities govern.

Sons and daughters steward differently because they practice reverence that orders motives, and Proverbs teaches that the fear of the Lord is the beginning of wisdom (Proverbs 1:7). Their planning is prayerful and their governance is humble, resisting the temptation to manipulate systems for personal gain. This reverent stewardship invites divine partnership and human trust. Early fathers counseled that reverent stewardship was the hallmark of mature discipleship and public witness. Discipleship forms reverence through prayer, Scripture, and communal practice so that stewardship remains aligned with Heaven's priorities. When sons and daughters steward reverently, covenant access is honored.

Sons and daughters steward differently because they submit plans to counsel, testing strategies against many advisors, and Proverbs commends many counselors for safety (Proverbs 11:14; 15:22). Their governance is communal rather than unilateral, and their plans carry the weight of tested confirmation. This communal stewardship reduces error and preserves relational trust. Early church councils modeled the practice of communal discernment for governance and resource allocation. Discipleship institutionalizes testing so that stewardship is accountable. When sons and daughters steward with counsel, resources are entrusted wisely.

Sons and daughters steward differently because they prioritize justice and restoration in allocation, ensuring that resources repair harm and protect the vulnerable, and Proverbs links justice with blessing (Proverbs 14:31; 21:3). Their stewardship designs systems that prevent exploitation and that build institutions of care rather than personal empires. This justice-centered stewardship prevents the misuse of transferred wealth and secures communal trust. Early Christian practice integrated care for widows and orphans into institutional planning. Discipleship forms the moral imagination that pairs stewardship with restoration. When sons and daughters steward for justice, covenant increase is redemptive.

Sons and daughters steward differently because they build margin intentionally—financial, temporal, and relational—so that generosity can be sustained and crises weathered, and Proverbs commends the prudent who prepare (Proverbs 6:6–8; 21:20). Their stewardship balances bold initiative with prudent reserves, enabling both risk and resilience. This margin-aware stewardship prevents panic decisions and preserves long-term capacity. Early church communities practiced communal stores and mutual aid to sustain mission. Discipleship forms the discipline of margin that makes generosity sustainable. When sons and daughters steward with margin, covenant flow deepens.

Sons and daughters steward differently because they invest in formation as the primary asset, funding discipleship, training, and institutional capacity that multiply stewardship across generations, and Proverbs values instruction and the passing of wisdom (Proverbs 4:1–9). Their stewardship converts present resources into future leaders and multiplied care. This formation-centered stewardship compounds influence through trained hands. Early Christian catechesis and mentoring ensured continuity of care and mission. Discipleship institutionalizes formation so that stewardship is reproducible. When sons and daughters steward for formation, covenant increase becomes generational.

Sons and daughters steward differently because they design accountable systems—transparent reporting, oversight, and succession—that protect legacy and invite partnership, and Proverbs links faithfulness with entrustment (Proverbs 28:20; 27:23–27). Their stewardship institutionalizes trust so that resources can be scaled without collapse. This accountable stewardship sustains donor confidence and enables long-term collaboration. Early church governance included elders and deacons to ensure transparent care. Discipleship trains stewards to report faithfully and to receive correction. When sons and daughters steward with accountability, covenant resources are entrusted widely.

Sons and daughters steward differently because they measure success by legacy and communal flourishing rather than by personal accumulation, and Proverbs honors leaving an inheritance for children's children (Proverbs 13:22). Their stewardship invests in institutions, families, and practices that outlast a single lifetime. This legacy-oriented stewardship converts present sacrifice into future capacity. Historical Christian institutions testify to stewardship that served societies for centuries. Discipleship forms the foresight and disciplines necessary for legacy planning. When sons and daughters steward for legacy, the covenant continues to bless.

Sons and daughters steward differently because they practice restorative economics—prioritizing restitution, care, and rebuilding—so that transferred resources heal rather than harm, and Scripture models restitution and prophetic restoration (Exodus 22; Isaiah 58). Their stewardship pairs prophetic release with ethical obligations to repair past wrongs and to build equitable systems. This restorative stewardship prevents the perpetuation of injustice under the guise of blessing. Early prophetic and apostolic practice emphasized restitution and care as signs of true blessing. Discipleship forms the frameworks that make restoration integral to stewardship. When sons and daughters steward restoratively, covenant transfer becomes healing.

Sons and daughters steward differently because they cultivate teachability and humility, remaining open to correction and formation, and Proverbs links teachability with life and favor (Proverbs 9:9; 12:1). Their stewardship is adaptive because they learn from counsel, failure, and communal wisdom rather than assuming infallibility. This teachable stewardship preserves relevance and prevents the pride that destroys influence. Early church leaders emphasized lifelong formation and accountability as safeguards for stewardship. Discipleship creates environments where humility is practiced and where leaders are formed for endurance. When sons and daughters steward with teachability, covenant increase is entrusted.

Sons and daughters steward differently because they integrate worship into governance, framing stewardship as sacred trust and aligning daily management with devotion, and Proverbs links reverence with wisdom (Proverbs 1:7; 3:9–10). Their stewardship treats resources as instruments for worshipful care rather than commodities for personal gain. This worshipful stewardship invites divine partnership and preserves the sacred purpose of provision. Early Christian liturgies and practices embedded stewardship within worship, shaping institutions that served both God and neighbor. Discipleship forms the habit of offering work as devotion. When sons and daughters steward in worship, Heaven's economy is honored.

Sons and daughters steward differently because they steward speech as a tool for formation—teaching, blessing, commissioning, and restoring—so that language becomes a vehicle for multiplying stewardship, and Proverbs emphasizes instruction as the pathway to life (Proverbs 4:1–9; 18:21). Their stewardship uses words to build culture, to mobilize partners, and to transmit values across generations. This speech-shaped stewardship converts vision into practiced habits. Early church catechesis and public benedictions transmitted identity and practice across communities. Discipleship institutionalizes formative language so that stewardship is reproducible. When sons and daughters steward with speech, covenant capacity multiplies.

CHAPTER ELEVEN — THE RIGHTEOUS PATH: AVOIDING THE TRAPS OF MAMMON

Proverbs' Warnings about Greed

The book of Proverbs repeatedly warns that greed corrodes the heart and destroys legacy, teaching that the pursuit of gain apart from wisdom leads to ruin rather than blessing (Proverbs 15:27; 28:22). Sons and daughters who heed these warnings learn that accumulation without formation produces brittle wealth that fractures under pressure and invites moral compromise. Greed distorts imagination, turning stewardship into possession and service into self-exaltation, and Proverbs contrasts the anxious hoarder with the generous steward who is made rich in life (Proverbs 11:24–25). Early church writers observed the same pattern: Augustine warned that disordered love of riches displaces love of God, and Chrysostom condemned the idolization of wealth that silences compassion. Discipleship reframes desire by forming motives toward covenant priorities rather than toward accumulation, teaching that true prosperity is measured by faithfulness and fruitfulness. When Proverbs' warnings are taken seriously, sons and daughters avoid the slow corrosion that greed brings.

Proverbs exposes the spiritual logic of greed by showing how it narrows vision to immediate gain and blinds the heart to long-term consequences (Proverbs 21:6; 13:11). Sons and daughters who fall into this trap often rationalize compromise as prudence, confusing expedience with wisdom and thereby eroding trust. The text calls readers to a different economy—one where patience, integrity, and justice produce durable increase rather than quick, unstable profit. Early Christian communities that prioritized formation over fortune preserved witness and multiplied care precisely because they resisted the cultural seduction of wealth. Discipleship trains the soul to recognize the subtle shifts of motive that precede compromise so that integrity is preserved before loss occurs. When the spiritual logic of greed is exposed, the path of righteousness becomes clearer.

Proverbs warns that the lover of money will never be satisfied, and this insatiable appetite produces restlessness that undermines stewardship and relationships (Proverbs 27:20). Sons and daughters who chase more without formation find themselves in a treadmill of anxiety that consumes joy and erodes generosity. The covenant counters this by rooting identity in belonging rather than in bank balances, and by teaching that contentment flows from reverence and trust (Proverbs 30:8–9). Early fathers taught that contentment is a spiritual discipline that protects against the tyranny of desire and preserves communal resources for care. Discipleship cultivates contentment through rhythms of gratitude, simplicity, and communal accountability. When contentment is formed, the traps of Mammon lose their power.

Proverbs links dishonest gain with sudden loss, warning that shortcuts often produce temporary advantage followed by ruin (Proverbs 13:11; 20:17). Sons and daughters who are tempted by schemes that promise rapid wealth must remember that integrity preserves reputation and long-term capacity. The covenant economy rewards faithfulness and prudence rather than cunning and manipulation, and the text calls believers to steward resources in ways that honor justice. Early church leaders insisted that means matter as much as ends, refusing to justify unethical methods by desirable outcomes. Discipleship forms the conviction that righteous means produce sustainable ends. When the community refuses dishonest shortcuts, stewardship remains trustworthy.

Proverbs exposes how greed corrodes relationships by turning people into instruments for gain rather than persons to be loved, and the text condemns oppression and exploitation as antithetical to covenant life (Proverbs 22:16; 14:31). Sons and daughters who prioritize accumulation over care fracture the social fabric that sustains long-term prosperity and invite social instability. The covenant calls for economies that protect the vulnerable and distribute resources in ways that preserve dignity and community. Early Christian institutions—hospitals, orphan care, and communal relief —were practical responses to the social damage greed produces. Discipleship forms hearts to see stewardship as communal care rather than private advantage. When relationships are protected, the traps of Mammon are avoided.

Proverbs warns that the pursuit of wealth can harden the heart and blind one to correction, and the text links pride with downfall while honoring humility as the path to life (Proverbs 16:18; 22:4). Sons and daughters who allow wealth to define them become resistant to counsel and correction, losing the very formation that secures stewardship. The covenant counters this by rooting identity in sonship and daughtership, which invites teachability and communal accountability. Early fathers counseled that humility is the safeguard of leaders entrusted with resources, and they modeled structures of oversight to preserve character. Discipleship institutionalizes correction so that wealth does not become a teacher of pride. When humility governs, the heart remains open to formation.

Proverbs teaches that greed often disguises itself as prudence, and the text calls for discernment to distinguish wise provision from covetous clutching (Proverbs 21:20; 28:25). Sons and daughters must learn to read motives honestly, recognizing when caution becomes fear and when prudence becomes hoarding. The covenant invites a posture of trust that balances preparation with generosity, allowing for margin without succumbing to scarcity thinking. Early Christian practice demonstrated that prudent reserves and generous sharing can coexist when motives are rightly ordered.

Discipleship trains the inner witness to name motive and to align action with covenant priorities. When discernment is practiced, the subtle traps of Mammon are exposed.

Proverbs warns that the love of money can lead to injustice and the oppression of the poor, and the text repeatedly calls for righteous commerce and fair scales (Proverbs 11:1; 22:16). Sons and daughters who steward within covenant responsibility design systems that protect the vulnerable and prevent exploitation. This ethical stance is not sentimental but practical: stable societies and sustainable economies require justice in exchange and care for the weak. Early church leaders insisted that economic life must reflect moral commitments, and they organized care systems to ensure fairness. Discipleship forms the moral imagination to embed justice into commerce. When justice governs exchange, Mammon's traps are dismantled.

Proverbs warns that greed breeds secrecy and isolation, and the text commends counsel and communal life as antidotes to the loneliness of accumulation (Proverbs 11:14; 15:22). Sons and daughters who isolate themselves with wealth lose the corrective voice of community and become vulnerable to deception and moral drift. The covenant invites shared stewardship —accountability, counsel, and mutual aid—that preserves integrity and multiplies capacity. Early Christian households practiced communal life precisely to prevent the isolation that wealth can produce. Discipleship creates the relational structures that keep leaders connected and accountable. When community is prioritized, the isolating traps of Mammon are avoided.

Proverbs warns that greed can lead to short-term thinking that sacrifices legacy for immediate gain, and the text honors those who leave an inheritance for future generations (Proverbs 13:22). Sons and daughters who chase immediate profit often forfeit the ability to bless posterity and to build institutions that outlast them. The covenant calls for generational stewardship that invests in formation, institutions, and relationships that compound blessing across time. Early Christian founders built schools, hospitals, and care systems with a horizon beyond their own lives. Discipleship forms the patience and foresight necessary for generational planning. When legacy is prioritized, Mammon's short-term seductions lose their appeal.

Proverbs warns that greed can corrupt worship by turning devotion into a transaction, and the text calls for offerings of the heart rather than bargaining with God (Proverbs 3:9–10). Sons and daughters who allow economic motives to dominate spiritual life risk reducing covenant to commerce and faith to formula. The covenant invites worshipful stewardship—giving that flows from reverence and gratitude rather than from calculation. Early Christian liturgies embedded generosity within worship to preserve its sacred character. Discipleship forms the heart so that stewardship remains an act of devotion. When worship governs wealth, the traps of Mammon are transformed into opportunities for blessing.

THE SPIRIT OF MAMMON VERSUS COVENANT

The spirit of Mammon is a posture that elevates material security above covenant relationship, and Proverbs exposes its logic by contrasting the anxious hoarder with the one who trusts the Lord (Proverbs 10:22; 3:5–6). Sons and daughters who live under Mammon's sway measure life by accumulation and fear, while covenant life measures by belonging and stewardship. This spiritual contrast is not merely theological but practical: Mammon produces short-term thinking, exploitation, and isolation, whereas covenant produces generosity, justice, and communal resilience. Early church writers identified Mammon as a rival lord and urged believers to choose allegiance to the Father rather than to wealth. Discipleship reorients allegiance through formation that reshapes desire and practice. When covenant allegiance is chosen, Mammon's claims are broken.

The spirit of Mammon promises security through possession but delivers insecurity through anxiety, and Proverbs warns that anxious toil produces little while the blessing of the Lord brings wealth without painful toil (Proverbs 10:22; 12:11). Sons and daughters who trust in possessions find themselves perpetually unsettled, always seeking the next acquisition to quiet fear. Covenant trust, by contrast, anchors the heart in relationship and invites stewardship that multiplies without the corrosive anxiety of clutching. Early Christian testimony shows communities that thrived under shared trust rather than private accumulation. Discipleship forms the trust that frees hands to give and hearts to rest. When covenant trust replaces Mammon's promise, provision becomes peaceful.

The spirit of Mammon corrupts motives by turning stewardship into self-preservation, and Proverbs exposes this by linking righteous motives with blessing and crooked motives with ruin (Proverbs 21:3; 16:8). Sons and daughters who steward for self-preservation are tempted to cut corners, exploit others, and hoard for imagined safety. Covenant stewardship reframes resources as entrusted for communal flourishing and for the Father's purposes, which protects against self-protective distortion. Early church leaders taught that true security is found in obedience and communal care rather than in private hoards. Discipleship forms motives through repeated practice of generosity and accountability. When motives are reordered, Mammon's corruption loses its grip.

The spirit of Mammon isolates leaders by encouraging secrecy and unilateral control over resources, and Proverbs warns that many counselors bring safety while isolation invites error (Proverbs 11:14; 15:22). Sons and daughters who centralize control for the sake of security cut off the corrective voice of community and increase the risk of abuse. Covenant structures distribute responsibility through counsel, oversight, and shared stewardship, preventing the concentration of power that Mammon favors. Early Christian governance—elders, deacons, and communal oversight—was designed to prevent such isolation. Discipleship institutionalizes shared responsibility so that resources are stewarded transparently. When stewardship is communal, Mammon's isolating tactics fail.

The spirit of Mammon seduces by promising identity through accumulation, and Proverbs counters this by rooting identity in the fear of the Lord and in belonging to the household of faith (Proverbs 1:7; 22:4). Sons and daughters who find identity in possessions become vulnerable to comparison, envy, and the need for constant validation. Covenant identity secures the heart in relationship, freeing people to steward without needing wealth to prove worth. Early fathers emphasized identity formation as the antidote to status-driven living. Discipleship forms identity through belonging, service, and mutual recognition. When identity is secured in covenant, Mammon's identity trap is dismantled.

The spirit of Mammon distorts worship by turning giving into bargaining, and Proverbs teaches that honor and firstfruits invite blessing when offered from reverence rather than calculation (Proverbs 3:9–10). Sons and daughters who give as a transaction miss the formative power of generosity and risk reducing worship to a ledger. Covenant worship frames giving as devotion and trust, and it forms hearts to give sacrificially rather than strategically for return. Early Christian liturgies embedded giving within worship to preserve its sacred character. Discipleship forms the habit of worshipful stewardship that resists transactional distortion. When worship shapes giving, Mammon's bargaining loses its appeal.

The spirit of Mammon encourages exploitation by normalizing dishonest scales and unjust gain, and Proverbs condemns dishonest weights and calls for fair commerce (Proverbs 11:1; 20:10). Sons and daughters who yield to Mammon's logic rationalize exploitation as necessary for survival, thereby undermining social trust and long-term prosperity. Covenant economics insist on just exchange and protection for the vulnerable, recognizing that sustainable prosperity requires fairness. Early Christian institutions modeled equitable care and fair practice as signs of covenant life. Discipleship forms the ethical frameworks that make justice nonnegotiable. When justice governs commerce, Mammon's exploitative logic is exposed.

The spirit of Mammon fosters impatience for results, pushing toward quick schemes and risky shortcuts, while covenant patience values steady formation and generational fruit (Proverbs 13:11; 21:5). Sons and daughters who succumb to impatience often sacrifice integrity for speed and lose the capacity to steward across seasons. Covenant patience invests in institutions, training, and relationships that compound blessing over time. Early Christian founders built enduring institutions precisely because they valued patient formation over immediate gain. Discipleship cultivates the endurance to steward across decades rather than quarters. When patience governs, Mammon's urgency is resisted.

The spirit of Mammon breeds comparison and envy,

which fracture communities and redirect resources toward status rather than care, and Proverbs warns that envy rots the bones (Proverbs 14:30). Sons and daughters who measure themselves by others' accumulation become competitors rather than collaborators, draining communal capacity. Covenant life cultivates gratitude and mutual honor, turning comparison into celebration and rivalry into partnership. Early church communities practiced mutual commendation and shared resources to prevent envy from taking root. Discipleship forms the habits of gratitude and honor that protect against comparison. When gratitude prevails, Mammon's divisive work is undone.

The spirit of Mammon resists accountability because it fears exposure, and Proverbs links faithfulness with entrustment while exposing the folly of secretive gain (Proverbs 28:20; 27:23–27). Sons and daughters who hide practices to protect wealth invite scandal and eventual collapse. Covenant structures insist on transparency, oversight, and communal review to preserve trust and to prevent abuse. Early church governance included roles and councils to ensure accountability and to protect the vulnerable. Discipleship forms the courage to be transparent and the humility to receive correction. When accountability is practiced, Mammon's secrecy is defeated.

The spirit of Mammon reduces people to instruments of profit, and Proverbs calls for honor, justice, and care for the poor as markers of covenant life (Proverbs 3:27; 14:31). Sons and daughters who resist Mammon design economies that restore dignity and empower contribution rather than creating dependency or exploitation. This restorative approach preserves social capital and multiplies sustainable prosperity. Early Christian institutions—schools, hospitals, and relief systems—were practical embodiments of economies that honored persons. Discipleship forms the practices that make restoration central to stewardship. When dignity is preserved, Mammon's dehumanizing logic is overturned.

The spirit of Mammon promises autonomy through wealth but delivers bondage to fear and to the very systems it seemed to master, and Proverbs teaches that the wise are freed by reverence and counsel rather than by accumulation (Proverbs 1:7; 11:14). Sons and daughters who choose covenant freedom trade the illusion of autonomy for the reality of relational trust and delegated responsibility. This covenant freedom enables shared stewardship and multiplies capacity without the loneliness of self-reliance. Early church communities found freedom in mutual dependence and shared care. Discipleship forms the relational habits that convert autonomy into accountable partnership. When covenant freedom is embraced, Mammon's bondage is broken.

QUICK GAIN VERSUS SLOW GAIN

Proverbs repeatedly contrasts quick gain with slow, steady increase, warning that sudden riches often vanish while patient stewardship yields durable wealth (Proverbs 13:11; 21:5). Sons and daughters who are tempted by schemes promising rapid profit must weigh the cost to character, reputation, and legacy. Quick gain often requires compromise—dishonest scales, exploitation, or risky speculation—that undermines long-term capacity and invites collapse. Slow gain, by contrast, is the fruit of diligence, discipline, and wise planning; it compounds through faithful stewardship and preserves relational capital. Early Christian practice favored steady institution building and formation over speculative ventures, recognizing that durable blessing requires time and testing. Discipleship trains patience and the habits that produce slow, sustainable increase. When slow gain is chosen, covenant prosperity endures.

Quick gain seduces by offering immediate validation and visible success, and Proverbs warns that such allure often masks moral cost and future ruin (Proverbs 20:21;

28:20). Sons and daughters who chase immediate applause risk trading integrity for applause and losing the trust that enables future stewardship. The covenant calls for a different metric of success—faithfulness, formation, and generational fruit—rather than the flash of sudden wealth. Early church leaders counseled restraint and long-term thinking, building institutions that served communities for centuries rather than chasing transient acclaim. Discipleship forms the inner metrics that value legacy over limelight. When long-term metrics govern, quick gain loses its appeal.

Quick gain often depends on leverage that amplifies both upside and downside, and Proverbs counsels prudence and foresight to avoid catastrophic loss (Proverbs 21:5; 24:3–4). Sons and daughters who use leverage without governance risk rapid collapse when conditions shift, whereas slow gain builds reserves, governance, and training that absorb shocks. This structural difference is practical: slow gain creates systems that can sustain generosity and mission across seasons. Early Christian communities that invested in governance and training survived persecution and scarcity because they had built durable structures. Discipleship forms the prudence to use leverage wisely and to prioritize resilience. When structural prudence is practiced, slow gain prevails.

Quick gain often bypasses formation by rewarding results over character, and Proverbs links faithfulness in small things with greater trust and responsibility (Proverbs 28:20; 27:23–27). Sons and daughters who skip formation for rapid expansion risk entrusting resources to untested hands and fracturing legacy.

Slow gain invests in people—training, mentoring, and accountability—so that stewardship can scale without collapse. This human investment compounds over generations and preserves institutional integrity. Early church catechesis and mentoring ensured that leaders were formed before being entrusted with larger responsibilities. Discipleship institutionalizes formation so that growth is matched by competence. When people are formed, slow gain becomes sustainable.

Quick gain often produces envy and rivalry because visible success invites comparison, and Proverbs warns that envy destroys while honor preserves peace (Proverbs 14:30; 15:18). Sons and daughters who pursue rapid prominence can fracture communities and divert resources into competition rather than care. Slow gain, built through shared stewardship and mutual honor, cultivates collaborative networks that multiply capacity. This cooperative approach reduces wasteful rivalry and preserves relational capital. Early Christian networks multiplied care precisely because they prioritized shared increase over individual glory. Discipleship forms the habits of honor that prevent rivalry. When collaboration is chosen, slow gain multiplies.

Quick gain can create fragile dependence on a single revenue stream or personality, and Proverbs values building and establishing the house with wisdom and counsel (Proverbs 24:3–4). Sons and daughters who rely on one source of income or on charismatic leadership risk collapse when that source fails. Slow gain diversifies capacity—training leaders, building institutions, and creating reserves—so that stewardship is not person-dependent. This diversification is practical: it preserves mission through transitions and seasons. Early church institutions that distributed responsibility endured beyond any single leader's tenure. Discipleship forms the systems that make stewardship reproducible. When diversification is practiced, slow gain secures legacy.

Quick gain often neglects justice because speed can rationalize exploitation, and Proverbs condemns dishonest gain while commending fair scales (Proverbs 11:1; 13:11). Sons and daughters who accept rapid profit at the expense of justice undermine the social foundations that sustain prosperity. Slow gain embeds justice into practice, ensuring that prosperity is redemptive rather than extractive. This ethical stance preserves social capital and invites long-term partnership. Early Christian care systems integrated justice into planning to prevent exploitation. Discipleship forms the moral frameworks that make justice nonnegotiable. When justice is embedded, slow gain blesses many.

Quick gain often lacks margin and reserves because immediate consumption follows sudden influx, and Proverbs commends the prudent who prepare and store for seasons (Proverbs 6:6–8; 21:20). Sons and daughters who fail to build margin after windfalls are vulnerable to future shocks and to the temptation to spend impulsively. Slow gain institutionalizes reserves and disciplined allocation so that generosity can be sustained and crises weathered. This fiscal prudence is practical: it smooths volatility and enables strategic giving. Early Christian communities used communal stores to preserve capacity across lean seasons. Discipleship forms the discipline of saving and planned generosity. When margin is built, slow gain endures.

Quick gain often produces short memories and weak institutional learning because success can mask structural flaws, and Proverbs values instruction and remembrance as safeguards for future generations (Proverbs 4:1–5). Sons and daughters who experience sudden success without documenting lessons risk repeating mistakes and losing hard-won wisdom. Slow gain institutionalizes learning—recording counsel, outcomes, and tested practices—so that future leaders inherit a living library of wisdom. This memory compounds stewardship capacity across generations. Early church letters and councils preserved lessons that guided later communities. Discipleship ensures that counsel becomes curriculum. When learning is institutionalized, slow gain becomes generational.

Quick gain can tempt leaders to centralize control to protect perceived advantage, and Proverbs commends many counselors and shared responsibility as safeguards (Proverbs 11:14; 27:17). Sons and daughters who centralize control after sudden success risk creating brittle systems dependent on a few individuals. Slow gain distributes authority through training, delegation, and accountable structures so that stewardship can scale without collapse. This distributed model multiplies care and preserves continuity. Early church governance created roles and councils to distribute responsibility. Discipleship forms the pathways for progressive entrustment. When authority is shared, slow gain multiplies.

Quick gain often neglects formation of the vulnerable because immediate profit can distract from steady care, and Proverbs links care for the poor with communal stability (Proverbs 14:31; 19:17). Sons and daughters who chase rapid wealth may deprioritize the steady work of restoring dignity and building institutions of care. Slow gain invests in the vulnerable through sustained programs and training that restore capacity and multiply resilience. This restorative investment is practical: it preserves social cohesion and prevents long-term costs of neglect. Early Christian institutions sustained communities by prioritizing steady care. Discipleship forms the commitment to consistent support rather than episodic charity. When the vulnerable are prioritized, slow gain blesses society.

Quick gain often produces brittle reputations because shortcuts and compromises surface over time, and Proverbs links a good name with favor that opens doors (Proverbs 22:1). Sons and daughters who pursue rapid prominence risk losing the trust that enables future partnerships and stewardship. Slow gain builds reputation through consistent integrity and transparent practice, attracting long-term partners and donors. This reputational capital is economic: it opens networks and multiplies access. Early Christian communities that maintained honorable witness became trusted partners in civic life. Discipleship forms the habits that preserve reputation. When reputation is built slowly, covenant access widens.

AVOIDING SNARES AND ENTANGLEMENTS

Avoiding snares requires vigilance because Proverbs warns that hidden traps often accompany the promise of gain, and the text calls for discernment and counsel to navigate them (Proverbs 22:3; 11:14). Sons and daughters must learn to test offers, to ask hard questions, and to consult trusted advisors before committing resources. This vigilance prevents entanglement in deals that compromise integrity or bind future generations to unjust obligations. Early church elders modeled such prudence by vetting proposals and by protecting communal resources from risky ventures. Discipleship forms the habits of scrutiny and communal review that expose snares early. When vigilance is practiced, entanglements are avoided.

Avoiding snares requires clear boundaries because Proverbs teaches that guarded speech and honest scales preserve life and commerce (Proverbs 4:23; 11:1). Sons and daughters who set transparent policies for partnerships, contracts, and resource use reduce ambiguity that predators exploit. These boundaries are practical protections: they prevent mission drift, favoritism, and the slow corrosion of trust. Early Christian communities used written agreements and public accountability to protect communal assets. Discipleship forms the discipline to create and enforce boundaries with both firmness and compassion. When boundaries are clear, snares lose their foothold.

Avoiding snares requires testing of prophetic words and promises because Scripture calls for testing spirits and for communal confirmation of prophetic speech (1 Thessalonians 5:20–21; Deuteronomy 18:21–22). Sons and daughters who receive prophetic encouragement about transfer or opportunity must bring such words into counsel and seek confirmation before acting. This testing prevents presumption and ensures that prophetic release is matched by wisdom and governance. Early church councils provided mechanisms for testing prophetic claims and for protecting communities from deception. Discipleship institutionalizes testing so that prophetic words are accountable. When prophetic words are tested, snares are exposed.

Avoiding snares requires ethical clarity because entanglements often arise when moral lines are blurred for gain, and Proverbs links righteousness with blessing while exposing the ruin of crooked gain (Proverbs 21:3; 13:11). Sons and daughters must insist on justice in commerce and on restoration where harm has been done, refusing to accept blessings that perpetuate injustice. This ethical clarity protects reputation and preserves the social foundations of prosperity. Early Christian practice insisted that blessing must be redemptive and restorative rather than exploitative. Discipleship forms the moral imagination to refuse tainted gain.

When ethics govern decisions, snares are avoided.

Avoiding snares requires legal and relational diligence because contracts and partnerships can carry hidden liabilities, and Proverbs commends the prudent who consider the path of their feet (Proverbs 4:26–27). Sons and daughters who conduct due diligence—legal review, background checks, and relational references—reduce the risk of entanglement. This diligence is practical: it prevents costly remediation and preserves momentum. Early Christian communities used elders and councils to vet external proposals and to protect communal assets. Discipleship forms the habit of careful inquiry and communal review. When diligence is practiced, snares are minimized.

Avoiding snares requires humility because pride invites overreach and blind spots, and Proverbs warns that pride precedes ruin while humility precedes honor (Proverbs 16:18; 22:4). Sons and daughters who remain teachable invite correction that exposes hidden risks and prevents reckless commitments. This humility is practical: it preserves relationships and prevents the isolation that leads to entanglement. Early church leaders modeled humility by submitting plans to counsel and by accepting correction. Discipleship forms the posture that keeps leaders open to wise input. When humility governs, snares are less likely to ensnare.

Avoiding snares requires financial transparency because secrecy invites suspicion and enables abuse, and Proverbs links honest scales with blessing (Proverbs 11:1). Sons and daughters who maintain open books, clear reporting, and independent review reduce the chance that hidden liabilities will surface later. This transparency is practical: it sustains donor confidence and prevents the erosion of trust that collapses movements. Early Christian institutions practiced public accountability to preserve unity and witness. Discipleship forms the discipline of transparent stewardship. When transparency is practiced, snares are exposed early.

Avoiding snares requires relational wisdom because entanglements often begin with flattering speech and seductive promises, and Proverbs warns against the flatterer who conceals danger (Proverbs 29:5; 26:28). Sons and daughters who cultivate honest counsel and who test offers against communal priorities avoid being seduced by charm. This relational wisdom is practical: it prevents the isolation that allows deception to flourish. Early church elders guarded communities by exposing flattering counsel and by insisting on tested relationships. Discipleship forms the discernment to see through flattery and to value tested loyalty. When relational wisdom is practiced, snares are avoided.

Avoiding snares requires structural safeguards because systems that lack checks and balances are vulnerable to capture, and Proverbs commends many counselors and shared responsibility (Proverbs 11:14; 27:17). Sons and daughters who design oversight—committees, audits, and succession plans—prevent the concentration of power that enables entanglement. These safeguards are practical: they preserve institutional integrity and enable recovery when mistakes occur. Early church governance included roles and councils to provide such protections. Discipleship forms the governance practices that make safeguards relational rather than merely bureaucratic. When structures protect, snares are less dangerous.

Avoiding snares requires a commitment to restoration because entanglements often leave harm in their wake, and Proverbs calls for correction that leads to life rather than exclusion that destroys (Proverbs 3:11–12; 9:8). Sons and daughters who build restorative pathways—restitution, reconciliation, and training—repair damage and prevent cycles of abuse. This restorative commitment is practical: it preserves human capital and prevents the loss of gifted people through shame. Early church practice emphasized reconciliation as a means of preserving leaders and communities. Discipleship creates the relational pathways for correction that heals and prepares. When restoration is practiced, snares become opportunities for renewal.

Avoiding snares requires a long-term horizon because short horizons make risky entanglements attractive, and Proverbs honors those who plan for future generations (Proverbs 13:22). Sons and daughters who think generationally refuse deals that promise immediate gain at the cost of future capacity. This horizon protects legacy and preserves the ability to bless posterity. Early Christian founders built institutions with a view beyond their own lifetimes, ensuring continuity of care. Discipleship forms the patience and foresight necessary for generational stewardship. When the long view governs, snares lose their appeal.

Avoiding snares requires the cultivation of inner integrity because external systems fail when the heart is compromised, and Proverbs links the heart with life and with the mouth (Proverbs 4:23; 18:21). Sons and daughters who guard the inner life—through prayer,

Scripture, silence, and communal accountability—are less likely to be lured into entanglements that betray covenant values. This inner integrity is the primary safeguard because it shapes motives and choices before external systems are tested. Early church formation prioritized the inner life as the foundation for public trust. Discipleship forms the disciplines that keep the heart aligned with covenant priorities. When inner integrity is cultivated, snares are resisted.

PURITY OF MOTIVE IN HEAVEN'S ECONOMY

Purity of motive is central to Heaven's economy because Proverbs repeatedly links right motive with blessing and wrong motive with ruin, teaching that the heart's orientation determines the fruit of stewardship (Proverbs 16:2; 21:2). Sons and daughters who steward from pure motives—reverence, love, and responsibility—invite covenant favor that multiplies resources without sorrow. Motive shapes method: when the heart seeks communal flourishing rather than personal elevation, decisions preserve reputation and legacy. Early church teachers insisted that inner purity is the prerequisite for trustworthy stewardship and that external success without inward formation is hollow. Discipleship forms motive through repeated practice, confession, and communal correction so that stewardship flows from identity rather than from insecurity. When motive is pure, Heaven's economy is accessed rightly.

Purity of motive resists the temptation to use spiritual language as a cover for personal gain, and Proverbs warns against those who cloak selfish ambition in piety (Proverbs 21:27; 30:12). Sons and daughters who guard motive refuse to weaponize faith for advantage and instead let worship shape stewardship. This integrity preserves communal trust and prevents the cynicism that corrodes witness. Early church fathers condemned those who used spiritual authority for personal enrichment and modeled servant leadership as the antidote. Discipleship forms the humility to serve without seeking status. When motive is transparent, Heaven's economy flows without scandal.

Purity of motive prioritizes justice and restoration because a heart aligned with covenant seeks to repair harm rather than to profit from it, and Proverbs links care for the poor with blessing (Proverbs 14:31; 19:17). Sons and daughters who steward with pure motive design systems that restore dignity and prevent exploitation. This restorative priority ensures that transferred resources heal communities rather than perpetuate cycles of harm. Early prophetic and apostolic practice emphasized restitution and care as signs of true blessing. Discipleship forms the moral imagination that pairs blessing with repair. When motive is restorative, Heaven's economy becomes redemptive.

Purity of motive embraces generosity as a formative practice rather than as a transactional tactic, and Proverbs teaches that the generous soul is made rich (Proverbs 11:24–25). Sons and daughters who give from identity rather than from calculation cultivate hearts that attract relational returns and divine partnership. This generous posture preserves joy and prevents the clutching that erodes legacy. Early Christian communities practiced radical sharing as an expression of family identity and as a safeguard against scarcity thinking.

Discipleship forms the habit of sacrificial giving so that generosity becomes natural. When motive is generous, Heaven's economy multiplies.

Purity of motive demands accountability because good intentions without oversight can still produce harm, and Proverbs links faithfulness with entrustment (Proverbs 28:20; 27:23–27). Sons and daughters who pair pure motive with transparent governance ensure that blessing is stewarded responsibly and that mistakes are corrected. This accountability protects both reputation and resources. Early church governance provided oversight to ensure that charitable acts were effective and just. Discipleship forms the practices of reporting and review that make motive and method congruent. When motive is accountable, Heaven's economy is preserved.

Purity of motive cultivates humility because those who steward for the common good recognize their dependence on the Father and on community, and Proverbs honors humility as the path to honor (Proverbs 22:4; 11:2). Sons and daughters who steward humbly invite correction and partnership rather than seeking control. This humility preserves relational capital and prevents the pride that destroys influence. Early Christian leaders modeled servant humility as the foundation for trustworthy stewardship. Discipleship forms the posture that keeps leaders teachable and accountable. When motive is humble, Heaven's economy is entrusted.

Purity of motive aligns speech with action because words that bless must be matched by deeds that care, and Proverbs links truthful lips with enduring favor

(Proverbs 12:22; 11:3). Sons and daughters who speak blessing and then act to implement care build credibility and invite partnership. This congruence between word and deed is practical: it mobilizes volunteers, donors, and collaborators who see integrity in action. Early church benedictions were often accompanied by practical care that demonstrated sincerity. Discipleship forms the discipline to match declarations with implementation. When motive is congruent, Heaven's economy is activated.

Purity of motive protects against entitlement because those who steward from identity understand blessing as trust rather than as personal right, and Proverbs warns that entitlement breeds ruin (Proverbs 16:18; 28:6). Sons and daughters who reject entitlement steward with gratitude and responsibility, preserving legacy for future generations. This posture prevents the squandering of resources and the fracturing of communities. Early Christian households taught that inheritance is stewardship, not a private trophy. Discipleship forms the ethic of stewardship that resists entitlement. When motive is stewardship, Heaven's economy endures.

Purity of motive fosters teachability because those who seek to serve rather than to be served remain open to correction and formation, and Proverbs links teachability with life and favor (Proverbs 9:9; 12:1). Sons and daughters who steward with a learner's heart adapt to changing seasons and preserve relevance. This teachability prevents the pride that isolates leaders from counsel and from communal wisdom. Early church formation emphasized lifelong learning as the safeguard for leaders. Discipleship institutionalizes learning so that stewardship evolves with wisdom. When motive is teachable, Heaven's economy is entrusted.

Purity of motive integrates worship and work because stewardship becomes an act of devotion rather than a secular task, and Proverbs links reverence with wisdom and blessing (Proverbs 1:7; 3:9–10). Sons and daughters who offer their labor and resources as worship invite divine partnership that multiplies provision beyond human calculation. This integration prevents the secularization of stewardship and preserves its sacred purpose. Early Christian liturgies embedded stewardship within worship to shape institutions that served both God and neighbor. Discipleship forms the habit of offering work as devotion. When motive is worshipful, Heaven's economy is honored.

Purity of motive secures legacy because resources stewarded with right motive build institutions and practices that bless future generations, and Proverbs commends leaving an inheritance for children's children (Proverbs 13:22). Sons and daughters who steward with purity invest in formation, governance, and care that outlast them and multiply blessing across time. This legacy orientation converts present sacrifice into generational capacity. Early Christian institutions that prioritized formation and justice left enduring testimonies of covenant care. Discipleship forms the foresight and disciplines necessary for legacy planning. When motive is pure, the covenant continues to bless.

CHAPTER TWELVE — THE LEGACY OF WISDOM: BUILDING FOR GENERATIONS

Inheritance for Children's Children

Inheritance in Proverbs is framed as more than transfer of assets; it is the passing of formed character, tested practices, and covenant patterns that enable future stewardship (Proverbs 13:22). Sons and daughters who steward with legacy in view invest in training, governance, and relationships that outlast a single lifetime rather than merely accumulating for consumption. This kind of inheritance secures continuity because it couples resources with formation—teaching, mentoring, and institutional rhythms that reproduce stewardship. Early Christian households practiced intentional transmission of faith and practice, ensuring that children learned both doctrine and daily disciplines that sustained communities. Discipleship is the primary vehicle by which inheritance becomes living capacity rather than inert wealth. When inheritance is planned as formation plus provision, future generations inherit competence as well as capital.

Inheritance for children's children requires intentional structures: wills, trusts, training programs, and institutional governance that translate personal stewardship into communal capacity. Sons and daughters who neglect structures risk leaving resources without the habits and leaders needed to steward them well. Proverbs commends leaving an inheritance for descendants as a mark of wisdom and foresight, and the text repeatedly links prudent planning with stability (Proverbs 21:5; 13:22). Early Christian communities institutionalized formation—catechesis, mentoring, and communal oversight—to ensure that spiritual and practical inheritance was transmitted. Discipleship programs that combine teaching with hands-on responsibility create heirs who can manage both resources and relationships. When structures accompany inheritance, legacy is preserved.

Inheritance for children's children includes moral capital—reputation, honor, and relational trust—that often proves more valuable than material transfer alone. Sons and daughters who protect reputation through integrity and transparent stewardship bequeath networks and credibility that open doors for their heirs. Proverbs links a good name with favor and influence, showing that reputation functions as relational currency (Proverbs 22:1). Early church leaders guarded communal reputation through public accountability and consistent care for the vulnerable, creating trust that outlived individual leaders. Discipleship forms reputational habits—honesty, fairness, and faithful reporting—that become part of the inheritance. When moral capital is preserved, material inheritance finds fertile soil.

Inheritance for children's children must be paired with education in stewardship because resources without competence often lead to waste. Sons and daughters who invest in training—financial literacy, governance, vocational skill, and spiritual formation—prepare heirs to steward wisely. Proverbs emphasizes instruction and correction as life, and the passing of wisdom is central to generational flourishing (Proverbs 4:1–9). Early Christian catechesis combined doctrinal teaching with practical formation so that new generations could sustain institutions and care systems. Discipleship models that include apprenticeships, mentoring, and progressive responsibility ensure that inheritance is matched by capacity. When education accompanies inheritance, legacy multiplies.

Inheritance for children's children includes the transmission of values and rituals that shape identity and practice across generations. Sons and daughters who embed rhythms—regular teaching, communal meals, stewardship practices—create cultural continuity that orients heirs toward covenant priorities. Proverbs shows that repeated instruction forms the heart and secures life, and ritualized practices become the scaffolding of legacy (Proverbs 4:1–5). Early Christian households used liturgy, catechesis, and communal rhythms to pass on identity and practice. Discipleship institutionalizes these rituals so that they survive leadership transitions and cultural shifts. When values and rituals are transmitted, inheritance becomes living tradition.

Inheritance for children's children requires humility from the giver because legacy is entrusted, not owned; sons and daughters who steward with humility model teachability and service for their heirs. Proverbs links humility with honor and warns against pride that destroys, teaching that the posture of the giver shapes the heart of the receiver (Proverbs 22:4; 16:18). Early church fathers counseled that those who give must do so with a servant's heart, modeling dependence on God rather than self-exaltation. Discipleship forms humility through correction, accountability, and communal practice so that inheritance is not a vehicle for entitlement. When humility shapes inheritance, legacy becomes stewardship rather than trophy.

Inheritance for children's children must include mechanisms for accountability and review so that resources are stewarded according to covenant priorities rather than personal whim. Sons and daughters who build oversight—boards, mentors, and reporting—protect legacy from misuse and ensure continuity of purpose. Proverbs values many counselors and planned governance as safeguards for the house (Proverbs 11:14; 24:3–4). Early Christian institutions developed roles like elders and deacons to provide such oversight and to preserve communal trust. Discipleship trains both givers and heirs in accountability practices that make stewardship transparent and relational. When accountability is institutionalized, inheritance remains faithful to its intended purpose.

Inheritance for children's children should be designed to empower rather than to enable dependency, because true legacy equips heirs to contribute rather than to consume. Sons and daughters who pair resources with training and responsibility create heirs who can multiply stewardship rather than squander it. Proverbs commends leaving an inheritance that secures future capacity, not mere comfort (Proverbs 13:22). Early Christian care models combined relief with training so recipients became contributors to communal life. Discipleship provides pathways for heirs to prove faithfulness through small responsibilities that grow into larger trusts. When inheritance empowers, legacy becomes generative.

Inheritance for children's children must be framed within covenant ethics—justice, mercy, and honor—so that wealth serves redemptive ends rather than perpetuating harm. Sons and daughters who embed ethical commitments into legacy planning ensure that transferred resources build institutions of care and restoration. Proverbs links justice for the poor with blessing and stability, showing that righteous use of resources secures communal flourishing (Proverbs 14:31). Early Christian legacies—schools, hospitals, and care systems —were expressions of ethical inheritance that served society. Discipleship forms the moral imagination to design legacies that heal and restore. When ethics govern inheritance, legacy blesses many.

Inheritance for children's children requires foresight about cultural change and adaptability so that institutions remain relevant across shifting contexts. Sons and daughters who build flexible governance and training systems enable heirs to adapt practices without abandoning core covenant priorities. Proverbs values wisdom that considers the path of one's feet and watches ways, encouraging prudence in planning (Proverbs 4:26–27). Early church institutions survived cultural shifts by preserving core teachings while adapting practices for new contexts. Discipleship forms leaders who can steward continuity and change with discernment. When adaptability is built into inheritance, legacy endures.

Inheritance for children's children includes spiritual inheritance—prayer, testimony, and covenant memory—that orients future generations toward dependence on the Father rather than on resources alone. Sons and daughters who pass on stories of faith, answered prayer, and communal testimony create a spiritual soil where stewardship is practiced as worship. Proverbs links the fear of the Lord with the beginning of wisdom and life, anchoring legacy in reverence (Proverbs 1:7). Early Christian testimony preserved spiritual memory that guided communities through trials. Discipleship embeds spiritual practices into family and institutional life so that faithfulness is transmitted. When spiritual inheritance is prioritized, material legacy serves eternal ends.

Inheritance for children's children must be stewarded with joy and gratitude so that heirs receive legacy as blessing rather than burden. Sons and daughters who model grateful stewardship teach heirs to steward with generosity and contentment rather than entitlement. Proverbs commends contentment and warns against insatiable desire, shaping motives for stewardship (Proverbs 30:8–9). Early Christian formation cultivated gratitude as a safeguard against the corrosive effects of wealth. Discipleship forms the habit of thanksgiving so that legacy is received with humility and used for blessing. When gratitude shapes inheritance, legacy multiplies joy.

GENERATIONAL WEALTH IN PROVERBS

Generational wealth in Proverbs is portrayed as the fruit of wisdom, diligence, and righteous practice rather than mere luck or exploitation, and the text repeatedly links steady increase with prudent stewardship (Proverbs 10:4; 13:11). Sons and daughters who pursue generational wealth invest in character, institutions, and relationships that compound over time. This biblical vision reframes wealth as a tool for blessing and continuity rather than as an end in itself. Early church witnesses modeled this by building enduring institutions—schools, hospitals, and care systems—that served communities across centuries. Discipleship trains leaders to think in terms of stewardship that multiplies across generations. When generational wealth is pursued through wisdom, it becomes a vehicle for lasting blessing.

Generational wealth in Proverbs requires the integration of spiritual and practical disciplines: reverence, counsel, planning, and faithful labor all contribute to durable increase (Proverbs 3:5–6; 21:5). Sons and daughters who neglect any of these elements risk creating brittle wealth that collapses under pressure. The covenant economy values formation as the multiplier of resources, teaching that wisdom precedes riches (Proverbs 8:10–11). Early Christian formation combined spiritual disciplines with practical governance to sustain institutions through hardship. Discipleship forms the habits that convert present labor into generational capacity. When spiritual and practical disciplines unite, generational wealth endures.

Generational wealth in Proverbs is protected by justice and fair commerce, because exploitative gain corrodes social trust and undermines long-term prosperity (Proverbs 11:1; 16:8). Sons and daughters who build wealth through righteous exchange preserve the social fabric that sustains markets and institutions. This ethical foundation prevents the social costs of exploitation —resentment, rebellion, and reputational collapse. Early Christian communities insisted on fair treatment of workers and care for the vulnerable as integral to sustainable prosperity. Discipleship forms the moral frameworks that make justice nonnegotiable in wealth creation. When justice undergirds wealth, generational blessing is secure.

Generational wealth in Proverbs is multiplied through networks and counsel because many counselors bring safety and open collaborative opportunities that scale impact (Proverbs 11:14; 15:22). Sons and daughters who cultivate wise networks gain access to resources, partnerships, and mentorship that accelerate stewardship capacity. This network effect is practical: it converts individual stewardship into communal multiplication. Early church networks of house churches and elders multiplied care and mission across regions. Discipleship forms relational capital that enables generational multiplication. When networks are cultivated, generational wealth expands responsibly.

Generational wealth in Proverbs is sustained by margin and reserves that protect against volatility and enable strategic generosity, and the text commends the prudent who prepare (Proverbs 6:6–8; 21:20). Sons and daughters who build reserves avoid panic decisions and maintain the ability to give sacrificially in lean seasons. This fiscal prudence smooths volatility and preserves capacity for long-term investment. Early Christian communal stores and mutual aid systems exemplified how margin sustains mission through hardship. Discipleship forms the discipline of saving and planned generosity that secures legacy. When margin is maintained, generational wealth becomes resilient.

Generational wealth in Proverbs is transmitted through tested responsibility: faithfulness in small things leads to greater trust and entrustment, creating a ladder of stewardship across generations (Proverbs 28:20; 27:23–27). Sons and daughters who prove reliable with small trusts are more likely to be given larger responsibilities that expand capacity. This progressive entrustment is the covenantal mechanism by which stewardship scales. Early church practice of progressive responsibility prepared leaders to receive and exercise authority wisely. Discipleship provides the testing ground where faithfulness is proven. When responsibility is earned, generational wealth is entrusted wisely.

Generational wealth in Proverbs is invested in formation because people are the primary multiplying asset; training leaders multiplies stewardship capacity beyond any single lifetime (Proverbs 4:1–9). Sons and daughters who fund discipleship, education, and vocational training convert present resources into future leaders who sustain institutions. This human investment compounds influence across generations. Early Christian catechesis and mentoring ensured continuity of care and mission. Discipleship institutionalizes formation so that capacity grows beyond a single generation. When people are invested in, generational wealth becomes generative.

Generational wealth in Proverbs is guarded by transparent governance and accountability that preserve trust and prevent abuse, and the text links faithfulness with entrustment (Proverbs 28:20; 27:23–27). Sons and daughters who institutionalize oversight attract partners willing to invest in long-term projects because they see stewardship competence. This accountability sustains funding and partnership by demonstrating responsible management. Early church governance included elders and deacons to ensure transparent care. Discipleship trains stewards to report faithfully and to receive correction. When governance is transparent, generational wealth is entrusted more widely.

Generational wealth in Proverbs is used to build institutions that serve public good—schools, hospitals, and care systems—so that blessing multiplies beyond family lines and benefits society, and the text honors those who build for future generations (Proverbs 13:22; 24:3–4). Sons and daughters who invest in public goods convert private blessing into communal flourishing. This institutional investment compounds impact across time and preserves legacy. Early Christian institutions became enduring testimonies of covenant care because they served common needs. Discipleship forms the vision and governance to build institutions that outlast founders. When wealth builds public goods, generational blessing spreads.

Generational wealth in Proverbs is protected by cultural practices that transmit values—honor, generosity, and justice—so that institutions remain faithful to covenant priorities across leadership changes. Sons and daughters who embed values into rituals and curricula ensure continuity of purpose. This cultural protection prevents mission drift and preserves identity. Early Christian liturgies and catechesis transmitted values that guided communities through upheaval. Discipleship institutionalizes cultural practices so that values are lived rather than merely stated. When culture preserves values, generational wealth serves eternal ends.

Generational wealth in Proverbs is stewarded with humility because those who steward for posterity recognize their role as trustees rather than owners, and the text warns against pride that destroys (Proverbs 16:18; 22:4). Sons and daughters who steward with humility model teachability and service for heirs, preventing entitlement and misuse. This humble stewardship preserves relational capital and invites continued trust. Early church leaders modeled servant leadership as the foundation for trustworthy stewardship. Discipleship forms the posture that keeps leaders teachable and accountable. When humility governs stewardship, generational wealth is entrusted rightly.

Generational wealth in Proverbs is oriented toward restoration and justice because sustainable prosperity requires repairing past harms and building equitable systems, and the text links justice with blessing (Proverbs 14:31; Isaiah 58). Sons and daughters who use wealth to restore dignity and to build fair structures ensure that prosperity is redemptive rather than extractive. This restorative orientation secures social capital and preserves the moral foundation of stewardship. Early prophetic and apostolic practice emphasized restitution and care as signs of true blessing. Discipleship forms the ethical frameworks that make restoration integral to generational planning. When restoration guides wealth, generational blessing heals communities.

COVENANT CONTINUITY

Covenant continuity is the practice of aligning successive generations with the same relational commitments—reverence, justice, honor, and stewardship—so that the economy of Heaven flows through families and institutions across time. Sons and daughters who cultivate continuity do not merely pass assets; they pass covenant practices that reproduce identity and capacity. Proverbs teaches that instruction and correction secure life, and continuity depends on repeated formation rather than one-time transfers (Proverbs 4:1–9). Early church communities preserved covenant continuity through catechesis, liturgy, and communal oversight that kept successive generations aligned. Discipleship is the engine of continuity, creating rhythms that survive cultural change. When covenant continuity is practiced, the hidden covenant remains active across generations.

Covenant continuity requires intentional mentoring relationships where elders invest time and authority in younger leaders, transmitting both wisdom and reputation. Sons and daughters who facilitate such mentoring ensure that heirs inherit tested judgment and relational networks. Proverbs values the company of the prudent and the passing of counsel as safeguards for the house (Proverbs 13:20; 15:22). Early Christian mentorship—apostles to elders, elders to deacons—created chains of formation that preserved doctrine and practice. Discipleship formalizes mentoring pathways so that continuity is relational and reproducible. When mentoring is institutionalized, covenant continuity is secured.

Covenant continuity depends on institutional memory—records, curricula, and archived counsel—that future leaders can consult to avoid repeating mistakes and to inherit tested practices. Sons and daughters who preserve memory create a living library of wisdom that shortens learning curves for heirs. Proverbs commends remembrance and instruction as life, emphasizing the value of transmitted counsel (Proverbs 4:1–5). Early church letters, councils, and catechetical materials preserved institutional memory that guided later communities. Discipleship ensures that counsel is recorded and taught so that formation continues beyond a single leader's tenure. When memory is preserved, covenant continuity deepens.

Covenant continuity requires governance that balances stability with adaptability so institutions can remain faithful while responding to new contexts. Sons and daughters who design governance with clear roles, review processes, and adaptive mechanisms prevent both ossification and drift. Proverbs links wise counsel and ordered building with stability, suggesting that governance is the architecture of continuity (Proverbs 24:3–4). Early church councils provided governance that preserved core commitments while allowing contextual practice. Discipleship forms leaders who can steward continuity with discernment. When governance balances stability and adaptability, covenant continuity thrives.

Covenant continuity is sustained by shared rituals and liturgies that rehearse identity and priorities across generations, embedding values into daily life. Sons and daughters who maintain formative rituals—prayer, teaching, communal meals—create cultural continuity that orients heirs toward covenant practice. Proverbs emphasizes repeated instruction as formative, and ritualized practices become the scaffolding of legacy (Proverbs 4:1–5). Early Christian liturgies and household practices transmitted identity across dispersed communities. Discipleship institutionalizes rituals so that they survive leadership transitions. When rituals are preserved, covenant continuity is embodied.

Covenant continuity requires economic practices that prioritize stewardship over consumption, ensuring that resources are allocated to formation, care, and institutional capacity rather than fleeting comforts. Sons and daughters who budget for discipleship, reserves, and institutional maintenance protect legacy from erosion. Proverbs commends prudent provision and warns against squandering wealth, linking stewardship with continuity (Proverbs 21:20; 13:11). Early Christian communities practiced communal stores and planned giving to sustain mission. Discipleship forms the financial disciplines that make continuity possible. When economics prioritize stewardship, covenant continuity is funded.

Covenant continuity depends on succession planning that prepares new leaders through progressive responsibility and testing, ensuring that authority is transferred to proven stewards. Sons and daughters who create clear pathways for entrustment prevent the collapse that follows personality-dependent leadership. Proverbs links faithfulness in small things with greater trust, illustrating the ladder of stewardship (Proverbs 28:20; 27:23–27). Early church ordination and mentoring prepared leaders to receive and exercise authority wisely. Discipleship institutionalizes succession so that stewardship is reproducible. When succession is planned, covenant continuity is assured.

Covenant continuity is protected by a culture of accountability that keeps leaders humble and teachable, preventing pride from undermining legacy. Sons and daughters who embed mutual oversight and correction preserve the integrity of institutions across generations. Proverbs warns that pride precedes ruin and honors humility as the path to lasting honor (Proverbs 16:18; 22:4). Early church councils and communal oversight provided corrective mechanisms that preserved witness. Discipleship forms the practices of confession, counsel, and restoration that sustain accountability. When accountability is practiced, covenant continuity remains healthy.

Covenant continuity is strengthened by cross-generational collaboration where elders and youth work together, blending experience with innovation to keep institutions relevant and faithful. Sons and daughters who foster such collaboration prevent generational silos and ensure mutual learning. Proverbs values many counselors and the exchange of wisdom across ages (Proverbs 11:14; 27:17). Early Christian communities combined elder wisdom with youthful energy to expand mission. Discipleship creates forums for intergenerational exchange that renew institutions. When collaboration is cultivated, covenant continuity is renewed.

Covenant continuity requires a theology of stewardship that frames resources as entrusted for communal flourishing rather than personal entitlement, shaping motives across generations. Sons and daughters who teach stewardship as vocation rather than reward form heirs who steward with responsibility and generosity. Proverbs links the fear of the Lord with wisdom and life, anchoring stewardship in reverence (Proverbs 1:7). Early Christian formation taught stewardship as devotion and service, not as a path to status. Discipleship embeds this theology into curricula and practice so that motives remain aligned. When stewardship is taught as vocation, covenant continuity is sustained.

Covenant continuity is preserved by public testimony and storytelling that keep covenant memory alive, passing on examples of faithfulness and cautionary tales that orient future decision-making. Sons and daughters who tell stories of tested faith and wise stewardship create a moral imagination for heirs. Proverbs uses narrative and proverb to transmit wisdom across generations, showing the power of story in formation (Proverbs 1–9). Early Christian testimonies and letters preserved memory that guided communities through trials. Discipleship institutionalizes storytelling as a formation tool. When testimony is preserved, covenant continuity is vivid.

Covenant continuity culminates in a communal identity that transcends individual lifespans, where sons and daughters see themselves as part of an ongoing household of faith entrusted with care for future generations. This identity orients decisions toward legacy, justice, and formation rather than immediate gratification. Proverbs honors those who build for posterity and who leave an inheritance for children's children (Proverbs 13:22). Early Christian communities embodied such identity, creating institutions that served society for centuries. Discipleship forms this communal identity through repeated practice and shared memory. When identity is communal, covenant continuity becomes the living reality of Heaven's economy.

SONS AND DAUGHTERS WHO BUILD BEYOND THEMSELVES

Sons and daughters who build beyond themselves think institutionally rather than individually, investing in structures that multiply care and formation beyond their own tenure. They prioritize schools, training centers, and care systems that outlast a single leader and serve many generations. Proverbs commends building and establishing the house with wisdom and counsel, linking institutional design with stability (Proverbs 24:3–4). Early Christian founders invested in institutions precisely because they understood stewardship as generational work. Discipleship equips leaders to design institutions that balance mission, governance, and formation. When builders think institutionally, legacy becomes scalable.

Sons and daughters who build beyond themselves cultivate teams and distributed leadership so that stewardship is not person-dependent but reproducible through trained hands. They create pathways for progressive responsibility that test and prepare new stewards. Proverbs links faithfulness in small things with greater trust, illustrating the ladder of entrustment (Proverbs 28:20). Early church governance distributed responsibility among elders and deacons to sustain care across communities. Discipleship institutionalizes delegation and training so that institutions can scale without collapse. When leadership is distributed, stewardship multiplies.

Sons and daughters who build beyond themselves invest in durable governance—charters, bylaws, oversight bodies—that preserve mission and prevent capture by short-term interests. They design accountability mechanisms that protect legacy and ensure ethical use of resources. Proverbs values many counselors and planned building as safeguards for the house (Proverbs 11:14; 24:3–4). Early Christian councils and communal oversight provided such governance to protect communal trust. Discipleship forms the governance literacy needed to create resilient institutions. When governance is durable, legacy is protected.

Sons and daughters who build beyond themselves fund formation as the primary asset, allocating resources to discipleship, vocational training, and leadership development that produce multiplying capacity. They understand that people, not things, are the multiplying agents of stewardship. Proverbs emphasizes instruction and the passing of wisdom as central to life (Proverbs 4:1–9). Early Christian catechesis and mentoring ensured continuity of care and mission. Discipleship institutionalizes formation funding so that leaders are produced, not merely appointed. When formation is funded, institutions thrive.

Sons and daughters who build beyond themselves design for justice and restoration, ensuring that institutions serve the vulnerable and repair past harms rather than perpetuate inequality. They embed ethical commitments into mission and practice so that wealth becomes redemptive. Proverbs links justice with blessing and stability, showing that righteous systems sustain prosperity (Proverbs 14:31). Early Christian institutions—hospitals, orphan care—were expressions of restorative stewardship. Discipleship forms the moral imagination to design institutions that heal. When justice is central, institutions bless society.

Sons and daughters who build beyond themselves create cultural practices—rituals, stories, and rhythms—that transmit identity and priorities across generations, making institutions resilient to leadership change. They embed liturgies and curricula that form hearts and habits. Proverbs teaches that repeated instruction forms life and secures wisdom (Proverbs 4:1–5). Early Christian liturgies and household practices transmitted identity across dispersed communities. Discipleship institutionalizes cultural formation so that institutions remain faithful. When culture is formed, institutions endure.

Sons and daughters who build beyond themselves steward resources with prudence, maintaining margin and reserves that enable generosity and resilience, and they avoid boom-and-bust cycles that erode trust. They plan for seasons and build contingency into budgets. Proverbs commends the prudent who prepare and store for lean times (Proverbs 6:6–8; 21:20). Early Christian communal stores and mutual aid systems exemplified such prudence. Discipleship forms the financial disciplines that secure long-term capacity. When prudence guides stewardship, institutions weather storms.

Sons and daughters who build beyond themselves practice transparent governance that invites partnership and public trust, understanding that reputation is a multiplier for institutional impact. They report openly, invite review, and welcome counsel. Proverbs links a good name with favor that opens doors (Proverbs 22:1). Early Christian communities preserved trust through public accountability and fair distribution. Discipleship forms the habits of transparency that sustain partnerships. When governance is transparent, institutions attract support.

Sons and daughters who build beyond themselves prioritize succession and mentorship, creating clear pathways for new leaders to be trained, tested, and entrusted, preventing collapse when founders step down. They institutionalize progressive responsibility so that authority is earned. Proverbs links faithfulness in small things with greater trust, illustrating the ladder of stewardship (Proverbs 28:20). Early church ordination and mentoring prepared leaders for continuity. Discipleship provides the testing ground for entrustment. When succession is planned, institutions continue.

Sons and daughters who build beyond themselves integrate worship and work, framing institutional labor as devotion so that stewardship remains sacred rather than merely managerial. They embed prayer, thanksgiving, and spiritual formation into institutional life. Proverbs links reverence with wisdom and life, anchoring stewardship in the fear of the Lord (Proverbs 1:7).

Early Christian liturgies shaped institutions to serve both God and neighbor. Discipleship forms the habit of offering work as worship. When worship informs institutions, legacy serves eternal ends.

Sons and daughters who build beyond themselves measure success by communal flourishing and generational impact rather than by short-term metrics, aligning incentives with long-term stewardship. They track formation, care delivered, and institutional health rather than mere financial growth. Proverbs honors those who leave an inheritance for future generations and values steady increase over sudden riches (Proverbs 13:22; 13:11). Early Christian founders prioritized enduring impact over immediate acclaim. Discipleship forms the metrics that matter for covenant legacy. When success is measured by flourishing, institutions bless many.

Sons and daughters who build beyond themselves leave an eternal impact because they root institutions in covenant priorities—justice, honor, generosity, and formation—so that their work participates in Heaven's economy beyond their lifetime. Their stewardship becomes a conduit for blessing that multiplies across generations and into eternity. Proverbs teaches that wisdom produces lasting fruit and that the fear of the Lord is the beginning of life (Proverbs 8:10–11; 1:7). Early Christian legacies testify that covenantal institutions can shape societies for centuries. Discipleship is the means by which such legacies are formed and sustained. When sons and daughters build beyond themselves, the eternal impact of wisdom-based living is realized.

CHAPTER THIRTEEN — PROPHETIC TRANSFER: WHEN THE WORD OPENS THE DOOR TO WEALTH

The Nature of Prophetic Transfer

Prophetic transfer is the movement of resources, influence, or opportunity that follows a credible word from God and the communal confirmation of that word, and it is distinct from magical thinking because it always functions within covenant relationships and tested wisdom. In Scripture prophetic words often precede structural openings—Joseph's interpretation of Pharaoh's dreams led to an administrative appointment that preserved Egypt and surrounding nations during famine, showing how revelation and governance can intersect to release provision. This biblical pattern demonstrates that prophetic insight can catalyze legal and institutional authority to reallocate resources for survival and flourishing. Prophetic transfer is therefore not a private entitlement but a public authorization that must be stewarded with justice and accountability. The early church recognized prophetic utterance as a gift to the body that required testing and oversight, and fathers like Irenaeus and Augustine insisted that prophetic speech be judged by fruit and conformity to Scripture. Discipleship prepares communities to receive prophetic words by forming character, governance, and practices that can translate a word into sustainable stewardship.

Prophetic transfer in the biblical imagination often accompanies a reversal of fortunes where covenant faithfulness and divine timing converge, and the Exodus narrative and Jubilee legislation provide the theological backdrop for redistribution that protects families and restores access to means of production. The Jubilee year in Leviticus frames economic reordering as a covenantal safeguard so that land and freedom are not permanently lost to cycles of debt, indicating that God's economy includes structural resets for justice. This legal framework shows that prophetic or priestly pronouncements in Israel were embedded in statutes designed to prevent permanent dispossession and to preserve generational capacity. Prophetic transfer therefore must be read against a scriptural ethic that pairs release with restitution and systemic repair. Early interpreters debated the historical observance of Jubilee, but they consistently affirmed its theological intent: God's people are stewards of a land that ultimately belongs to the Lord. Discipleship translates Jubilee principles into contemporary practices by insisting that transfer be tethered to restoration and long-term formation.

Prophetic transfer is visible in the narratives of Elijah and Elisha where prophetic words produce ongoing provision for widows and households, demonstrating that prophetic speech can unlock daily sustenance as well as larger structural openings. Elijah's word to the widow at Zarephath that her jar of flour and jug of oil would not be exhausted until the drought ended shows how prophetic promise can secure immediate survival for the vulnerable and thereby preserve human capital for future flourishing. Such episodes teach that prophetic transfer often arrives through relational channels—hospitality, trust, and the willingness of the vulnerable to act on a word of faith. The early church read these stories as models of God's care that moved through prophetic mediation and human obedience, and they used them to justify communal support for those in need. Discipleship forms the posture to receive such words: obedience, tested faith, and communal confirmation rather than impulsive presumption.

Prophetic transfer is not a guarantee that every spoken word will produce material change; rather it is a covenantal mechanism that operates when revelation aligns with justice, stewardship, and communal confirmation. The prophetic word functions as a kind of authorization that opens doors—legal, relational, and institutional—when it is received by those who have the capacity and character to steward what is released. This means prophetic transfer requires both heavenly initiative and earthly competence: the word may open a door, but human wisdom, governance, and networks must walk through it responsibly. The early church insisted that prophetic utterances be tested by elders and by Scripture to prevent deception and to ensure that any transfer served the common good. Discipleship therefore trains both prophetic gifting and administrative competence so that openings become sustainable institutions rather than fleeting windfalls.

Prophetic transfer often surfaces where corrupt systems have hoarded resources or where injustice has concentrated wealth, and the prophetic word can function as a divine summons to reallocate for restoration and covenant flourishing. Scripture contains prophetic indictments of unjust accumulation and promises of reversal for those who align with God's justice, indicating that transfer can be part of God's corrective work in history. Yet the biblical pattern always pairs prophetic release with ethical obligations: restitution, care for the poor, and the building of structures that prevent future exploitation. The early church fathers warned against using prophetic language to justify personal enrichment and insisted that prophetic fruit be measured by justice and mercy. Discipleship forms the moral imagination to ensure that transfer repairs rather than repeats past harms.

Prophetic transfer is relational at its core because prophetic words typically move through networks of trust —hosts, patrons, rulers, and communities—so that what is released is integrated into existing stewardship channels rather than dispersed chaotically. Joseph's rise involved Pharaoh's court and administrative structures;

Elijah's provision moved through a widow's household; Elisha's miracles often resulted in communal testimony that opened further doors. These patterns show that prophetic transfer rarely bypasses human systems; it reorients them. The early church institutionalized this insight by combining prophetic ministry with diaconal care and governance, ensuring that prophetic openings were matched by accountable distribution. Discipleship trains communities to receive prophetic words into structures that can steward resources for long-term flourishing.

Prophetic transfer is not a substitute for wisdom; rather it amplifies wisdom when the prophetic word is tested and integrated into counsel and planning. Proverbs repeatedly insists that many counselors bring safety, and prophetic words that bypass counsel risk presumption and harm. The biblical pattern therefore requires that prophetic insight be submitted to communal discernment, legal prudence, and ethical planning before resources are reallocated. Early church practice reflected this: prophetic utterances were weighed by elders and councils to ensure alignment with Scripture and justice. Discipleship forms the humility to bring prophetic impressions into advisory contexts so that revelation and prudence cohere.

Prophetic transfer can be catalytic for mission when it releases resources into formation, hospitality, and institutions that multiply care and witness, as seen in biblical examples where prophetic provision sustained prophets and enabled wider ministry. When prophetic words lead to the funding of schools, care systems, or training centers, the initial transfer becomes a seed for generational capacity rather than a one-time miracle. The early church's use of prophetic insight to mobilize resources for hospitals, catechesis, and relief demonstrates how prophetic openings can be institutionalized for long-term impact. Discipleship ensures that prophetic release is paired with formation so that new resources produce multiplying leaders and sustainable institutions.

Prophetic transfer is accountable to Scripture because the prophetic word must be measured against the revealed character and priorities of God—justice, mercy, humility, and the fear of the Lord—so that any release of wealth serves covenant ends rather than personal ambition. The prophets of Israel consistently tied material reordering to covenant fidelity, calling for repentance and justice as prerequisites for blessing. The early church appealed to Scripture as the final arbiter of prophetic claims, insisting that words that contradicted the law and the prophets be rejected. Discipleship forms the habit of Scripture-testing so that prophetic transfer remains tethered to God's revealed will.

Prophetic transfer is often accompanied by testimony that multiplies trust and opens further networks, because when a prophetic word is confirmed by fruit—provision, restoration, or justice—others are more willing to entrust resources and influence to those who steward well. The Shunammite woman's hospitality to Elisha led to blessing and testimony that enhanced her household's standing and capacity, illustrating how prophetic encounters can produce reputational capital that unlocks further opportunity. Early Christian communities used testimony to mobilize support for mission, recognizing that credible stories of provision invite partnership. Discipleship forms the practices of testimony and accountability so that stories of transfer are accompanied by transparent stewardship.

Prophetic transfer is ultimately a means to an end: the expansion of covenant life—justice, formation, and worship—rather than an end in itself. The prophetic word that releases wealth is meant to fund institutions of mercy, training, and witness that embody Heaven's economy on earth. The biblical pattern shows that God's provision is often directed toward sustaining the vulnerable, training leaders, and preserving generational capacity. Early church practice affirmed that prophetic provision should be used to build hospitals, schools, and care systems that outlast a single generation. Discipleship ensures that prophetic transfer is converted into structures that bless many and endure.

Prophetic transfer requires a posture of stewardship from recipients: gratitude, accountability, and a commitment to justice, because the prophetic word opens doors but the community must steward what is received for the common good. The biblical witness and early church practice converge on this point: prophetic release is not license for entitlement but a summons to faithful administration. Discipleship forms the disciplines—reporting, training, and restorative practice—that convert prophetic openings into generational blessing. When prophetic transfer is stewarded with humility and justice, Heaven's economy is both honored and extended.

COVENANT CONDITIONS FOR PROPHETIC TRANSFER

Reverence is foundational for prophetic transfer because the fear of the Lord orders motives and prevents the misuse of prophetic speech, and Proverbs teaches that the fear of the Lord is the beginning of wisdom. Sons and daughters who cultivate reverence align their desires with covenant priorities and resist the temptation to use prophetic language for personal gain. This posture protects communities from prophetic words that serve ego rather than justice. Early church fathers emphasized reverence as the soil in which genuine prophecy grows, warning that charismatic speech without holiness invites deception. Discipleship forms reverence through Scripture, prayer, and communal correction so that prophetic words issued from a humble heart are more likely to be trustworthy and fruitful.

Righteousness prepares the soil for prophetic transfer because God's economy favors just practices and condemns dishonest gain, and Proverbs repeatedly links righteous conduct with blessing and stability. Sons and daughters who live justly create environments where prophetic words can be implemented without perpetuating injustice. This ethical foundation ensures that any transfer repairs rather than repeats harm. Early Christian communities insisted that prophetic ministry be accompanied by righteous action—care for widows, fair commerce, and protection of the vulnerable. Discipleship forms the habits of justice that make prophetic release redemptive rather than extractive.

Honor is a covenant condition because prophetic words often move through networks of trust, and honor opens doors by creating reputational capital that invites partnership and entrustment. Sons and daughters who practice honor toward leaders, donors, and the vulnerable build credibility that makes prophetic recommendations actionable. This relational currency reduces friction when resources are reallocated and invites collaborative stewardship. Early church practice of public commendation and benediction functioned to release leaders and resources into wider networks. Discipleship forms the habit of honoring others so that prophetic words are received within a culture of trust.

Counsel is essential because prophetic impressions must be tested by many counselors to avoid presumption and error, and Proverbs commends the safety of many advisors. Sons and daughters who submit prophetic words to elders and peers ensure that revelation is weighed against wisdom and likely consequences. This communal testing prevents rash declarations from producing harm and ensures that any transfer is matched by governance. Early church councils modeled this practice by vetting prophetic claims and providing corrective guidance. Discipleship institutionalizes counsel so that prophetic words are not isolated pronouncements but communal decisions.

Generosity prepares the soil for prophetic transfer because a generous community demonstrates that resources will be used for covenant ends rather than personal aggrandizement, and Proverbs teaches that the generous soul is made rich. Sons and daughters who practice sacrificial giving create a culture where prophetic release is likely to be stewarded for formation and care. This generosity signals to heaven and to human partners that resources will circulate for the common good. Early Christian households practiced radical sharing, and their generosity often preceded multiplied provision and influence. Discipleship forms generous habits so that prophetic openings are matched by a culture of giving.

Integrity in speech and measurement is a covenant condition because prophetic words that lead to transfer require transparent accounting and truthful testimony to preserve trust, and Proverbs condemns dishonest scales. Sons and daughters who maintain integrity in reporting and in public testimony ensure that transferred resources are tracked and used as intended. This transparency sustains donor confidence and prevents scandal that would close doors. Early church governance included oversight roles to ensure integrity in distribution. Discipleship trains stewards in honest reporting and public accountability so that prophetic transfer is credible.

Teachability is a covenant condition because prophetic transfer often requires recipients to learn new practices of stewardship, and Proverbs links teachability with life and favor. Sons and daughters who remain learners adapt to new responsibilities and receive correction that refines their capacity to steward larger trusts. This posture prevents pride from turning prophetic release into entitlement. Early church formation emphasized catechesis and mentorship to prepare new leaders for entrusted resources. Discipleship institutionalizes progressive responsibility so that prophetic openings are matched by growing competence.

Justice in allocation is a covenant condition because prophetic transfer must not perpetuate inequality or harm, and Proverbs repeatedly ties justice for the poor to communal stability. Sons and daughters who design distribution with justice in view ensure that transferred wealth repairs structural wrongs and builds capacity for the vulnerable. This ethical tether prevents prophetic release from becoming a vehicle for private enrichment. Early prophetic practice often accompanied calls for restitution and care, and the early church echoed that prophetic ethic. Discipleship forms the frameworks that pair transfer with restorative action.

Prayerful discernment is a covenant condition because prophetic words require spiritual confirmation and timing, and Scripture models seasons of waiting and confirmation before action. Sons and daughters who pray for clarity and for communal confirmation avoid premature enforcement of prophetic words that may be misinterpreted. This rhythm of prayer and waiting preserves integrity and prevents impulsive decisions. Early church practice combined prayer with counsel to confirm prophetic direction. Discipleship forms the spiritual rhythms that make prophetic reception sober and communal.

Accountability structures are a covenant condition because prophetic transfer must be stewarded within systems that can report, correct, and sustain, and Proverbs values many counselors and ordered building. Sons and daughters who create oversight—boards, audits, mentorship—protect transferred resources from misuse and ensure continuity. This institutional scaffolding converts prophetic momentum into durable institutions. Early church governance provided such structures to preserve communal trust. Discipleship trains communities to build accountable systems that steward prophetic release responsibly.

Restorative commitment is a covenant condition because prophetic transfer often intersects with past injustices, and any release must include plans for restitution and repair, following biblical patterns of restoration. Sons and daughters who insist on restoration as part of prophetic outcomes ensure that transfer heals communities rather than perpetuating harm. This restorative posture aligns prophetic release with covenant justice. Early prophetic and apostolic practice emphasized restitution and care as signs of true blessing. Discipleship forms the moral imagination to embed restoration into transfer.

Formation pathways are a covenant condition because prophetic transfer must be matched by training and mentoring so that new stewards can manage resources wisely, and Proverbs links instruction with life and favor. Sons and daughters who pair prophetic release with discipleship convert sudden openings into long-term capacity. This pairing is practical: it equips recipients to govern, to report, and to multiply blessing. Early church catechesis and mentoring ensured that new leaders were formed to steward entrusted resources. Discipleship institutionalizes follow-through so that prophetic transfer becomes generational.

THE MECHANICS OF TRANSFER

Prophetic words intersect with human networks because testimony and reputation mobilize relational capital that translates prophetic promise into practical openings, and biblical narratives show how testimony about prophetic provision invited further partnership. When a prophetic word is confirmed by fruit, networks mobilize—neighbors, patrons, civic leaders—creating pathways for resources to move into covenant hands. Sons and daughters who steward networks well translate prophetic momentum into institutional support rather than isolated windfalls. Early church practice used testimony to gather resources for mission, recognizing that credible stories invite partnership. Discipleship forms the relational skills to steward networks responsibly so that transfer is multiplied through trusted channels.

Prophetic transfer often requires legal openings—permissions, titles, or administrative authority—that convert a word into enforceable change, as seen when Joseph's interpretation led to Pharaoh's decree to store grain and appoint officials. Human law and governance are the mechanisms by which prophetic insight becomes structural provision, and prophetic words that ignore legal realities risk producing chaos rather than restoration. Sons and daughters who understand legal processes can translate prophetic openings into durable policy and institutional practice. Early biblical examples show prophets working within or alongside rulers to effect change. Discipleship trains leaders in governance and legal prudence so that prophetic release is implemented lawfully and sustainably.

Prophetic transfer moves through testimony because credible witnesses amplify a word's reception and invite others to entrust resources, and the Shunammite narrative shows how hospitality and prophetic blessing produced testimony that enhanced household capacity. When communities can point to confirmed words and accountable outcomes, donors and partners are more willing to invest in the vision. Sons and daughters who document and testify to faithful stewardship create the credibility that unlocks further transfer. Early church communities preserved testimonies in letters and liturgies to mobilize support for care and mission. Discipleship forms the discipline of transparent storytelling that accompanies stewardship.

Prophetic transfer can dismantle unjust structures when prophetic speech exposes exploitation and calls for restitution, prompting legal and social reforms that reallocate resources toward covenant ends. The prophetic tradition in Scripture often functions as a critique of systems that hoard wealth and oppress the poor, and prophetic words can catalyze corrective policy when received by leaders with authority. Sons and daughters who pair prophetic critique with practical proposals—legal redress, land restoration, institutional reform—translate prophetic urgency into systemic change. Early prophets called for justice that restructured society; the early church implemented care systems that mitigated exploitation. Discipleship forms the capacity to move from prophetic indictment to constructive reform.

Prophetic transfer intersects with testimony and networks to create reputational capital that invites investment, because those known for honoring prophetic words with faithful stewardship attract partners who value integrity. Reputation becomes a multiplier: trustworthy stewards receive more opportunities to steward. Sons and daughters who protect reputation through transparent governance and consistent care build the relational currency that sustains transfer. Early Christian leaders guarded reputation through accountability and public reporting to preserve trust. Discipleship trains communities to steward reputation as a strategic asset for covenant work.

Prophetic transfer requires administrative competence because resources released into mission must be managed—budgets, teams, training, and reporting—to convert blessing into sustainable institutions. Prophetic words open doors, but administrative systems keep them open. Sons and daughters who invest in governance, accounting, and formation ensure that transfer becomes institutional capacity rather than ephemeral advantage. Early church institutions developed roles like deacons and elders to manage care and resources responsibly. Discipleship forms administrative competence through apprenticeships and progressive responsibility.

Prophetic transfer often leverages hospitality and local networks because prophets frequently moved through households and local leaders, and hospitality created relational platforms for provision and testimony. The Shunammite woman's hospitality to Elisha produced blessing that strengthened her household and community witness. Sons and daughters who cultivate hospitality and local partnerships create the grassroots channels through which prophetic provision can be distributed and multiplied. Early Christian households practiced hospitality as a means of mission and care. Discipleship trains communities to use hospitality strategically for formation and distribution.

Prophetic transfer can be amplified by strategic generosity that seeds formation and institutions—schools, clinics, training centers—so that initial release multiplies through capacity building. When prophetic words lead to investments in formation, the return is generational rather than momentary. Sons and daughters who direct prophetic provision into training and institutional development convert blessing into multiplying leaders. Early church philanthropy funded institutions that served society for centuries. Discipleship ensures that prophetic release is paired with strategic investment in human capital.

Prophetic transfer interacts with markets when prophetic words open commercial opportunities that can be stewarded for communal benefit, but such interactions require ethical guardrails to prevent exploitation. When prophetic openings create business opportunities, sons and daughters must design fair commerce that benefits workers and communities rather than extracting value. Proverbs' insistence on honest scales and fair treatment of laborers provides the moral framework for such enterprise. Early Christian practice included fair labor and care for workers as part of covenant economics. Discipleship forms the ethical frameworks for market engagement that bless rather than harm.

Prophetic transfer often requires translation into policy when systemic change is needed—land restitution, debt relief, or regulatory reform—and prophetic words can catalyze political will when they are received by leaders committed to justice. Sons and daughters who can translate prophetic urgency into policy proposals increase the likelihood that transfer will be institutionalized. Early prophetic voices sometimes influenced kings and rulers to enact reforms; the prophetic tradition includes both critique and constructive counsel. Discipleship trains leaders to craft policy that embodies prophetic priorities while respecting legal processes.

Prophetic transfer is sustained by accountability mechanisms that track outcomes and ensure that resources serve intended purposes, because without oversight prophetic release can be dissipated or misused. Sons and daughters who implement audits, reporting, and mentorship protect transferred wealth and preserve donor confidence. Early church governance included oversight roles to ensure faithful distribution. Discipleship forms the disciplines of transparent stewardship that make prophetic transfer durable.

Prophetic transfer requires cultural translation because prophetic language and symbolic acts must be made intelligible to civic and institutional partners for practical implementation, and this translation often involves testimony, legal framing, and strategic communication. Sons and daughters who can translate prophetic claims into policy language, budgets, and program design enable prophetic openings to be received by secular institutions. Early Christian leaders translated theological commitments into social programs that civic partners could support. Discipleship forms the communicative skills necessary to bridge prophetic vision and institutional practice.

SAFEGUARDS AND DISCERNMENT

Testing prophetic words is the first safeguard because Scripture commands testing of prophets and the early church practiced communal confirmation to prevent deception, and Proverbs warns that the way of the fool is right in his own eyes. Sons and daughters must bring prophetic impressions into counsel, prayer, and scriptural scrutiny before acting on them materially. This testing prevents presumption and ensures that any transfer aligns with covenant priorities. Early church councils and elders provided mechanisms for such testing, and contemporary discipleship structures should replicate those safeguards. When prophetic words are tested, communities protect themselves from entanglement and misuse.

Avoiding entitlement is a safeguard because prophetic transfer must not become a license for personal enrichment; recipients are stewards, not owners, and Scripture repeatedly warns against the corruption of wealth. Sons and daughters who receive prophetic release must adopt a posture of stewardship—accountability, generosity, and service—rather than entitlement. This ethic prevents the conversion of prophetic blessing into private gain and preserves communal trust. Early church fathers condemned the use of spiritual language to justify personal enrichment and modeled servant leadership as the proper posture for those entrusted with resources. Discipleship forms the humility that resists entitlement.

Ensuring justice is a safeguard because prophetic transfer must repair injustice and protect the vulnerable rather than perpetuate harm, and Levitical and prophetic texts insist that economic reordering be tethered to restitution and care. Sons and daughters who steward prophetic release must include plans for restitution where wrongs have occurred and for ongoing care of those harmed by prior systems. This justice requirement prevents prophetic release from becoming a vehicle for repeating past exploitation. Early prophetic practice and apostolic teaching emphasized restitution and care as integral to blessing. Discipleship forms the frameworks to operationalize justice in transfer.

Restoring what was taken unjustly is a safeguard because prophetic transfer often intersects with historical dispossession, and Scripture models restitution as part of covenant restoration. Sons and daughters who steward prophetic release must prioritize returning what was unjustly taken and building systems that prevent recurrence. This restorative focus aligns prophetic release with God's concern for the oppressed and secures communal legitimacy for transfer. Early prophetic calls often included demands for restitution; the early church practiced care that sought to repair social harm. Discipleship trains leaders to design restorative pathways that accompany transfer.

Guarding against manipulation is a safeguard because

prophetic language can be misused by those who seek influence, and communities must protect themselves with transparent processes and independent review. Sons and daughters should require written stewardship plans, independent audits, and public reporting before significant transfers are enacted. This transparency deters manipulation and preserves donor and public confidence. Early church governance included oversight to prevent abuses of authority. Discipleship forms the institutional habits that make manipulation difficult and accountability normal.

Embedding discipleship with transfer is a safeguard because prophetic release without formation often leads to misuse; pairing transfer with training, mentoring, and progressive responsibility converts openings into sustainable capacity. Sons and daughters who require formation pathways for new stewards ensure that resources are matched by competence. This pairing is practical: it equips recipients to manage budgets, governance, and relational complexity. Early church catechesis and mentoring prepared leaders to steward entrusted resources. Discipleship institutionalizes follow-through so that prophetic release becomes generational.

Legal diligence is a safeguard because prophetic transfer that ignores legal realities risks collapse; due diligence—title checks, contract review, and regulatory compliance—protects both givers and recipients. Sons and daughters who insist on legal review before implementing transfer reduce the risk of future litigation and ensure that resources are used lawfully. This prudence preserves momentum and prevents costly remediation.

Early biblical examples show prophets working within legal and royal frameworks to effect change. Discipleship trains leaders to integrate legal counsel into prophetic implementation.

Covenantal covenants and written agreements are safeguards because formalizing expectations, restoration plans, and governance prevents ambiguity that predators exploit, and Proverbs values clear planning and many counselors. Sons and daughters who document stewardship commitments create enforceable pathways for accountability and continuity. This formalization protects legacy and ensures that transfer serves intended covenant ends. Early church letters and canons provided written norms that guided practice across communities. Discipleship forms the habit of covenantal documentation that preserves trust.

Community oversight is a safeguard because distributed authority reduces the risk of unilateral capture of resources, and Proverbs commends many counselors and shared responsibility as safeguards for the house. Sons and daughters who create oversight committees, boards, and mentorship networks distribute responsibility and create relational checks that deter abuse. This distributed model multiplies care and preserves continuity. Early church governance used elders and deacons to distribute stewardship. Discipleship institutionalizes shared oversight so that prophetic transfer is stewarded by many hands.

Ethical auditing is a safeguard because independent review of outcomes ensures that transferred resources achieve intended restorative and formation goals, and public reporting sustains donor confidence. Sons and daughters who commission ethical audits and publish results demonstrate commitment to transparency and justice. This practice deters misuse and invites continued partnership. Early Christian communities practiced public accountability in resource distribution to preserve unity and witness. Discipleship forms the discipline of reporting and review that makes audits constructive rather than punitive.

Restorative dispute resolution is a safeguard because conflicts over transfer can arise, and having agreed mechanisms for mediation, restitution, and reconciliation prevents fractures that drain capacity. Sons and daughters who build restorative processes into transfer plans ensure that disputes are resolved in ways that preserve dignity and communal trust. This approach prevents litigation and preserves human capital. Early church councils often mediated disputes to preserve unity. Discipleship trains communities in peacemaking and restorative justice practices.

Spiritual humility and ongoing testing are final safeguards because prophetic transfer must be continually evaluated by fruit, counsel, and Scripture to ensure it remains aligned with covenant priorities. Sons and daughters who remain teachable and who welcome periodic review prevent the ossification of error and ensure that transfer continues to serve justice and formation. This ongoing testing keeps prophetic release accountable to the living God and to the community. Early church practice combined prophetic boldness with elder oversight and periodic correction. Discipleship forms the rhythms of testing and renewal that sustain faithful stewardship over time.

CHAPTER FOURTEEN — SOZO BLESSING: WHOLENESS, COVENANT PROSPERITY, AND THE PROSPERING HAND

Sozo as Wholeness the Foundation of Prosperity

Sozo describes holistic salvation and restoration that touches spirit, soul, and body, and this wholeness becomes the soil in which sustainable prosperity grows because healed people steward well. Scripture links wholeness with fruitfulness, as Jesus proclaimed freedom and healing that released people into mission and provision, and Proverbs ties life to wisdom and the fear of the Lord (Proverbs 3:13–18; Luke 4:18–19). Sons and daughters who experience inner restoration are less likely to make fear-driven economic choices and more likely to steward with clarity and generosity. Early church teachers emphasized healing and formation together; they practiced pastoral care that restored leaders so communities could flourish rather than fracture under pressure. Discipleship that pursues sozo attends to wounds, patterns, and identity so that outward increase is matched by inward health. When wholeness precedes enterprise, the prosperity that follows carries life rather than sorrow.

Sozo begins with identity because being made whole reorients a person from scarcity to belonging, and identity determines economic posture more than technique, as Proverbs teaches that the heart directs the course of life (Proverbs 4:23). Sons and daughters who know they belong steward resources as trustees rather than as anxious owners, and this posture produces generosity and long-term thinking. The New Testament links identity in Christ with new patterns of living that include care for the poor and faithful stewardship, and early Christian formation prioritized identity work before public ministry. Discipleship practices—confession, mentoring, and spiritual direction—repair identity wounds so that stewardship flows from rootedness. When identity is healed, sozo blessing becomes the engine of sustainable provision.

Sozo includes emotional restoration because unresolved fear and shame distort decision-making and invite compromise, and Proverbs warns that anxious hearts make poor choices (Proverbs 12:25; 14:30). Sons and daughters who receive emotional healing gain clarity and resilience, enabling them to plan, give, and lead without the corrosive influence of shame. Early church pastoral care addressed sorrow and trauma as part of formation, recognizing that leaders must be whole to steward well. Discipleship integrates emotional formation with practical training so that healed hearts produce wise hands. When emotions are tended, the sozo blessing protects legacy and multiplies fruit.

Sozo embraces relational healing because broken relationships fracture networks that sustain provision, and Scripture models reconciliation as a prerequisite for blessing and witness (Matthew 5:23–24; Romans 12:18). Sons and daughters who pursue reconciliation restore trust and relational capital that open doors for partnership and stewardship. The early church practiced reconciliation as communal discipline, restoring leaders and preserving unity so resources could be pooled for care. Discipleship teaches peacemaking skills and restorative practices that repair relationships and preserve institutional capacity. When relationships are healed, sozo blessing expands the channels through which Heaven's economy flows.

Sozo includes vocational restoration because wholeness aligns gifts with calling, enabling hands to prosper in work that fits identity and season, and Proverbs links skillful work with provision (Proverbs 22:29; 10:4). Sons and daughters who receive vocational clarity steward their labor as worship and invest in formation that multiplies capacity. Early Christian formation connected calling with training so that ministries and enterprises were staffed by competent, formed people.

Discipleship provides apprenticeships and mentoring that translate calling into competence and sustainable practice. When vocation is restored, the sozo blessing makes labor fruitful and generational.

Sozo requires spiritual renewal because inner transformation opens the heart to wisdom and to covenant priorities, and Proverbs teaches that the fear of the Lord is the beginning of wisdom (Proverbs 1:7). Sons and daughters who cultivate reverence align motives with Heaven's economy and resist the seductions of Mammon. The early church emphasized spiritual disciplines —prayer, Scripture, fasting—as the context for renewal that produced faithful stewardship. Discipleship embeds these disciplines into daily life so that spiritual renewal is habitual rather than episodic. When spiritual life is renewed, sozo blessing becomes the foundation for righteous increase.

Sozo includes physical restoration because bodily health affects capacity to work, to lead, and to serve, and Scripture honors bodies as part of God's good creation to be stewarded (1 Corinthians 6:19–20). Sons and daughters who attend to physical well-being preserve stamina for long-term stewardship and avoid the collapse that follows neglect. Early Christian communities cared for the sick and established hospitals as expressions of holistic concern that preserved human capital. Discipleship encourages rhythms of rest, nutrition, and care that sustain leaders and communities. When bodies are tended, sozo blessing supports enduring productivity.

Sozo involves financial healing because patterns of scarcity, debt, and fear can be addressed through teaching, counseling, and covenant support, and Proverbs commends prudent provision and wise counsel (Proverbs 21:20; 15:22). Sons and daughters who receive financial formation break cycles of scarcity and steward resources with margin and generosity. Early church practice included mutual aid and training in stewardship to prevent chronic poverty and to enable sustainable giving. Discipleship provides practical financial discipleship—budgeting, saving, and ethical commerce—so that provision is stable. When financial wounds are healed, sozo blessing enables faithful investment in mission.

Sozo cultivates moral formation because inner wholeness produces integrity that preserves reputation and invites entrustment, and Proverbs links righteousness with honor and long life (Proverbs 11:3; 22:4). Sons and daughters who are formed morally attract trust and responsibility, and trust becomes relational capital that opens doors for stewardship. The early fathers insisted that character precedes capacity and that leaders must be tested in small things before larger trusts are given. Discipleship forms moral habits through accountability and correction so that integrity becomes visible. When moral formation is present, sozo blessing secures legacy.

Sozo fosters resilience because healed people recover from setbacks without losing identity or vision, and Proverbs teaches that wisdom and counsel prepare the heart for trials (Proverbs 2:1–6; 3:11–12). Sons and daughters who are whole respond to loss with restoration rather than despair, preserving networks and capacity for future increase. Early Christian communities that practiced mutual care sustained resilience through famine and persecution by restoring leaders and sharing resources. Discipleship builds resilience through communal rhythms, mentoring, and practical training. When resilience is cultivated, sozo blessing sustains stewardship across seasons.

Sozo culminates in a posture of stewardship rather than entitlement because wholeness reorients desire from possession to trust, and Scripture models stewardship as the faithful management of what is entrusted (Luke 12:42–48). Sons and daughters who are whole steward resources for communal flourishing and for the Father's purposes rather than for personal aggrandizement. Early church formation taught that blessing is a trust to be used for mercy and formation. Discipleship embeds stewardship as vocation so that sozo blessing becomes the engine of generational care. When stewardship is embraced, sozo blessing multiplies into legacy.

COVENANT PRACTICES THAT PRODUCE SOZO BLESSING

Discipleship rhythms—Scripture, prayer, silence, and communal formation—create the inner conditions for sozo because repeated practice rewires desire and forms character, and Proverbs links instruction with life (Proverbs 4:1–9). Sons and daughters who commit to these rhythms cultivate the humility and wisdom that invite holistic blessing rather than quick fixes. Early church catechesis combined doctrinal teaching with spiritual disciplines to form leaders who could steward resources faithfully. Discipleship programs that integrate inner formation with practical training produce stewards who can manage prophetic release and institutional responsibility. When rhythms are practiced, sozo blessing becomes the fruit of formation.

Confession and restoration are covenant practices that produce sozo because honest admission of brokenness opens the way for healing and for communal support, and Scripture models confession as a pathway to restoration (James 5:16; Galatians 6:1–2). Sons and daughters who practice confession receive correction and care that repair identity and restore capacity. Early Christian communities practiced mutual confession and restoration to preserve leaders and to prevent scandal. Discipleship creates safe spaces for confession and for the disciplined work of repair so that wounds do not calcify into dysfunction. When confession is practiced, sozo blessing heals and equips.

Mentoring and apprenticeship are covenant practices that produce sozo because formation requires relational transmission of wisdom and skill, and Proverbs values the company of the prudent (Proverbs 13:20). Sons and daughters who enter mentoring relationships inherit tested judgment and practical competence that enable them to steward resources well. Early church mentorship—apostles to elders, elders to deacons—ensured continuity of practice and character. Discipleship institutionalizes apprenticeship so that formation is reproducible and accountable. When mentoring is prioritized, sozo blessing becomes generational capacity.

Communal care and mutual aid are covenant practices that produce sozo because shared responsibility prevents isolation and preserves margin for generosity, and Proverbs commends generosity that refreshes others (Proverbs 11:24–25). Sons and daughters who participate in mutual aid networks experience provision that is both practical and formative. Early Christian households pooled resources to care for widows and the poor, demonstrating how communal structures sustain mission. Discipleship forms the habits of mutual aid—regular giving, shared counsel, and accountable distribution—that make sozo blessing communal rather than individual. When communal care is practiced, sozo blessing circulates.

Teaching in stewardship disciplines is a covenant practice that produces sozo because financial literacy, governance training, and ethical commerce equip heirs to manage resources without repeating past mistakes, and Proverbs links instruction with life (Proverbs 4:1–9). Sons and daughters who receive practical training break cycles of scarcity and steward with margin and generosity. Early church formation included practical instruction in care and distribution to prevent mismanagement. Discipleship programs that include budgeting, governance, and ethical enterprise prepare leaders for entrusted resources. When stewardship is taught, sozo blessing is sustained.

Hospitality and service are covenant practices that produce sozo because welcoming the stranger and caring for the vulnerable create relational platforms for provision and testimony, and Scripture repeatedly commends hospitality as a mark of covenant life (Hebrews 13:2; Romans 12:13). Sons and daughters who practice hospitality open channels for prophetic encounters and for communal blessing. Early Christian households practiced hospitality as mission and as a means of mutual support. Discipleship trains communities to use hospitality strategically for formation and distribution. When hospitality is habitual, sozo blessing flows through relationships.

Accountability and transparent governance are covenant practices that produce sozo because oversight preserves trust and prevents misuse, and Proverbs values many counselors and ordered building (Proverbs

11:14; 24:3–4). Sons and daughters who institutionalize accountability attract partners and donors who value reliability. Early church governance—elders, deacons, and councils—protected communal resources and preserved witness. Discipleship forms the practices of reporting, auditing, and review that make stewardship credible. When governance is transparent, sozo blessing is entrusted widely.

Justice and restitution are covenant practices that produce sozo because repairing past harms aligns transfer with God's concern for the oppressed, and Levitical and prophetic texts insist on restoration as part of covenant life (Leviticus 25; Isaiah 58). Sons and daughters who prioritize restitution ensure that blessing heals communities rather than perpetuating injustice. Early prophetic tradition called for justice as the condition of blessing, and the early church practiced care that sought to restore dignity. Discipleship forms the frameworks to operationalize restitution in transfer. When justice is central, sozo blessing becomes redemptive.

Sabbath rhythms and rest are covenant practices that produce sozo because rest preserves leaders and prevents the moral erosion that accompanies relentless striving, and Scripture commands rhythms of rest as part of covenant life (Exodus 20:8–11; Mark 6:31). Sons and daughters who honor Sabbath rhythms sustain clarity and endurance for long-term stewardship. Early Christian monastic and communal rhythms institutionalized rest as a safeguard for formation and mission. Discipleship forms the habit of Sabbath so that labor remains life-giving. When rest is practiced, sozo blessing carries joy.

Prayerful discernment and communal confirmation are covenant practices that produce sozo because prophetic impressions require testing and timing, and Scripture models seasons of waiting and confirmation before action (1 Thessalonians 5:20–21; Acts 13:1–3). Sons and daughters who seek communal confirmation avoid presumption and ensure that openings are matched by wisdom. Early church practice combined prayer with counsel to confirm prophetic direction. Discipleship forms the spiritual rhythms that make prophetic reception sober and communal. When discernment is practiced, sozo blessing is responsibly received.

Formation pathways and progressive responsibility are covenant practices that produce sozo because entrustment must be earned through faithful service in small things, and Proverbs links faithfulness with increased trust (Proverbs 28:20; 27:23–27). Sons and daughters who are given progressive responsibility prove competence and character before larger trusts are conferred. Early church structures tested servants through deaconship and eldership progression. Discipleship institutionalizes progressive entrustment so that transfer is matched by proven stewardship. When formation pathways exist, sozo blessing becomes sustainable.

THE PROMISE AND THE PRACTICE HANDS THAT PROSPER

Scripture promises that God prospers the work of faithful hands when those hands are aligned with covenant priorities, and Deuteronomy and Proverbs connect blessing with obedience and wise labor (Deuteronomy 28; Proverbs 16:3). Sons and daughters who commit their labor to covenant purposes experience provision that carries peace and preserves joy. The early church taught that God's blessing often accompanies faithful service and that prosperity is not merely material but relational and spiritual. Discipleship trains hands through apprenticeships, vocational formation, and ethical enterprise so that prosperity is both practical and holy. When hands are aligned with Heaven, the promise of prospering labor is realized.

Practical stewardship disciplines make hands prosper because budgeting, saving, and ethical commerce create margin and enable strategic generosity, and Proverbs commends prudent provision (Proverbs 21:20; 6:6–8). Sons and daughters who practice these disciplines avoid the cycles of boom and bust that erode trust and capacity. Early Christian communities used communal stores and planned giving to sustain mission through lean seasons. Discipleship provides practical training in financial stewardship so that prosperity is sustainable. When disciplines are practiced, hands prosper without compromise.

Skill development and vocational excellence make hands prosper because competence attracts trust and opportunity, and Proverbs honors the diligent worker who stands before leaders (Proverbs 22:29). Sons and daughters who invest in skill and craft are more likely to be entrusted with responsibility and resources. The early church valued learned leaders who combined spiritual formation with practical competence. Discipleship includes apprenticeships and vocational training that prepare hands for entrusted tasks. When skill is cultivated, hands prosper and multiply stewardship.

Ethical enterprise makes hands prosper because businesses that honor justice and fair treatment build reputational capital that invites partnership and long-term customers, and Proverbs condemns dishonest scales while commending fair commerce (Proverbs 11:1; 16:8). Sons and daughters who run enterprises with integrity attract sustainable growth and civic trust. Early Christian merchants and patrons who practiced fair trade contributed to communal stability and witness. Discipleship forms the moral frameworks for enterprise so that profit serves people rather than exploiting them. When enterprise is ethical, hands prosper and bless society.

Generosity as investment makes hands prosper because

strategic giving into formation, mission, and institutions multiplies influence and opens networks that return relational and practical fruit, and Proverbs teaches that scattering often precedes increase (Proverbs 11:24–25). Sons and daughters who give strategically seed training centers, care systems, and leadership pipelines that produce multiplying returns. Early Christian philanthropy funded schools and hospitals that served communities for generations. Discipleship guides strategic generosity so that gifts produce long-term capacity. When generosity is strategic, hands prosper through multiplied stewardship.

Network stewardship makes hands prosper because relationships and testimony mobilize resources and opportunities, and Scripture shows how testimony about provision invites partnership (Acts 4:32–37). Sons and daughters who steward networks with honor and transparency unlock collaborative ventures and pooled resources. Early church networks of house churches multiplied care and mission across regions. Discipleship forms relational skills that translate testimony into trustworthy partnerships. When networks are stewarded, hands prosper through shared capacity.

Adaptive planning makes hands prosper because scenario thinking and contingency preserve capacity through volatility, and Proverbs commends the prudent planner (Proverbs 21:5; 24:3–4). Sons and daughters who plan for seasons avoid panic decisions and position resources for strategic deployment. Early Christian communities prepared for famine and persecution through communal stores and training. Discipleship forms the foresight to steward across cycles rather than react to them. When planning is adaptive, hands prosper steadily.

Restorative investment makes hands prosper because directing resources to repair past harms builds social capital and prevents future liabilities, and prophetic and Levitical texts tie restoration to covenant health (Leviticus 25; Isaiah 58). Sons and daughters who invest in restitution and rebuilding create stable communities that attract long-term support. Early prophetic calls for justice often led to reforms that stabilized societies. Discipleship forms the ethical imagination to pair prosperity with restoration. When restoration is prioritized, hands prosper redemptively.

Teaching and multiplying leaders make hands prosper because investing in formation converts present resources into future stewards who expand capacity, and Proverbs values instruction and the passing of wisdom (Proverbs 4:1–9). Sons and daughters who fund discipleship and training multiply their impact through trained hands. Early church catechesis and mentoring produced leaders who sustained institutions across generations. Discipleship institutionalizes formation so that prosperity becomes generational. When leaders are multiplied, hands prosper through multiplied stewardship.

Accountable distribution makes hands prosper because transparent reporting and oversight preserve donor confidence and enable scaling, and Proverbs links faithfulness with entrustment (Proverbs 28:20; 27:23–27). Sons and daughters who implement accountability attract partners willing to invest in long-term projects. Early church governance included roles to ensure faithful distribution and to protect communal trust. Discipleship forms the disciplines of reporting and review that make stewardship credible. When distribution is accountable, hands prosper with sustained partnership.

Sabbath stewardship makes hands prosper because rhythms of rest and renewal sustain creativity and prevent burnout, and Scripture models rest as part of covenant life (Exodus 20:8–11; Mark 6:31). Sons and daughters who honor Sabbath rhythms return to labor with renewed clarity and endurance. Early Christian rhythms preserved leaders and multiplied witness by preventing exhaustion. Discipleship forms the habit of rest that sustains long-term productivity. When Sabbath is practiced, hands prosper without losing soul.

Legacy investment makes hands prosper because directing resources to institutions and practices that outlast a lifetime compounds blessing across generations, and Proverbs commends leaving an inheritance for children's children (Proverbs 13:22). Sons and daughters who invest in schools, clinics, and training centers convert present prosperity into generational capacity. Early Christian founders built institutions that served societies for centuries. Discipleship forms the governance and curricula that make legacy sustainable. When legacy is invested, hands prosper into eternity.

JUSTICE RESTORATION AND THE ETHICAL USE OF TRANSFERRED WEALTH

Justice is the ethical foundation for using transferred wealth because prophetic release must repair rather than repeat past harms, and Scripture repeatedly ties blessing to right treatment of the vulnerable (Proverbs 14:31; Isaiah 58). Sons and daughters who steward transferred resources must prioritize restitution, fair allocation, and systems that prevent future exploitation. Early prophetic tradition insisted that material reordering accompany repentance and reform. Discipleship forms the frameworks to operationalize justice in distribution so that transfer becomes healing. When justice governs transfer, sozo blessing restores communities.

Restitution is a necessary practice when transfer intersects with historical dispossession because returning what was taken aligns action with covenant repair, and

Levitical statutes and prophetic calls model restoration as part of covenant life (Leviticus 25; Amos 5). Sons and daughters who insist on restitution ensure that prophetic release does not perpetuate injustice under the guise of blessing. Early prophetic voices demanded restitution as evidence of true repentance and reform. Discipleship trains leaders to design practical restitution pathways that accompany transfer. When restitution is practiced, transfer becomes redemptive.

Transparency is an ethical imperative because open reporting and independent review prevent misuse and build trust, and Proverbs condemns dishonest scales while commending honest testimony (Proverbs 11:1; 12:22). Sons and daughters who steward transferred wealth must publish plans, audits, and outcomes so that communities can verify justice and impact. Early church governance included public accountability to preserve unity and witness. Discipleship forms the habit of transparent stewardship that sustains donor and civic confidence. When transparency is upheld, transfer is credible and sustainable.

Community participation is essential because those affected by transfer must have voice and agency in how resources are used, and Scripture models communal discernment and care (Acts 6:1–7). Sons and daughters who include local leaders and beneficiaries in planning ensure that transfer meets real needs and builds capacity rather than dependency. Early Christian care systems integrated local input to preserve dignity and effectiveness. Discipleship trains leaders to facilitate participatory processes that empower recipients. When communities participate, transfer becomes empowering.

Legal and relational repair must accompany transfer because structural change often requires titles, policy reform, and institutional redesign to secure long-term access, and prophetic openings that ignore legal realities risk reversal. Sons and daughters who pair prophetic release with legal mechanisms—land titles, regulatory compliance, and institutional charters—protect gains for future generations. Early biblical examples show prophets working with rulers to effect durable change. Discipleship forms the competence to translate prophetic urgency into lawful, lasting structures. When legal repair is done, transfer endures.

Ethical enterprise is a responsible use of transferred wealth because businesses that honor workers and community multiply blessing without exploitation, and Proverbs links fair scales with stability (Proverbs 11:1). Sons and daughters who invest in enterprises that pay fair wages and build local capacity convert transfer into sustainable livelihoods. Early Christian practice included fair commerce as part of covenant economics. Discipleship forms the ethical frameworks for enterprise that bless rather than extract. When enterprise is ethical, transfer builds resilient economies.

Formation funding secures transfer by investing in training, governance, and leadership development so that new stewards can manage resources wisely, and Proverbs values instruction as life (Proverbs 4:1–9). Sons and daughters who allocate a portion of transferred wealth to formation ensure that blessing multiplies through trained hands. Early church institutions used endowments and communal resources to fund catechesis and care. Discipleship institutionalizes formation funding so that transfer becomes generational capacity. When formation is funded, transfer yields multiplying leaders.

Safeguards against entitlement protect transfer from corruption because recipients must steward with humility and accountability rather than assuming ownership, and Scripture warns against the pride that destroys (Proverbs 16:18). Sons and daughters who receive prophetic release must adopt stewardship covenants that include reporting, mentorship, and restorative obligations. Early church practice required accountability for those entrusted with communal resources. Discipleship forms the posture of stewardship that resists entitlement. When safeguards are in place, transfer remains faithful.

Restorative dispute resolution preserves unity when conflicts arise over transfer by providing agreed mechanisms for mediation, restitution, and reconciliation, and Proverbs teaches that correction given in love leads to life (Proverbs 3:11–12). Sons and daughters who build restorative processes into transfer plans prevent fractures that drain capacity. Early church councils mediated disputes to preserve communal trust. Discipleship trains communities in peacemaking and restorative justice practices. When disputes are resolved restoratively, transfer continues to bless.

Ethical auditing and impact evaluation ensure that transferred wealth achieves intended restorative and formation goals, and public reporting sustains confidence and invites further partnership. Sons and daughters who commission independent reviews demonstrate commitment to justice and effectiveness. Early Christian governance included oversight to ensure faithful distribution. Discipleship forms the discipline of evaluation so that learning informs future practice. When auditing is ethical, transfer is accountable and scalable.

Covenantal covenants formalize expectations by documenting restoration plans, governance, and succession so that transfer is not ambiguous and can be enforced for continuity, and Proverbs values clear planning and many counselors (Proverbs 11:14; 24:3–4). Sons and daughters who create written covenants protect legacy and ensure that resources serve intended covenant ends. Early church letters and canons provided written norms that guided practice across communities. Discipleship forms the habit of covenantal documentation that preserves trust. When covenants are formalized, transfer is durable.

Ongoing discipleship is the final ethical safeguard because prophetic transfer without formation often leads to misuse; pairing release with continuous mentoring, accountability, and training converts openings into sustainable stewardship. Sons and daughters who commit to lifelong formation ensure that transferred wealth builds institutions, trains leaders, and restores communities. Early church catechesis and mentoring prepared leaders to steward entrusted resources across generations. Discipleship institutionalizes follow-through so that prophetic transfer becomes a conduit for generational blessing. When discipleship continues, sozo blessing matures into enduring legacy.

CHAPTER FIFTEEN — PROPHETIC DECREES: DECLARING COVENANT INCREASE WITH DISCERNMENT

The Nature and Authority of Decrees

A prophetic decree is covenantal speech that seeks to align human action with Heaven's will, and it functions as an instrument of relational authority rather than as a magical formula. Sons and daughters who learn to decree responsibly understand that words carry weight because they both reflect inner formation and invite communal response. Decrees in Scripture often accompany covenant responsibility—blessings pronounced by patriarchs, prophetic declarations before kings, and apostolic directives that shaped early church life. The authority of a decree rests on three pillars: alignment with Scripture, confirmation by community, and the moral credibility of the speaker. Early church practice treated authoritative speech with caution, requiring elders and councils to weigh public declarations before institutional action. Discipleship forms the character and competence that make decrees credible and effective.

Decrees derive authority from covenant identity because heirs speak not as autonomous agents but as representatives of a household under God's rule. Sons and daughters who decree from identity avoid the posture of entitlement and instead adopt stewardship language that invites partnership with the Father. This representative quality means decrees are relational instruments: they call communities to act, they authorize stewardship, and they open doors when matched by faithful practice. The New Testament language of binding and loosing frames communal speech as exercised within accountable structures rather than as private fiat. Early fathers emphasized that authoritative speech must be rooted in obedience and humility, not in charisma alone. Discipleship trains heirs to speak as representatives, not as self-appointed rulers.

Decrees are effective when they are consonant with God's revealed priorities—justice, mercy, humility, and the flourishing of the vulnerable—because Heaven's economy advances where covenant values are honored. Sons and daughters who decree for increase must ensure that their words do not contradict the scriptural ethic of restoration and care. A decree that promises transfer without plans for restitution or formation risks becoming a self-serving wish rather than a covenantal instrument. The prophetic tradition in Scripture consistently ties material reordering to moral renewal, showing that words of release are meant to repair and to build. Early church councils tested prophetic claims against Scripture and communal ethics to prevent misuse. Discipleship forms the moral imagination that keeps decrees tethered to justice.

Decrees function as catalysts when they are matched by human competence—administration, legal prudence, and relational networks—that can implement the declared intention. Sons and daughters who decree must also prepare the structures that will receive and steward what is released. A prophetic word can open a door, but competent hands must walk through it with governance, accounting, and training. The biblical pattern shows prophets working alongside rulers and administrators to effect durable change rather than leaving outcomes to chance. Early church practice combined prophetic utterance with diaconal systems to ensure provision was distributed wisely. Discipleship trains both prophetic gifting and administrative skill so decrees produce sustainable fruit.

Decrees carry risk when uttered without communal confirmation because unchecked declarations can produce division, entitlement, or legal entanglement. Sons and daughters who value covenant health submit prophetic impressions to elders and peers for testing and refinement. This communal testing is not a denial of prophetic voice but a safeguard that preserves unity and prevents harm. The early church institutionalized such testing through councils and elder oversight to protect communities from charismatic excess. Discipleship forms the humility to receive correction and the discipline to bring words into advisory contexts. When decrees are confirmed, they function as communal instruments of blessing.

Decrees are not a substitute for justice; they are a means to enact justice when paired with concrete plans for restitution and systemic repair. Sons and daughters who decree for transfer must include mechanisms that restore what was taken unjustly and that protect the vulnerable from further harm. The prophetic tradition in Scripture often calls for both denunciation of injustice and practical measures to repair it, indicating that words must be followed by action. Early prophetic and apostolic practice insisted that blessing be tethered to ethical outcomes. Discipleship forms the capacity to translate prophetic urgency into restorative policy and practice. When decrees are justice-oriented, they become instruments of redemptive change.

Decrees gain traction when they are accompanied by testimony and evidence of prior faithfulness, because reputation functions as relational capital that opens doors for entrustment. Sons and daughters who have proven integrity in small things are more likely to be heard and supported when they declare a word for increase. This pattern appears in Scripture where trusted servants are given authority and where communities respond to credible testimony. Early church leaders guarded reputation through transparent reporting and public accountability to sustain trust. Discipleship forms the track record of faithfulness that makes decrees believable. When testimony precedes decree, doors open more readily.

Decrees must be framed with humility because the posture of the speaker shapes reception; arrogant pronouncements repel while humble declarations invite partnership. Sons and daughters who approach decreeing with teachability and dependence on God create a relational climate where words can be received and acted upon. The prophets of Scripture often coupled bold speech with repentance and humility, modeling a balance of courage and submission. Early church practice emphasized the need for prophetic speech to be accompanied by a humble life. Discipleship forms the inner posture that keeps decrees accountable to God and community. When humility governs speech, decrees serve rather than dominate.

Decrees are temporal instruments that require sensitivity to timing; prophetic words often unfold across seasons rather than instantaneously. Sons and daughters who decree must discern the season and prepare for the long arc of implementation. Scripture models seasons of waiting, preparation, and harvest, indicating that prophetic timing matters. Early church leaders counseled patience and confirmation before acting on prophetic impressions. Discipleship forms the endurance to steward a word across time and to adapt plans as circumstances evolve. When timing is honored, decrees mature into sustainable outcomes.

Decrees should invite participation rather than coercion because prophetic speech that mobilizes communal action multiplies stewardship capacity. Sons and daughters who decree in ways that invite collaboration create networks that can implement and sustain the declared vision. This participatory approach prevents concentration of power and ensures shared ownership of outcomes. The early church practiced communal discernment and shared mission to implement prophetic initiatives. Discipleship trains leaders to translate decrees into mobilizing language that gathers partners. When decrees invite many hands, covenant increase is multiplied.

Decrees must be accountable to Scripture as the final arbiter, because prophetic speech that contradicts God's revealed character cannot be trusted. Sons and daughters who test decrees against Scripture avoid declarations that serve private agendas or that undermine covenant priorities. The prophets of Israel were judged by their conformity to the law and the prophets, and the early church appealed to Scripture in evaluating prophetic claims. Discipleship forms the habit of Scripture-testing so that decrees remain faithful. When Scripture governs speech, prophetic authority is rightly exercised.

DISCERNMENT TESTING AND COMMUNAL CONFIRMATION

Testing prophetic words is a biblical imperative because Scripture instructs communities to examine prophets and to weigh their words against truth and fruit. Sons and daughters who receive prophetic impressions must bring them into prayerful counsel and scriptural scrutiny before acting materially. This process prevents presumption and ensures that any transfer aligns with covenant priorities. The early church formalized testing through elders and councils to protect communities from deception and error. Discipleship trains believers to practice sober discernment and to welcome correction as part of formation. When prophetic words are tested, communities preserve unity and integrity.

Communal confirmation requires multiple voices because many counselors bring safety and reduce the risk of idiosyncratic error, and Proverbs commends collective wisdom for sound decisions. Sons and daughters who submit prophetic words to elders, peers, and trusted advisors allow diverse perspectives to surface potential pitfalls and to refine implementation plans. This communal process transforms private impressions into accountable communal directives. Early church councils exemplified this practice by vetting prophetic claims and issuing communal guidance. Discipleship forms the relational networks that provide wise counsel and mutual oversight. When confirmation is communal, decrees carry institutional legitimacy.

Discernment includes testing for alignment with Scripture because the Word of God is the measuring rod for prophetic speech, and any declaration that contradicts Scripture must be rejected. Sons and daughters who measure prophetic impressions against Scripture protect their communities from words that would distort covenant priorities. The prophets of Israel were judged by their fidelity to the law and the prophets, and the early church continued this practice. Discipleship forms the habit of Scripture-testing so that prophetic speech remains tethered to revealed truth. When Scripture is the standard, discernment is anchored.

Discernment requires attention to fruit because genuine prophetic words produce life—justice, restoration, and formation—rather than division or greed. Sons and daughters who observe outcomes before fully implementing a decree can confirm whether the word bears covenant fruit. This fruit test is practical: it evaluates whether a prophetic release leads to restored dignity, multiplied formation, and sustained stewardship. Early church leaders looked for evidence of fruit as a sign of authenticity. Discipleship trains communities to monitor outcomes and to adjust plans in light of observed fruit. When fruit is the test, prophetic words are validated by life.

Discernment includes evaluating motives because prophetic speech can be co-opted by personal ambition, and Scripture warns against those who cloak selfish ends in spiritual language. Sons and daughters who probe motives—both of the speaker and of potential beneficiaries—prevent prophetic release from becoming a vehicle for private enrichment. This moral scrutiny preserves communal trust and prevents exploitation. Early church fathers warned against the misuse of spiritual authority for gain and modeled servant leadership as the antidote. Discipleship forms the inner witness that names motive and aligns action with covenant ethics. When motives are examined, prophetic release remains redemptive.

Discernment requires legal and practical due diligence because prophetic openings often intersect with civic systems that require lawful implementation. Sons and daughters who conduct title searches, regulatory reviews, and contractual planning reduce the risk of reversal or litigation. This prudence ensures that prophetic release becomes durable policy rather than temporary advantage. Biblical examples show prophets working with rulers to effect structural change, indicating the need for legal translation. Discipleship trains leaders to integrate legal counsel into prophetic implementation. When due diligence is done, decrees are implemented lawfully.

Discernment includes community voice because those affected by transfer must have agency in decisions that impact their lives, and Scripture models communal participation in covenant decisions. Sons and daughters who include beneficiaries in planning ensure that transfer meets real needs and builds capacity rather than dependency. This participatory approach preserves dignity and effectiveness. Early church practice integrated local input into care systems to ensure relevance. Discipleship forms the skills to facilitate participatory processes that empower recipients. When community voice is honored, decrees become empowering.

Discernment requires transparency because open processes reduce suspicion and invite broader partnership, and Proverbs links honest scales with trust. Sons and daughters who publish stewardship plans, audits, and outcomes demonstrate integrity and invite continued support. This transparency deters manipulation and sustains donor confidence. Early Christian governance included public accountability to preserve unity and witness. Discipleship forms the habit of transparent reporting that makes stewardship credible. When transparency is practiced, confirmation is strengthened.

Discernment includes testing prophetic timing because words often require seasons to manifest and premature enforcement can cause harm. Sons and daughters who wait for confirmation and for the right season avoid forcing outcomes that compromise integrity. This patience preserves resources and prevents the waste of impulsive action. Scripture models seasons of preparation before provision arrives, and early church leaders counseled patience. Discipleship forms the endurance to steward prophetic words across time. When timing is respected, decrees unfold rightly.

Discernment requires independent review because

third-party evaluation of plans and outcomes reduces conflicts of interest and increases credibility. Sons and daughters who commission independent audits and ethical reviews demonstrate commitment to justice and effectiveness. This practice deters misuse and invites continued partnership. Early church structures included oversight to ensure faithful distribution. Discipleship forms the discipline of independent review so that learning informs future practice. When independent review is used, confirmation gains public trust.

Discernment includes restorative safeguards because disputes and unintended harms can arise, and agreed mechanisms for mediation and restitution prevent fractures that drain capacity. Sons and daughters who build restorative processes into transfer plans ensure that conflicts are resolved in ways that preserve dignity and communal trust. This approach prevents litigation and preserves human capital. Early church councils often mediated disputes to preserve unity. Discipleship trains communities in peacemaking and restorative justice practices. When restorative safeguards exist, decrees are implemented with care.

Discernment culminates in ongoing evaluation because prophetic release must be continually assessed by fruit, counsel, and Scripture to ensure it remains aligned with covenant priorities. Sons and daughters who welcome periodic review prevent the ossification of error and ensure that transfer continues to serve justice and formation. This ongoing testing keeps prophetic release accountable to the living God and to the community. Early church practice combined prophetic boldness with elder oversight and periodic correction. Discipleship forms the rhythms of testing and renewal that sustain faithful stewardship over time. When evaluation is ongoing, decrees remain faithful.

DECREES JUSTICE AND THE TRANSFER OF WEALTH

Decrees can catalyze transfer when they align with justice because prophetic words that call for redistribution must repair structural wrongs and protect the vulnerable. Sons and daughters who decree for transfer must include restitution plans and equitable allocation to ensure that blessing heals communities. The Jubilee and prophetic calls in Scripture model economic resets tied to covenant fidelity, showing that transfer without justice is incomplete. Early prophetic tradition insisted that material reordering accompany repentance and reform. Discipleship forms the frameworks to operationalize justice in transfer so that decrees become instruments of restoration. When justice is central, transfer becomes redemptive.

Decrees that prompt legal reform translate prophetic urgency into durable policy by engaging rulers, legislators, and administrators to enact structural change. Sons and daughters who can craft policy proposals and build coalitions increase the likelihood that prophetic words will be institutionalized. Biblical prophets sometimes influenced kings to enact reforms, demonstrating the interface between prophetic speech and governance. Early church leaders worked with civic authorities to establish care systems and protections for the vulnerable. Discipleship trains leaders to translate prophetic priorities into lawful, lasting structures. When policy follows decree, transfer is secured.

Decrees that mobilize networks convert prophetic momentum into pooled resources because testimony and relational capital invite partners to invest in shared vision. Sons and daughters who steward networks with honor and transparency unlock collaborative ventures and pooled funding that scale impact. The early church multiplied care through networks of house churches and patrons who responded to credible testimony. Discipleship forms the relational skills to translate testimony into trustworthy partnerships. When networks are mobilized, transfer becomes communal capacity.

Decrees that seed institutions multiply transfer by directing resources into schools, clinics, and training centers that produce generational capacity rather than one-time relief. Sons and daughters who prioritize institutional investment convert prophetic openings into multiplying structures. Early Christian philanthropy funded institutions that served societies for centuries, demonstrating the multiplying effect of institutional transfer. Discipleship ensures that prophetic release is paired with formation so that new resources produce leaders and sustainable programs. When institutions are seeded, transfer yields long-term blessing.

Decrees that require restitution repair historical dispossession by returning land, titles, or compensation to those wronged, aligning prophetic release with covenant repair. Sons and daughters who insist on restitution ensure that transfer does not perpetuate injustice under the guise of blessing. The Levitical statutes and prophetic calls model restoration as part of covenant life, indicating that material reordering must include repair. Early prophetic voices demanded restitution as evidence of true repentance and reform. Discipleship trains leaders to design practical restitution pathways that accompany transfer. When restitution is enacted, transfer heals communities.

Decrees that promote ethical enterprise convert transfer into sustainable livelihoods by investing in businesses that pay fair wages and build local capacity. Sons and daughters who fund ethical enterprises create jobs and preserve dignity while generating resources for communal care. Proverbs' insistence on honest scales provides the moral framework for enterprise that blesses rather than exploits. Early Christian merchants and patrons who practiced fair trade contributed to communal stability and witness. Discipleship forms the ethical frameworks for enterprise that serve people. When enterprise is ethical, transfer builds resilient economies.

Decrees that pair transfer with formation ensure that new stewards are trained to manage resources wisely, preventing misuse and enabling multiplication. Sons and daughters who allocate a portion of transferred wealth to discipleship, governance training, and vocational education convert blessing into capacity. Early church institutions used endowments and communal resources to fund catechesis and care, ensuring continuity. Discipleship institutionalizes formation funding so that transfer becomes generational. When formation accompanies transfer, stewardship multiplies.

Decrees that embed accountability protect transfer from corruption by requiring audits, reporting, and independent review, thereby sustaining donor and public confidence. Sons and daughters who implement robust oversight demonstrate commitment to justice and effectiveness. Early church governance included oversight roles to ensure faithful distribution and to protect communal trust. Discipleship forms the disciplines of transparent stewardship that make prophetic release durable. When accountability is embedded, transfer remains credible.

Decrees that include community participation empower beneficiaries to shape outcomes, preserving dignity and ensuring relevance. Sons and daughters who facilitate participatory planning prevent paternalism and build local ownership of initiatives. Scripture models communal discernment and care, and early church practice integrated local input into care systems. Discipleship trains leaders to facilitate participatory processes that empower recipients. When communities participate, transfer becomes empowering rather than imposed.

Decrees that anticipate legal repair secure transfer by addressing titles, regulatory compliance, and institutional charters so that gains are protected for future generations. Sons and daughters who pair prophetic release with legal mechanisms reduce the risk of reversal and ensure continuity. Biblical examples show prophets working with rulers to effect durable change, indicating the need for legal translation. Discipleship forms the competence to translate prophetic urgency into lawful, lasting structures. When legal repair is done, transfer endures.

Decrees that prioritize restorative dispute resolution preserve unity by providing agreed mechanisms for mediation, restitution, and reconciliation when conflicts arise. Sons and daughters who build restorative processes into transfer plans prevent fractures that drain capacity and trust. Early church councils often mediated disputes to preserve communal life. Discipleship trains communities in peacemaking and restorative justice practices. When disputes are resolved restoratively, transfer continues to bless.

Decrees that are publicly accountable invite ongoing evaluation and learning, ensuring that transferred wealth achieves intended restorative and formation goals. Sons and daughters who commission independent evaluations and publish results demonstrate commitment to justice and invite further partnership. Early Christian governance practiced public accountability to preserve unity and witness. Discipleship forms the discipline of evaluation so that learning informs future practice. When accountability is public, transfer is scalable and trustworthy.

DECREEING WITH HUMILITY AND STEWARDSHIP

Decreeing with humility begins with a posture of dependence on God and on communal wisdom, because prophetic authority exercised without teachability invites error and pride. Sons and daughters who approach decreeing with humility invite correction and preserve relational trust, making their words more likely to be received and acted upon responsibly. The prophets of Scripture often coupled bold speech with repentance and submission, modeling a balance of courage and humility. Early church leaders emphasized servant posture as the safeguard for prophetic influence. Discipleship forms the inner life that keeps decrees accountable to God and community. When humility governs speech, decrees serve the common good.

Decreeing with stewardship requires clear implementation plans that translate words into accountable action, because prophetic release without governance risks dissipation. Sons and daughters who pair decrees with budgets, oversight, and training convert prophetic momentum into institutional capacity. This practical pairing ensures that transfer becomes sustainable rather than ephemeral. Early church practice combined prophetic insight with diaconal systems to manage provision responsibly. Discipleship trains leaders in administrative competence so that decrees are implemented wisely. When stewardship accompanies decree, blessing is preserved.

Decreeing with covenant covenants formalizes expectations by documenting restoration plans, governance, and succession so that transfer is not ambiguous and can be enforced for continuity. Sons and daughters who create written covenants protect legacy and ensure that resources serve intended covenant ends. Early church letters and canons provided written norms that guided practice across communities. Discipleship forms the habit of covenantal documentation that preserves trust. When covenants are formalized, decrees become durable commitments.

Decreeing with accountability establishes independent review and ethical auditing to ensure outcomes align with stated goals, because transparency sustains donor and public confidence. Sons and daughters who commission independent evaluations demonstrate commitment to justice and invite continued partnership. Early church governance included oversight to ensure faithful distribution and to protect communal trust. Discipleship forms the discipline of reporting and review that makes audits constructive rather than punitive. When accountability is institutionalized, decrees are implemented with integrity.

Decreeing with restorative obligations embeds restitution and repair into outcomes so that prophetic transfer heals historical wounds rather than perpetuating harm.

Sons and daughters who insist on restorative measures ensure that transfer aligns with covenant justice. The Levitical and prophetic traditions model restoration as part of covenant life, indicating that material reordering must include repair. Early prophetic voices demanded restitution as evidence of true repentance and reform. Discipleship trains leaders to design practical restitution pathways that accompany transfer. When restoration is required, decrees become redemptive.

Decreeing with participatory design includes beneficiaries in planning and governance so that transfer meets real needs and builds local capacity. Sons and daughters who facilitate participatory processes preserve dignity and effectiveness. Early Christian care systems integrated local input to ensure relevance and sustainability. Discipleship forms the skills to enable community voice and shared ownership. When participation is central, decrees empower rather than impose.

Decreeing with legal prudence secures outcomes by translating prophetic priorities into lawful instruments —titles, charters, and policy reforms—that protect gains for future generations. Sons and daughters who integrate legal counsel into implementation reduce the risk of reversal and ensure continuity. Biblical examples show prophets working with rulers to effect durable change, indicating the need for legal translation. Discipleship forms the competence to craft lawful, lasting structures. When legal prudence is applied, decrees endure.

Decreeing with formation funding allocates resources to training, governance, and leadership development so that new stewards can manage entrusted wealth wisely.

Sons and daughters who fund discipleship convert prophetic release into multiplying capacity. Early church institutions used communal resources to fund catechesis and care, ensuring continuity. Discipleship institutionalizes formation funding so that transfer becomes generational. When formation is funded, decrees yield multiplying leaders.

Decreeing with transparency publishes plans, audits, and outcomes so that communities can verify justice and impact, and public reporting sustains confidence and invites partnership. Sons and daughters who steward transparently deter manipulation and preserve donor trust. Early church governance practiced public accountability to preserve unity and witness. Discipleship forms the habit of transparent stewardship that sustains credibility. When transparency is upheld, decrees are trusted.

Decreeing with restorative dispute resolution provides agreed mechanisms for mediation and reconciliation when conflicts arise, preventing fractures that drain capacity. Sons and daughters who build restorative processes into transfer plans ensure that disputes are resolved in ways that preserve dignity and communal trust. Early church councils mediated disputes to preserve unity. Discipleship trains communities in peacemaking and restorative justice practices. When disputes are resolved restoratively, decrees continue to bless.

Decreeing with ongoing evaluation commits to periodic review of outcomes, counsel, and scriptural alignment so that prophetic release remains accountable and adaptive. Sons and daughters who welcome periodic assessment prevent the ossification of error and ensure that transfer continues to serve justice and formation. Early church practice combined prophetic boldness with elder oversight and periodic correction. Discipleship forms the rhythms of testing and renewal that sustain faithful stewardship over time. When evaluation is ongoing, decrees remain faithful instruments of covenant increase.

Decreeing with humility and stewardship culminates in a posture of grateful service: prophetic words that open doors are received as trust to be managed for the common good rather than as personal entitlement. Sons and daughters who steward with gratitude, accountability, and justice convert prophetic release into institutions, formation, and restoration that bless generations. The biblical and early church witness converge on this ethic: prophetic authority is exercised for the flourishing of the household of faith and the vulnerable beyond it. Discipleship remains the primary means by which prophetic speech is tested, formed, and stewarded. When decrees are matched by humble stewardship, Heaven's economy flows with justice, mercy, and enduring increase.

CONCLUSION — RETURNING TO THE ANCIENT PATHWAYS

THE REDISCOVERY OF THE HIDDEN COVENANT

The hidden covenant is not a secret formula but a recovered way of life where identity precedes activity and relationship governs resources. Sons and daughters rediscover this covenant by reorienting motives from possession to stewardship, practicing reverence, and embedding justice into daily decisions. This rediscovery reframes prosperity as relational and generational rather than transactional and immediate. The practical result is communities that plan, give, and govern with integrity so that blessing circulates rather than concentrates.

Rediscovery requires disciplined formation—Scripture, prayer, counsel, and communal practice—that rewires imagination from scarcity to stewardship. When covenant patterns are rehearsed in households, churches, and institutions, the hidden covenant becomes visible in policies, budgets, and rhythms of care. The recovery of covenant is therefore both inward and structural: hearts are formed and systems are redesigned to reflect Heaven's priorities.

SONS WALKING IN HEAVEN'S ECONOMY

Walking in Heaven's economy means living as heirs who steward rather than owners who hoard. Sons and daughters who walk this way speak with humility, give with generosity, plan with prudence, and lead with honor. Their decisions prioritize legacy, justice, and formation, and their daily practices—margin, Sabbath, counsel—create the conditions for sustainable increase.

Practically, walking in Heaven's economy looks like transparent governance, progressive entrustment, and investments in people and institutions that multiply care. It looks like prophetic words tested by elders, decrees paired with restitution, and generosity that seeds training and hospitals, schools, and care systems. The visible fruit is steady, generational blessing that preserves dignity and multiplies witness.

WISDOM AS THE FOUNDATION OF PROSPERITY

Wisdom is the soil in which prosperity rooted in covenant grows. Proverbs teaches that wisdom precedes riches, that counsel protects increase, and that character attracts entrustment. Sons and daughters who prioritize wisdom invest in formation, mentorship, and the slow work of character so that prosperity is durable and redemptive.

Wisdom disciplines include listening to many counselors, refusing shortcuts that compromise justice, and embedding practices that translate revelation into accountable action. When wisdom governs, prosperity becomes a byproduct of faithful stewardship rather than the object of anxious striving.

COVENANT AS THE KEY TO ACCESS

Covenant is the key that opens relational channels to Heaven's economy because it defines belonging, responsibility, and mutual obligation. Access is not earned by technique but received through identity and practiced through honor, generosity, and faithful stewardship. Sons and daughters who live covenantally unlock prophetic partnership, communal favor, and institutional trust.

Access requires both inward formation and outward structures: a heart formed by reverence and a community organized by transparent governance, restorative justice, and discipleship pathways. Together these make prophetic transfer and decrees accountable, restorative, and generational.

THE INVITATION TO LIVE DIFFERENTLY

This book closes with an invitation rather than a promise: live differently by choosing covenant over accumulation, formation over fame, and justice over expedience. Sons and daughters are called to practice small faithfulness—daily prayer, honest speech, disciplined planning, generous scattering—that compounds into institutional capacity and generational blessing.

Accepting the invitation means joining a long line of witnesses who built schools, hospitals, and care systems because they believed stewardship was sacred. It means testing prophetic words with counsel, pairing release with restitution, and stewarding every gift for the common good. The pathway is ancient, the stakes are eternal, and the fruit is a visible economy where Heaven's priorities are lived out on earth.

SOURCES, INFLUENCES, AND FURTHER READING

PRIMARY BIBLICAL TEXTS

The Holy Bible. English Standard Version. Wheaton, IL: Crossway, 2016. The Holy Bible. New American Standard Bible. La Habra, CA: Lockman Foundation, 1995. The Holy Bible. New King James Version. Nashville, TN: Thomas Nelson, 1982.

EARLY CHURCH AND PATRISTIC SOURCES

Augustine of Hippo. The City of God. Translated by Henry Bettenson. London: Penguin Classics, 2003.

Chrysostom, John. Homilies on the Gospel of Matthew. Translated by George Prevost. Nicene and Post-Nicene Fathers, First Series, Vol. 10. Peabody, MA: Hendrickson, 1994.

Irenaeus of Lyons. Against Heresies. Translated by Alexander Roberts and William Rambaut. Ante-Nicene Fathers, Vol. 1. Peabody, MA: Hendrickson, 1994.

The Didache. In The Apostolic Fathers, translated by Michael W. Holmes. Grand Rapids, MI: Baker Academic, 2007.

The Apostolic Constitutions. In Ante-Nicene Fathers, Vol. 7. Peabody, MA: Hendrickson, 1994.

BIBLICAL THEOLOGY AND OLD TESTAMENT SCHOLARSHIP

Brueggemann, Walter. The Prophetic Imagination. Minneapolis: Fortress Press, 2001.

Brueggemann, Walter. Theology of the Old Testament: Testimony, Dispute, Advocacy. Minneapolis: Fortress Press, 1997.

Wright, Christopher J. H. Old Testament Ethics for the People of God. Downers Grove, IL: InterVarsity Press, 2004.

Wright, Christopher J. H. The Mission of God. Downers Grove, IL: InterVarsity Press, 2006.

Goldingay, John. Old Testament Theology. Vols. 1–3. Downers Grove, IL: InterVarsity Press, 2003–2009.

NEW TESTAMENT THEOLOGY AND KINGDOM ECONOMICS

Wright, N. T. Jesus and the Victory of God. Minneapolis: Fortress Press, 1996.

Wright, N. T. Paul and the Faithfulness of God. Minneapolis: Fortress Press, 2013.

Fee, Gordon D. God's Empowering Presence: The Holy Spirit in the Letters of Paul. Peabody, MA: Hendrickson, 1994.

Blomberg, Craig L. Neither Poverty nor Riches: A Biblical Theology of Material Possessions. Downers Grove, IL: InterVarsity Press, 1999.

STEWARDSHIP, WEALTH, AND JUSTICE

Sider, Ronald J. Rich Christians in an Age of Hunger. Nashville: Thomas Nelson, 2005.

Keller, Timothy. Generous Justice. New York: Dutton, 2010.

Perkins, John M. With Justice for All. Ventura, CA: Regal Books, 1982.

Stott, John. Issues Facing Christians Today. Grand Rapids, MI: Zondervan, 2006.

DISCIPLESHIP, FORMATION, AND GOVERNANCE

Willard, Dallas. The Spirit of the Disciplines. San Francisco: HarperOne, 1998.

Foster, Richard J. Celebration of Discipline. San Francisco: HarperOne, 1998.

Bonhoeffer, Dietrich. Life Together. New York: Harper & Row, 1954.

Banks, Robert. Paul's Idea of Community. Peabody, MA: Hendrickson, 1994.

PROPHETIC MINISTRY AND DISCERNMENT

Green, Michael. I Believe in the Holy Spirit. Grand Rapids, MI: Eerdmans, 2004.

Grudem, Wayne. The Gift of Prophecy in the New Testament and Today. Wheaton, IL: Crossway, 2000.

Keener, Craig S. Gift and Giver. Grand Rapids, MI: Baker Academic, 2001.

CHAPTER-SPECIFIC SOURCE LISTS

Chapters 1–3 — Covenant, Wisdom, and Heaven's Economy

Proverbs (entire book)

Deuteronomy 8; 28

Brueggemann, Theology of the Old Testament

Wright, Old Testament Ethics for the People of God

Augustine, City of God

CHAPTERS 4–6 — STEWARDSHIP, PLANNING, AND GENERATIONAL WEALTH

Proverbs 6; 13; 21; 24

Blomberg, Neither Poverty nor Riches

Keller, Generous Justice

Sider, Rich Christians in an Age of Hunger

Chrysostom, Homilies

CHAPTERS 7–9 — SPEECH, DECREES, AND AUTHORITY

Proverbs 18; 21

Matthew 16; 18

Grudem, The Gift of Prophecy

Keener, Gift and Giver

The Didache

CHAPTERS 10–12 — LEGACY, INSTITUTIONS, AND COVENANT CONTINUITY

Proverbs 13; 22

Leviticus 25

Wright, The Mission of God

Banks, Paul's Idea of Community

Apostolic Constitutions

CHAPTER 13 — PROPHETIC TRANSFER

Genesis 41

Exodus 3–12

1 Kings 17; 2 Kings 4

Isaiah 58; Amos 5

Brueggemann, The Prophetic Imagination

Wright, Old Testament Ethics

CHAPTER 14 — SOZO BLESSING AND WHOLENESS

Luke 4; John 10

Proverbs 3; 4

Willard, The Spirit of the Disciplines

Foster, Celebration of Discipline

Bonhoeffer, Life Together

CHAPTER 15 — PROPHETIC DECREES AND DISCERNMENT

1 Thessalonians 5

Acts 13; 15

Grudem, The Gift of Prophecy

Green, I Believe in the Holy Spirit

Early Church Councils (Acts 15 model)

CONCLUSION — RETURNING TO THE ANCIENT PATHWAYS

Jeremiah 6:16

Proverbs (summary theology)

Augustine, City of God

Wright, Paul and the Faithfulness of God

AUTHOR INFORMATION

Dr. Russell "Rush" Welch is an apostolic teacher, prophetic reformer, and frontline Kingdom warrior whose testimony has ushered countless men and women into the liberating reality of life in Christ Jesus. His journey —marked by grace, forged through trial, and crowned with redemption—has become a living parable of the very Kingdom he so fiercely proclaims.

Through Spirit-breathed writings, apostolic teaching, personal mentorship, and compelling public ministry, he calls believers to rediscover the Gospel not as a passive doctrine, but as the vibrant, world-altering announcement of God's reign—just as Christ and His disciples taught it. Dr. Russ carries a distinct apostolic mantle to confront darkness, restore broken lives, and equip the Remnant to advance the Gospel of the Kingdom with boldness and clarity. His heart burns especially for America's veterans—those battle-scarred warriors, many living on the streets—whom he longs to see healed, restored, and re-commissioned as spiritual soldiers in the army of God.

Those who follow his work encounter a steady stream of prophetic insight, transformative stories, and practical encouragement, all offered with the clarity and candor reminiscent of C.S. Lewis's approach to truth. His voice is both a sword and a compass—cutting through confusion while pointing believers back to the King and His Kingdom.

Dr. Russ ministers with a rare blend of humility, wisdom, and militant devotion, refusing to dilute the message of Christ or compromise the call of discipleship. Whether addressing a congregation, speaking at a conference, gathering with a small group, or engaging in media conversations, he carries the same apostolic fire: to awaken identity, ignite purpose, and mobilize warriors for the advancing Kingdom of God. His ongoing journey can be followed at facebook.com/rush.welch, where he continues to equip, challenge, and inspire the Remnant.

For invitations, interviews, or speaking engagements, Dr. Welch may be contacted at: Email: dr.russwelch1964@gmail.com Phone: 904.322.0737

Made in the USA
Coppell, TX
05 November 2026

11281647R20212